GOOD MORNING, DISCIPLE

GOOD MORNING DISCIPLE

Daily Exercises for Spiritual Growth

VIC JACKOPSON

With a foreword by
Dick Lucas

MarshallPickering
An Imprint of HarperCollins*Publishers*

*This book is respectfully dedicated to my
dear friends Robert and Ruth Glaze of Dallas, Texas,
whose love and encouragement over many years
have warmed and enabled me.*

Marshall Pickering is an Imprint of
HarperCollins*Religious*
Part of HarperCollins*Publishers*
77–85 Fulham Palace Road, London W6 8JB

First published in Great Britain
in 1992 by Marshall Pickering

1 3 5 7 9 10 8 6 4 2

A catalogue record for this book is
available from the British Library

ISBN 0 551 02584 0

Typeset by Medcalf Type Ltd, Bicester, Oxon
Printed and bound in Great Britain by
HarperCollinsManufacturing Glasgow

CONTENTS

ACKNOWLEDGMENTS

Space does not permit a list of those folk who, with God's help, have reshaped and changed my life over the years from the young delinquent in Winchester Prison to a servant of the Lord writing these words. Without them this contribution would be very much the poorer.

No book, especially a Christian book, is the work of one man or woman. It is a team effort. Therefore, I would like to thank my dear wife, Sue, and my elder daughter, Christy, for the months of typing, correcting, changing, advising and for their never-ending patience.

I am indebted to the trustees of Hope Now International Ministries for a three-month sabbatical leave when the bulk of the writing was completed. This would never have been possible without the use of a delightful hideaway in the Cotswolds, loaned by a friend, to whom I am most grateful. Thanks are also due to the staff of Regent's Park College, Oxford, for the use of their library facilities.

I am further indebted to the reverends Canon Michael Botting of Chester, Andrew Rigden-Green of Torquay, Peter Jamieson of Woodford Green, Michael Quicke of Cambridge, and to Mr Robin Orr and Mrs Joanna Godfree of Highfield School, Liphook, for their care in reading the manuscript and making many helpful suggestions in the final stages of preparation.

My special thanks to Preb. Dick Lucas of St Helen's Church, Bishopsgate, for agreeing to enhance the book with his gracious Foreword. His constant challenge and encouragement to spend time in study has, I hope, paid dividends.

My thanks to the more than one thousand prayer partners who held me before the Father day after day.

Finally, God Himself who, by His Holy Spirit, spurred me on when I felt like giving up. His constant answers to my prayers, when faced with a blank sheet of paper, were an inspiration to my own faith.

Hallelujah!

FOREWORD

There are some Christian workers you (or at least I) cannot help loving for their straightforward and attractive Christian witness, their courage in active Christian outreach, and their steadfast love for the gospel and for those they seek to reach for Christ. Vic Jackopson is just such a person. A visit from him is always a tonic; a new book from him is always a treat; and a request from him to write a Foreword is a command I cannot refuse!

I delight in the wonderful way God called Vic to Himself from unpromising beginnings in order to make him a fisher of men. I delight in his concern for all sorts and conditions of people in their spiritual need, from the hippy traveller at Glastonbury to the worker here in the square mile of the City of London – few people can reach out to such different types so boldly, so wisely and so well. And I delight in his friendship.

Vic and I could not have had a more dissimilar start in life, except in this respect, that as young believers we were both given, early on, a book on doctrine, famous in its day, entitled *In Understanding Be Men*. Today I guess many would think it impossibly heavy for the new convert. Consequently, milk and water are so often served up, and feeble spiritual growth is the result. But true conversion means a voracious appetite that looks for better fare than slops. This book, *Good Morning, Disciple*, takes the young Christian seriously and the Christian life seriously. It offers fresh, wholesome and readable help in Bible study and Christian thinking. Those who use this material day by day will find great joy and benefit in a deeper understanding of the foundations of our most holy faith.

So my advice to the reader is to "wake up" each morning to Vic's cheerful greeting, and through this regular time with God, to "grow up" into Christ.

Prebendary Dick Lucas
St Helen's, Bishopsgate
June, 1991

A WORD FROM THE AUTHOR

Good Morning, Disciple,

Wherever you are and whatever time of the day you plan to read this book of letters, welcome to *Good Morning, Disciple*.

My purpose in writing this book is twofold. Firstly, to help you lay a deep foundation upon which you may grow to full Christian maturity.

Secondly, to help you develop a daily habit of Bible study, without which spiritual depth and maturity are merely an illusion.

Why the letter style? It probably goes back to my own early days as a Christian when I was given a copy of C.S. Lewis's *Screwtape Letters*. And, of course, there is good biblical precedent for epistles. Not that I claim any apostolic authority for what I write. The letter style does, however, give me the opportunity to address you personally.

Where necessary I have not hesitated to use technical terminology, and here the glossary in the back of the book will be useful. Sometimes I have used the original Greek (in which the New Testament was written) to clarify the meaning. The more serious student will want to go beyond my paltry grasp of Greek to the interpretive commentaries. I have asterisked these in the bibliography.

Don't be afraid of language. It is a friend to those who would grow deeper in their understanding. I well remember the first book which I was given after my conversion to Christ. *In Understanding Be Men* was not for the faint-hearted. Without a single examination to my name, unused to books and suffering from dyslexia, I ploughed through Hammond's introduction to Christian doctrine. How grateful I am to God for Donald Charlcraft who gave me that book. It raised my head, giraffe-like, to the highest branches and gave me a taste for the mysteries of God. If I may achieve that in some small measure in your life, then these months of writing will have been worth the effort.

These studies are all taken from Paul's letter to the Colossians. Each day I have taken a verse, or a part of a verse, to create a theme. As we work from the beginning through to the end of the epistle, in these six months we shall cover the major doctrines and themes of the New Testament. By the time you reach the end, a secure foundation of biblical understanding will be yours.

At the close of each letter I have recommended a passage of Scripture, and I would encourage you to spend time meditating on it. If you are not sure where to find a particular book of the Bible, do look up the page number on the contents page in the front of your Bible – it's not cheating! We've all had to do it. Indeed, I still do for certain books!

When I say meditate, I do not mean that you have to sit in a strange position or recite mantras, and I definitely don't advocate emptying your mind. Christian meditation is filling the mind with God's Word and anything which is noble, right, pure, lovely, admirable, excellent or praiseworthy (see Philippians 4.8). Find a place where you can sit comfortably, with your Bible and notebook open in front of you. Read the passage at least twice, noting especially its context. What did it mean to those who read it first? Then jot down in your notebook what it means to you in connection with the day's theme and your own personal walk with God. You may even want to note down what the passage teaches you about God, Jesus, the Holy Spirit, yourself, God's people, your family, your work and your witness to the world.

When you have done this, spend some time in prayer, asking especially if there is something God wants you to put into action as a result of reading His Word.

Some time ago I developed the diagram overleaf to help me focus on the three priorities of the Christian life: God, God's people and God's world.

Notice how, reading in an anti-clockwise direction, our relationship with God begins with salvation, which we receive as a gift from God, based upon what Christ has done upon the cross. That process of grace continues throughout the life of a believer as God gives and continues to give.

Sanctification is the life-long development of our relationship with God as we surrender more and more of our lives to Him, to be changed into Christ-like characters for His glory. It is the giving side of presenting our bodies as "living sacrifices, holy and pleasing to God" (Romans 12.1).

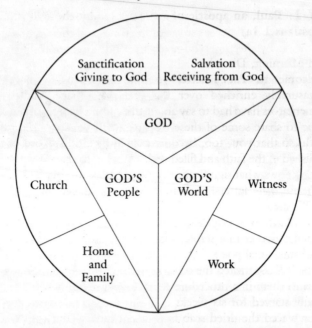

Once that relationship with God is established, in Christ, we enter into a new relationship with His people. All Christians, regardless of race, social status, wealth or any other factor, are now called brothers and sisters.

Because it is God's intention that you and your household be saved (Acts 16.31), you accept a new responsibility towards your immediate family, as far as in you lies, to create a Christian home.

From this secure base, I shall seek to share with you, from Colossians, how to develop a strategy for working and witnessing in the world.

You will see how, day by day, everything Paul has to say in his epistle, and indeed, everything you will read in God's Word, fits into this diagram. You may want to refer back to it from time to time. It will help you to keep a balanced view of what God wants to do in you and through you.

Do enjoy the book.

Yours in His glorious service,

Vic Jackopson
Southampton, 1991

DAY 1   Paul, an apostle of Christ Jesus by the will of God (Colossians 1.1a)

Good Morning, Disciple,

Welcome to Paul's letter to the Colossians. I have been immeasurably enriched over the years as I have studied what commentators have had to say about these four chapters of pure gold. I hope to share some of these treasures with you over the next six months so that you, too, become excited by God's Word of truth, established in the faith and filled with a longing to share it with others.

Who knows what significant event may shape your life, even as you read these daily letters? A chance event can direct the course of a person's life.

A small group of boys and girls, back in the summer of 1757, sat huddled together in a stable, weak and afraid. Most were to die of the dreaded smallpox.

None had contracted the contagious disease naturally. Their parents gave it to them in a procedure called "buying the pox". They were virtually starved for six weeks and bled by leeches, then the town doctor placed the dried scab from a smallpox victim over a scratch on each child's arm. If they survived they would never again catch the smallpox; if they died they had only hastened the inevitable.

One of the survivors from that stable was a lad called Edward Jenner. Haunted by the experience, he went on to discover vaccination, and his research has led to the eradication of smallpox, the killer of millions.

Another such world changing event occurred when a Jewish Pharisee called Saul met with the risen Lord Jesus Christ in a startling encounter. You can read about it in Acts 9.1-31. It made such an impression on Saul's life that he, a persecutor of the Christian Church, changed his name to Paul and became God's chief spokesman for the gospel.

This opening greeting demonstrates Paul's credentials. As Christ's representative, the Lord's ambassador, he would speak not on his own authority but that of the Lord Himself. He had been chosen to carry the name of the Lord beyond its Jewish confines into a Gentile world (Acts 9.15). This is why, 2,000 years later, we read it as the Word of God. God spoke it through his apostle for all time, to all people.

Read Acts 9.1-31 – and ask God to meet with you in a special way over the next six months.

Quote "If you had the talents of an angel, you could do no good with them till His hour is come, and till He leads you to the people He has determined to bless by your means" – John Newton, *Letters of John Newton* (Banner of Truth, 1960).

Promise "No eye has seen, no ear has heard, no mind has conceived what God has prepared for those who love Him" (1 Corinthians 2.9).

DAY 2 Timothy our brother (1.1b)

Good Morning, Disciple,

Why do I call you a disciple? Because, in the language of the Bible, a disciple is anyone who learns. When Jesus called the twelve disciples, He was really inviting them to become His pupils. He taught many others by the shore and on the hills overlooking Galilee and to all who would follow Him He said, "Learn from me" (Matthew 11.29). So, in a sense, anyone who wants to learn more about the Lord Jesus Christ and how to serve Him is as much a disciple as the original twelve.

At the end of His life on earth Jesus commissioned those who had been with Him for three years to "go and make disciples of all nations, baptising them . . . and teaching them . . ." (Matthew 28.19-20). What they had learned they must now teach.

There is no better example of this than the relationship between the apostle Paul and the younger Christian, Timothy. Apparently Timothy, the son of a Greek who was married to a Jewish Christian called Eunice, was already a believer when Paul met him in Lystra. The young man quickly became the travelling companion and disciple of the missionary apostle (Acts 16.1-3).

While there was never any doubt as to who was the teacher and who was the learner, we never sense anything but deep affection between the two. Here in Colossians they are described as brothers, elsewhere as father and son (Philippians 2.22). Paul writes, "I am sending to you Timothy, my son whom I love, who is faithful in the Lord. He will remind you of my way of life in Christ Jesus, which agrees with what I teach in every church" (1 Corinthians 4.17).

This verse gives us two foundation principles for discipleship: relationship and reality.

My prayer is that you, too, will find an older believer from whom you can learn the faith in the bond of a true Christian relationship, and that you in turn will become just such a teacher and friend to others. Without love discipleship is impossible. It is love which protects the young; love which leads, builds up and nurtures; love which understands, encourages and shares without holding anything back.

Where you have such closeness there must also be transparent reality. Why did Timothy become "faithful in the Lord"? Because he had seen his spiritual father's way of life – and it matched his teaching. Only such a man could say, "Whatever you have learned or received or heard from me . . . put it into practice" (Philippians 4.9).

Read 2 Timothy 1.8-2.7 and meditate on this theme of discipleship. Pray that you will become a good disciple.

Quote "A multiplier is a disciple who is training his spiritual children to reproduce themselves" – Gary W. Kuhne, *Discipleship*, ed. Billie Hanks Jr (Zondervan, 1981).

Promise "Everyone who is fully trained will be like his teacher" (Luke 6.40).

DAY 3 To the holy and faithful (1.2a)

Good Morning, Disciple,

We often joke in our family about the day a friend of my youngest daughter, Ruth, came to tea. They were just five years old. When Roxana returned home her father asked her, "What does Mr Jackopson do for a living?"

"I don't really know," replied Roxana. "He's something to do with the church. I think he's a saint."

In the true biblical sense of the word she was right. For all believers are saints.

The New Testament was originally written in Greek. If you have ever studied a foreign language you will know how often the same word may be translated in different ways to capture the various senses of the original. The Greek word used here, *hagioi*, is an example. It can mean in its noun form "the holy ones" or "the saints", but as an adjective as in this verse, it describes the believers as holy brothers in Christ.

The word holy conjures up pictures of benign-looking saints with haloes in stained glass windows or the kind of Holy Joe most of us simply wouldn't want to know. Nothing could be further from its real meaning. True holiness is set in the common affairs of ordinary life.

You may have heard the story of the young rascal vandalising the stained glass windows of a church. When his stone crashed through it knocked the "e" out of "highest". When the congregation gathered the next Sunday for worship they read, instead of the familiar words "Glory to God in the highest", "Glory to God in the high st".

That's where holiness belongs: in the High Street, and in every other street where the rubber hits the road.

Holiness means being set aside for God's purpose. Just as a gardener needs a spade or a hairdresser needs scissors, God needs you and me. We are His instruments.

Faithfulness is the other side of the same coin. When two people marry they vow to keep the "holy estate of matrimony". They say, in effect, "We are so much in love that we commit ourselves to serve each other for the rest of our lives." In this they are "holy" to each other and committed to faithfulness.

Our relationship with the Lord is of the same order. We are His holy saints: tools and instruments reserved for His use, called to be faithful believers.

As you meditate on 1 Peter 2.1-12 look for these two qualities – holiness and faithfulness – and face this new day as one of God's faithful saints.

Quote "God is calling out from the world a people for Himself, and the vocation of this people is to be 'holy' or different" – John Stott, *Issues Facing Christians Today* (Marshall Pickering, 1984).

Promise "Blessed are those who hunger and thirst for righteousness, for they will be filled" (Matthew 5.6).

DAY 4 Brothers in Christ at Colosse (1.2b)

Good Morning, Disciple,

If you were to ask me to sum up this epistle in two words, I would answer: "In Christ". Union with Christ is a constantly recurring theme in all four chapters, just as a melody might run through each movement of a symphony.

Over these months together we shall see how the Christian's relationship with God, His people and His world has its foundation in Christ. Our faith, forgiveness, freedom and peace are in Him. In Him we are dead and buried to the old sin life and raised to new life. Our fellowship, our family life, our work and our witness – all are in Him.

It may be helpful to see it in the form of a diagram with Christ as the centre to which everything is attached.

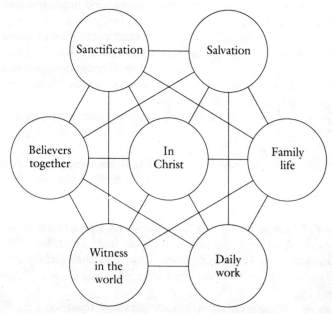

Notice how every issue is not only connected "in Christ" but is also connected to each other. Sanctification, living a life in Christ, affects every other area. Salvation brings me into a relationship with other believers. This is why Paul addresses the church as the "holy and faithful brothers in Christ at Colosse" (1.2).

Of course, not every person who heard the letter read out to the congregation was "in Christ". One may be in the church but not "in Christ", regularly in the choir or the congregation and yet not "in Christ". The important point is not whether we are members of a church, but whether we are "members of his body" (Ephesians 5.30).

Here is the acid test in a church like the one at Colosse where, as we shall see later, man-made ideas were being peddled by those who were in the church but not necessarily in Christ. Were they really brothers and sisters if their confidence was in anything other than Christ Himself and His completed work upon the cross? Could they say they were "sons (and daughters) of God through faith in Christ Jesus" (Galatians 3.26)? Could they affirm, "There is now no condemnation for those who are in Christ Jesus" (Romans 8.1)? If not, they could not lay claim to being included in this address to the "holy and faithful brothers (and sisters) in Christ at Colosse".

As you meditate on John 15.1-17, write down some of the privileges you have because you are united to Christ.

Quote "The unity of the Christian Church is not based on the oneness of human spirits, but upon the unity of the divine Spirit" – Dietrich Bonhoeffer, *Sanctorum Communio* (Collins, 1963).

Promise "If anyone is in Christ, he is a new creation; the old has gone, the new has come!" (2 Corinthians 5.17).

DAY 5   Grace and peace to you from God our Father (1.2c)

Good Morning, Disciple,

Have you begun to understand what grace and peace are? A story may help.

During the Irish potato famine in 1846 many poor tenant farmers lost everything. Bankruptcy forced those who were able to raise the fare to emigrate to America or England. Many more became homeless paupers.

Tenants of Canon Faucett wrote to their absentee landlord in England to beg for time to pay their rent arrears. Imagine their faces when eventually they read his reply. He told them the rent was not only fair but due and must be paid in full.

As they read on, however, their faces must have changed. Perhaps they even broke out into song and dance. Faucett had enclosed with each letter a cheque – enough to cover the rent, which must still be paid, and a surplus amount for each family to buy much-needed food.

The Canon knew the meaning of grace and demonstrated it more clearly than any sermon.

"By grace you have been saved, through faith," says Paul, "and this is not from yourselves, it is the gift of God – not by works, so that no one can boast" (Ephesians 2.8-9). The price of our salvation is too high for us to pay. We are before God as those peasant farmers to Canon Faucett. God Himself paid the price upon the cross as an act of grace. We didn't earn it, we didn't deserve it, but God gave it to us anyway.

Way back in the years before Christ, Jews would greet each other, as they still do today, with the word *Shalom*, peace. It meant not merely the absence of conflict but a general wellbeing, the source and giver of which was God alone. The New Testament fills out this gift of *Shalom* to show that Jesus is God's gift of peace. Paul says, "He himself is our peace" (Ephesians 2.14).

When Paul puts grace and peace together, as he does here, it is not merely as a casual greeting. It acts as a blessing, a prayer, and a reminder of the source of salvation.

Meditate this morning on Titus 3.1-8. You may even want to memorise verse 5 so that, if you are ever tempted to doubt your salvation or have an opportunity to share your faith, you have an anchor on God's promise.

Quote "The surest sign that God has done a work of grace in my heart is that I love Jesus best, not weakly and faintly, not intellectually, but passionately, personally and devotedly, overwhelming every other love of my life" – Oswald Chambers.

Promise "My grace is sufficient for you" (Corinthians 12.9).

DAY 6   We always thank God (1.3a)

Good Morning, Disciple,

Gratitude, like union with Christ, is one of the recurring themes of this letter. It crops up in the context of prayer, worship, work and salvation. In his very first epistle the apostle Paul had written, "Give thanks in all circumstances, for this is God's will for you in Christ Jesus" (1 Thessalonians 5.18). We need the reminder, for few of us are thankful even when things go well, let alone in all circumstances.

The story goes that Edward Spencer in his student days saved seventeen shipwrecked men from a sinking ship during a storm on Lake Michigan. Many years later the preacher, Dr Torrey, made reference to the event in a sermon. As he did so, a voice from the congregation rang out that the hero was present at the meeting. Dr Torrey asked Spencer, now an elderly man, for his recollections of what happened. "Only this, sir," he replied. "Of the seventeen I saved, not one of them thanked me."

Do you find that hard to believe? I would, if Luke had not recorded the healing by Jesus of ten men who had leprosy. When only one of them, a Samaritan, returned to say thank you, Jesus exclaimed, "Were not all ten cleansed? Where are the other nine? Was no one found to return and give praise to God except this foreigner?" (Luke 17.17, 18).

Without gratitude for what God has done there is no foundation for true worship, no lasting contentment and little appreciation of the worth of others. Thanksgiving is the oxygen of any lasting relationship.

There is no hint here that Paul is engaging in empty flattery or devious manipulation. He is genuinely, heart-warmingly open in his thanks to God for a group of believers whom he has never met. Perhaps their pastor, Epaphras, brother Timothy and Paul prayed together each day for the little church at Colosse.

As you read Romans 1.18-32, notice especially verse 21 and what happens when folk refuse to surrender themselves and say thank you to God for what He has done. It's rather like going down several flights of stairs to an ever-deepening darkness of ignorance, idolatry, impurity and ghastly depravity. A lack of thanksgiving leads to an ever diminishing level of contentment, which in turn leads to ever increasing lust for forbidden fruit.

If that is true, meditate on this. Where will gratitude lead you?

Quote "Little boy to the stars: 'Gosh! If heaven is that beautiful on the bottom, just think what it's like on the other side'" – source unknown.

Promise "Call upon me in the day of trouble; I will deliver you" (Psalm 50.15).

DAY 7 The father of our Lord Jesus Christ (1.3b)

Good Morning, Disciple,

How do you view God? Some think of Him as a cosmic force; an energy for good; not a Him at all, but an impersonal it. Simpler folk and children picture Him as a wise old man with a flowing white beard. Avant-garde modernists will say facetiously, "She's black." To animists and contemporary pagans He is in everything. To the Hindu of India He is not one but many. The Muslim wakens each morning to the chant, *Laa ilaaha illa Ilaah*, "There is no God but Allah". Your view of God determines not only your theology but every area of your life.

Bilquis Sheikh, a high-born Pakistani Muslim, demonstrates this in her fascinating autobiography *I Dared to Call Him Father*. She became disillusioned by the murder of Muslims who had converted to Christianity – murders sanctified by the Koran and carried out by members of the victims' own families.

She tells of her secret acquisition of a Bible, which she wanted to compare with the Koran. Matters came to a head when a Christian doctor encouraged her to pray directly to God for answers to her confusion. "Talk to Him as if He were your father," she counselled.

"Talk to God as if He were my father!" writes Bilquis. "The thought shook my soul in the peculiar way truth has of being at once startling and comforting."

The next night, with the Koran in one hand and the Bible in the other, she prayed, "I'm confused, Father. I have to get one thing straight right away . . . Which is your book?"

"In which one do you meet me as Father?" came the answer.

Several days later, knowing that her new faith in God as Father and in His Son as Lord might cost her life, Bilquis Sheikh became a Christian.

Though the focus of attention in Colossians is on Christ, it is always in the context of God's love and grace at work through Him. Jesus uniquely has the right to say "My Father" (Matthew 26.39), because He alone could say, "I and the Father are one" (John 19.30). Yet it is Jesus who introduces Him as "Our Father" (Matthew 6.9), because we have become God's adopted children. "You received the Spirit of sonship. And by Him we cry, Abba, Father. The Spirit himself testifies with our spirit that we are God's children" (Romans 8.15, 16).

As you meditate on Ephesians 1.1-14, jot down some of the gifts God the Father has given to you. How do you view Him now?

Quote "Our Lord Jesus Christ is the exclusive way to the Father. By His cross alone a man enters into the adoption of a son of God" – Oswald Chambers, *Christian Discipline*, Vol.1 (Christian Literature Crusade, 1936).

Promise "If anyone loves me, he will obey my teaching. My Father will love him, and we will come to him and make our home with him" (John 14.23).

DAY 8 When we pray for you (1.3c)

Good Morning, Disciple,

I wonder who is praying for you? I generally find that whenever a person comes to know Christ as Saviour someone, somewhere, has been praying: loving parents and most especially grandparents, a believing husband or wife or just a very good friend. Whenever we pray for somebody we are making a gift to that person via heaven.

In his book *Perestroika* Mikhail Gorbachev suddenly springs to life when he quotes from a number of letters sent to him by well-wishers. One, which cheered my heart, came from V. A. Brikovskis who encouraged her leader like this: "Every Sunday I go to church and pray that God refrain from punishing the world for our sins. I know you are an atheist, but through your efforts you have shown that some believers have something to learn from you. I want you to know that every Sunday I am in church from nine a.m. to one p.m. praying for you and your family.''

More letters like that to world leaders might have greater impact than the whingeing criticism they usually hear from the media and the public. Even the unbeliever, in my experience, is most appreciative when he knows someone is praying for him.

Once some Christian students at Southampton University went from room to room in the halls of residence, telling each student, ''We are going to have a special prayer meeting on Sunday to pray for members of the student body. Is there anything we can pray about for you?''

Two weeks later the Christians returned to the halls, this time to ask, ''Has the prayer we prayed for you been answered?'' This led to many interesting conversations. One self-professed agnostic was so impressed that anyone could be so genuinely caring that he asked them to stay and explain the Bible to him. That night Ian became a Christian.

We would not have been surprised if Paul had said, ''Look here, chums, I'm in a bit of a fix. Pray that I'll be released from prison.'' But no, that is not his first thought. In spite of his imprisonment Paul and his companions pray for the Colossians, rising above their own trials to pray for others.

As you read what Jesus says about prayer in Matthew 6.5-15, draw up a list of people known to you and pray for them.

Quote ''Prayer, like everything else in the Christian life, is for God's glory and for our benefit, in that order'' – R. C. Sproul, *Effective Prayer* (Tyndale House Publishers, 1984).

Promise ''Ask and it will be given to you; seek and you will find; knock and the door will be opened to you'' (Matthew 7.7).

DAY 9 Because we have heard of your faith in Christ Jesus (1.4a)

Good Morning, Disciple,

Have you ever heard anyone say, ''All you need is faith''? It doesn't matter what you have faith in, goes their argument, so long as you have faith in something. They may believe in the signs of the Zodiac, tarot cards, a rabbit's foot or some other lucky charm. "All roads lead to heaven." Do they?

Fifteen years ago I visited my foster father in hospital after he had suffered a heart attack. As I sat by his bed sharing some Scriptures with him he said to me, "That's what I like about you, Victor, you are such a man of faith. We are both men of faith, aren't we?"

You old rascal, I thought to myself, knowing full well that he was not a Christian. "What do you mean?" I quizzed.

"Well," says he, "you believe in God and I believe in my stone." He went on to tell me how, during the Second World War as a "desert rat" in North Africa, he had been given a week's leave in Jerusalem, where he picked up a stone which he kept as a sort of lucky charm.

"Where's your stone now?" I asked him.

"At home," he replied, looking up to the ceiling.

"No, that's not what I mean," I said. "Where is it now that you need it? What is it doing for you now?"

Pop took my point and later surrendered his life to Christ and put his faith in an object worthy of faith.

Does it work? That is the real test.

Millions in every generation and wherever the message of the gospel has been preached have transferred their trust from unworthy objects and from their own feeble efforts at doing good works, to trusting Christ alone for their salvation.

It is not so much that all roads and all faiths lead to heaven as that many come by different roads and a variety of faiths to the one way – Christ. Your faith in Him is thoroughly reliable and completely trustworthy. He said, "I am the way and the truth and the life. No one comes to the Father except through me" (John 14.6).

Meditate this morning on Philippians 3.4-21 and see how Paul transferred his trust to Christ alone.

Quote Christ is the master of my fate,
             Christ is the captain of my soul.

– Dorothea Day,
The Best Loved Poems of the American People, selected by Hazel
Felleman (Garden City, 1936).

Promise "For my Father's will is that everyone who looks to the Son and believes in him shall have eternal life, and I will raise him up at the last day" (John 6.40).

DAY 10   And of the love you have for all the saints (1.4b)

Good Morning, Disciple,

I wonder if you are having a good experience of fellowship with other believers? I do hope so. We all need to belong to a group, whether it is in a house church, a chapel or a more traditional church, where we can be accepted for what we are and in spite of what we are not. The key to true fellowship is the give and take of Christ-centred love.

I heard a lovely little parable when I was in Norway. Once, long ago, a stranger approached a wise old sage at the gateway to a city. "What kind of people live here?" he asked.

The old man replied with a question of his own. "What kind of people lived in the city whence you came?"

The traveller coloured with anger as he began blurting out his feelings. "Oh, them," he exploded, "they were just a bunch of hypocrites and mischief makers, the like of which you could never trust."

"Ah!" said the wise man knowingly, "I think you may well find that this town, too, is full of such residents and you'll never be happy here."

As the traveller resumed his journey another stranger approached and asked the same question. He received the same searching reply, "What kind of people lived in the city whence you came?"

The second traveller smiled as he recounted story after story of generosity, warm-hearted love and openness. The old man at the gate responded, "I think you may well find that this town is also full of such residents and you'll always be happy here." Both entered the city together.

Listen to how Aristides spoke about the second century Christians when he wrote to the Emperor Hadrian: "They love one another. They never fail to help widows: they save orphans from those who would hurt them. If they have something, they give freely to the man who has nothing; if they see a stranger they take him home, and are happy as though he were a real brother. They do not consider themselves brothers in the usual sense, but brothers instead through the Spirit of God."

Wherever true faith in Christ exists, love is the natural consequence, for love is the daughter of faith. See how this worked out as you read Acts 2.41-47, and take time to think through the implications for your own life.

Quote "Love apart from this oneness of faith is a fictitious bond . . . Nor is love stronger than the faith from which it emanates" – R. C. H. Lenski, *The Interpretation of St. Paul's Epistles* (Augsburg Publishing House, 1946).

Promise "All men will know that you are my disciples, if you love one another" (John 13.35).

DAY 11 The faith and love that spring from the hope (1.5a)

Good Morning, Disciple,

As you become more familiar with the Scriptures you will be fascinated by some of their recurring themes. Here's one – faith, hope and love. This trio is often to be found together, just like flowers which share the same season.

Perhaps the best known occasion is in Paul's famous chapter on the theme of love which ends, "Now these three remain: faith, hope and love. But the greatest of these is love" (1 Corinthians 13.13).

The greatest of these is love? How can this be if, as today's verse says, the faith and love spring from the hope?

In Jesus' parable about a sower whose seed fell on various kinds of soil, He states that the seed was the "word of God". Notice that while the places in which the seed fell differed, the seed never changed. It always had the same potential within it to bear a harvest.

Picture a seed being planted. What's the first thing that happens when it has germinated? It sends down roots. The same is true when a person reads the Bible. God's Spirit breathes upon the word and it creates in the heart of the reader hope – the hope of eternal life. Imagine the hope as roots reaching into every part of your life.

Hope without substance is mere wishful thinking. It is like a seed falling on the path or on shallow topsoil over rock where there is no place for the roots to take a hold. The plant withers and dies before it has a chance to grow. Seed which falls into good soil grows, with roots below the surface as well as a plant for all to see. This is like the person who receives God's Word of hope and puts his trust and confidence in Jesus Christ. The plant which grows up is like his faith – the life of faith.

If hope is the root and faith is the plant, love is the blossom, the fruit. The full flower of all true Christianity is love which demonstrates itself in what we do toward God and for one another.

So while love and faith spring from the hope, the greatest of the three is love, because love is what lasts for ever.

In today's longer reading, John 11.1-44, see if you can pick out the operation of faith, hope and love.

Quote "Take from a man his wealth and you hinder him; take from him his purpose and you slow him down. But take from a man his hope, and you stop him" – Neil C. Strait.

Promise "He who has the Son has life" (1 John 5.12).

DAY 12   That is stored up for you in heaven (1.5b)

Good Morning, Disciple,

Some months ago as I shared the gospel with a small group of army apprentices I mentioned the promise of eternal life. "Of course, none of you have given much thought to dying yet," I quipped in deference to their youth.

"Don't you believe it, sir," answered one of the lads. "When we are on guard duty in the wee hours of the morning and remember what has happened with recent IRA bombings and shootings, we all give some thought to dying."

His remarks spurred me on to an even greater boldness than usual, as I showed them from the Scripture how they could know about eternal life. "God has given us eternal life, and this life is in His son," I told them. "He who has the Son has life; he who does not have the Son of God does not have life" (1 John 5.11-12).

Such a hope is not mere wishful thinking or whistling in the dark.

It is the root of all Christian faith and love which conditions our behaviour in the light of eternity. "It teaches us to say 'No' to ungodliness and worldly passions, and to live self-controlled, upright and godly lives in this present age, while we wait for the blessed hope – the glorious appearing of our great God and Saviour Jesus Christ" (Titus 2.12-13).

This was brought home to me when Sue and I and our two daughters visited a dear friend of ours, Wilson Revill, then in his eighties, just before he died. He whispered "Susan . . . Victor . . . I am on my way to heaven. Soon I shall see Jesus."

Later with barely audible voice he called both girls to his side. They will never forget his words to them: "Trust in the Lord with all your heart – not a part of it, all of it. In all your ways acknowledge Him – not just in some of them, all of them, and He will direct your paths. When Satan strikes, and he will," he continued, his voice getting ever stronger, "call on the name of the Lord Jesus and say, 'Save me, Lord Jesus' and He will save you, as He has saved me many times."

Little over an hour later Wilson Revill's hope was realised. He died as he had lived. Nothing could destroy his hope, because nothing on earth could touch it. It was not here to touch. It was kept secure in heaven.

Meditate on that theme in 1 Peter 1.1-25 and thank God for this hope – secure in heaven.

Quote "Other men see only a hopeless end, but the Christian rejoices in endless hope" – Gilbert Beenken.

Promise "He who believes has everlasting life" (John 6.47).

DAY 13   That you have already heard about in the word of truth (1.5c)

Good Morning, Disciple,

Visiting his friend, a music teacher, a man once asked, "So what's the good news today?"

The musician struck a tuning fork. As the note hummed through the room he said, "That, my dear friend, is an A. It is an A today, it was an A 5,000 years ago, it will be an A 10,000 years on. The

soprano upstairs sings off key and the piano downstairs is out of tune.''
He struck the note again. "But that, my friend, is an A and that is
the good news for today.''

For Paul, the gospel was God's tuning fork. Everything must be
tested against it. The false teachers, whose heresies we shall meet in
chapter two, speculated about other ways to reach God. Not content
to believe Christ's own assertion that He was the way, the truth and
the life (John 14.6), they allowed their fertile imaginations to wander
into the mists of superstition and invented lie upon lie, error upon
error. Well did Montaigne say: "The reverse of truth has a hundred
thousand faces and an infinite field.''

Nietzsche argued from his distorted viewpoint: "There is only one
world, and that world is false, cruel, contradictory, misleading,
senseless . . . We need lies in order to live . . . Lying is a necessity
of life itself.''

In so far as the world is a reflection of Satan's dark influence,
Nietzsche was right, for Jesus said of that arch-deceiver, "There is
no truth in him'' (John 8.44). In a world ruled by Satan, truth is
what each one perceives it to be. Hence the confusion. Well has it
been said by Sissela Bok, "A society whose members are unable to
distinguish truthful messages from deceptive ones would collapse.''

And a church persuaded by heretics to depart from the true gospel
would also be vulnerable to collapse. Only the word of truth could
unmask these teachers of falsehood and expose the destructive nature
of their errors. So Paul endorses the gospel preached by Epaphras,
not simply as true, but as "the word of truth''.

God has spoken by His prophets but uniquely in His Son, who said,
"For this reason I was born . . . to testify to the truth. Everyone on
the side of truth listens to me'' (John 18.37).

Keep these things in mind as you meditate on 1 Timothy 3.

Quote "When regard for the truth has been broken down, or
even slightly weakened, all things will remain doubtful'' – St
Augustine.

Promise "My word . . . will not return to me empty, but will
accomplish what I desire and achieve the purpose for which I
sent it'' (Isaiah 55.11).

DAY 14 The gospel that has come to you (1.5d-6a)

Good Morning, Disciple,

Are you still in touch with the person who told you the good news about Jesus which, in our shorthand, we call the gospel? I do hope you have found an opportunity to thank not only God but also that person. We all need encouragement to keep on witnessing especially when there are so many who hear but don't hear, who understand but don't believe.

It always saddens me when someone decides not to accept the gospel. As Paul says, "The god of this age has blinded the minds of unbelievers, so that they cannot see the light of the gospel of the glory of Christ" (2 Corinthians 4.4).

One such celebrated atheist was the late Bertrand Russell. In 1918 he wrote to Lady Otteline Morrell these somewhat pathetic lines: "One is a ghost, floating through the world without any real contact. Even when one feels nearest to other people, something in one seems to obstinately belong to God, and to refuse to enter into any earthly communion – at least that is how I would express it if I thought there was a God. It is odd, isn't it? I care passionately for this world and many things and people in it, and yet – what is it all? There must be something more important, one feels, though I don't believe there is."

The gospel had come to Russell, but he had not come to the gospel. How desperately sad.

The other side of the coin, however, is thrilling. I have talked personally to thousands of individuals and preached to hundreds of thousands worldwide, and found that wherever the gospel is proclaimed clearly there are always some who are ready to receive it. That is what makes it so worthwhile.

I hope that before we reach the end of this six months studying Colossians together, you too will join the band of witnesses, able and willing to share your faith with others. Later on, in chapter four, we shall look at one way of doing this, using a simple Hope, Faith, Love acrostic. There is no surer evidence that you have appreciated the love and grace of God into your own life, than when you are inwardly motivated to tell someone else about it.

You will enjoy reading Acts 8 this morning. See how many

lessons you can learn from Philip the evangelist about sharing your faith.

Quote "Communicating the faith was not (in the first century) regarded as the preserve of the very zealous or the officially designated evangelist. Evangelism was the prerogative and duty of every church member" – Michael Green, *Evangelism in the Early Church* (Hodder & Stoughton, 1970).

Promise "Love never fails" (1 Corinthians 13.8).

DAY 15 All over the world the gospel is producing fruit and growing (1.6b)

Good Morning, Disciple,

As the scholar John Selden lay dying in 1654, he said to Archbishop Ussher, "I have surveyed most of the learning that is among the sons of men, and my study is filled with books and manuscripts (8,000 volumes) on various subjects. But at present, I cannot recollect any passage out of all my books and papers whereon I can rest my soul, save this from the sacred Scriptures: 'The grace of God that bringeth salvation hath appeared to all men'" (Titus 2.11).

Paul may have exaggerated when he asserted that "all over the world" the gospel was producing fruit and growing. But his claim has since come true. The gospel has been passed on to every generation, unlimited by class, education or wealth, and reached every part of the world. "I, if I am lifted up," promised Jesus, "will draw all men to myself" (John 12.32). All kinds and conditions of humanity have, like John Selden, rested their souls on this sure foundation.

No doubt Paul's bold statement was intended as a challenge to the elitist philosophies of the false teachers whom we shall meet in chapter two. They, like so many heretics after them, proposed other ways to God than through Jesus. But asceticism, good works, rites and rituals not only detract from the completed work of Christ, they limit salvation to those who can achieve their self-imposed standards. Such heresies distort and destroy believers' faith rather than producing fruit and growth, as the gospel does.

Fruitfulness and growth, however, are not measured by numbers.

Jesus told us that the gospel would never be accepted by everyone: "Wide is the gate and broad is the road that leads to destruction, and many enter through it. But small is the gate and narrow the road that leads to life, and only a few find it" (Matthew 7.13-14).

The productivity the apostle has in mind here is certainly the thirty, sixty and hundredfold multiplication the Lord forecast in His parable of the sower (Mark 4.20), but it is more than that. Surely it is also the harvest of lives changed for the better and preserved as the "fruit of righteousness" for "the day of Christ" (Philippians 1.10-11). It is those millions upon millions who in every age have borne the fruit of the Spirit (Galatians 5.22).

You will enjoy reading Acts 14. It is absolutely full of growth. I pray that you too will grow.

Quote "God's focus goes far beyond the minority who can make an intelligent verdict for or against Christ. He is targeted on earth's majority who have too little information to reach any verdict" – David Bryant, *In the Gap* (Regal Books, 1979).

Promise "Peacemakers who sow in peace raise a harvest of righteousness" (James 3.18).

DAY 16 Just as it has been doing among you since the day you heard it and understood God's grace in all its truth (1.6c)

Good Morning, Disciple,

As I share the gospel with folk I often tell them there are four steps in coming to Christ: to hear, understand, believe and surrender. Of course, what you hear and understand will determine what you believe and surrender to. Therefore it is vitally important to speak the gospel of grace and truth clearly.

"God's grace" is the unchangeable message. The undeserved love of God, demonstrated to us in Christ upon the cross as He took upon Himself the guilt and the punishment for our sin, is the only gospel. It is the "word of truth" which came to the Colossians and continues to spread worldwide.

I am reminded of the apostle's words: "You heard of him and were taught by him in accordance with the truth that is in Jesus" (Ephesians

4.21). John put it like this: "The Law was given through Moses; grace and truth came through Jesus Christ" (John 1.17).

Paul asks the question, "How can they believe in the one of whom they have not heard?" (Romans 10.14). The answer is plain – they cannot. But hearing alone is not enough! Jesus Himself said, "When anyone hears the message about the kingdom and does not understand it, the evil one comes and snatches away what was sown in his heart" (Matthew 13.19).

So we have a double obligation. First, our task is to tell the people of the world, who are "darkened in their understanding and separated from the life of God because of the ignorance that is in them" (Ephesians 4.18).

Secondly, we must do so in a way they can understand, without embellishing or obscuring God's grace. We are to speak "not in words taught us by human wisdom but in words taught by the Spirit, expressing spiritual truths in spiritual words" (1 Corinthians 2.13).

Our task can be achieved only in partnership with the Holy Spirit. "The man without the Spirit does not accept the things that come from the Spirit of God, for they are foolishness to him, and he cannot understand them, because they are spiritually discerned" (1 Corinthians 2.14). But when God's Spirit breathes upon anyone, he or she is able to respond to the words by understanding the message of grace and truth, believing in Christ and surrendering in love and obedience to Him.

As you read the story of Thomas in John 20.19-31, meditate especially on verse 29.

Quote "The gospel is neither a discussion nor a debate. It is an announcement" – Paul Rees.

Promise "Blessed . . . are those who hear the word of God and obey it" (Luke 11.28).

DAY 17 You learned it from Epaphras (1.7a)

Good Morning, Disciple,

Have you ever wondered what it would be like to get up in the morning and read your own obituary in the newspaper? A reporter in a British daily once expressed his delight that Sir Cyril Black, who had succeeded in getting the book *Last Exit to Brooklyn* banned, was no longer alive to challenge the release of the film of the book. It was Sir Cyril himself who showed me the article!

Back in the late 1800s a rich Swedish tycoon woke up to find he was dead. Well, not literally. The newspapers had confused him with his brother. In their headlines they called him the Dynamite King, for he had discovered blasting gelatin and invented detonators for explosives.

As he read, the premature obituaries had a profound effect upon him. Was he really to go down in history as the inventor of destructive devices? Was it too late to change? He decided not! From then on he put his wealth into a trust fund for the advancement of science, literature, medicine and world peace. To this day annual awards are given for service to humanity in these important fields. Few people today know of Alfred Nobel the Dynamite King, but all over the world the Nobel prizes are better known than most of the people who have won them.

Of the thousands who heard Paul preach the gospel in the city of Ephesus, some believed, but many more preferred to live with their obituaries already written – dead in sin and unbelief. Not so Epaphras! Whatever he was before that day, he would never be the same again. He would probably have remained in total obscurity but for three things: his conversion to Christ; his discipleship under Paul; and the ministry which he so effectively conducted at Colosse.

He was not only a remarkable evangelist and church planter in a place where other religions, superstitions and philosophies alien to Christianity held sway; that would have been enough. He went on to be the pastor/teacher of the Colossian flock. He knew that unless the preached word went beyond mere proclamation and persuasion, it would soon be suffocated by other teaching and by heretical doctrines. Emotion, feelings and ecstatic experience, however valid, were no substitute for learning the truth precept by precept.

The Scriptures give many warnings about false teachers. One of these you will find this morning in 2 John 1.1-13. Heed especially verses 8-9 and stay true to the teaching you are receiving from His Word.

Quote "The mediocre teacher tells. The good teacher explains.

The superior teacher demonstrates. The great teacher inspires'' –
William A. Ward.

Promise "Instruct a wise man and he will be wiser still"
(Proverbs 9.9).

DAY 18 Our dear fellow-servant, who is a faithful minister of Christ on our behalf (1.7b)

Good Morning, Disciple,

Are you ambitious? I imagine neither slave, nor servant, nor prisoner come very high on your list of aspirations. Yet these very terms are the words of endearment and commendation given to Pastor Epaphras, the founding father of the three churches at Colosse, Hierapolis and Laodicea.

In Philemon 23 Paul refers to him as his "fellow-prisoner". We cannot be sure whether the apostle is referring to an actual imprisonment at Ephesus or Rome, or if he means that Epaphras is so close to him as a daily visitor that it is virtually a self-imposed imprisonment. Whatever the case, these words are his medals of office.

Paul's reference to him as a "fellow-servant" and later as a "servant of Christ Jesus" (4.12) should be translated from the Greek *doulos* as "fellow-slave" or "slave of Christ". It is recognition that the one called by God to a specific task is owned by the one who called him. Hence, Abraham (Psalm 105.42), Moses (Psalm 105.26), David (Psalm 89.3) and Paul (Romans 1.1) are all called servants as a title of the highest honour.

The standards of the world are turned upside down when Paul uses yet another term for service, *diakonos*. The Greek word is, of course, close to our English word deacon, one who serves. But here it is rightly translated as minister. It is a useful reminder that the dignity of office in the kingdom is measured in acts of service.

Epaphras had earned the title "faithful minister" because he had not only preached the gospel by which folk could come to faith, but had also taught it, implying a systematic instruction into the doctrines of the gospel. Such knowledge is the only effective antidote to the onslaught of false doctrine such as invaded the Colossian church.

Discipleship was the most important principle Jesus established for the spontaneous expansion of His Church. He commissioned us to "Go and make disciples of all nations . . . teaching them to obey everything I have commanded you" (Matthew 28.19-20).

The faithful minister, by whatever name he is called, must "hold firmly to the trustworthy message as it has been taught, so that he can encourage others by sound doctrine and refute those who oppose it" (Titus 1.9).

In 1 Timothy 3.10-4.8, see how Timothy, the co-author of the Colossian letter, was charged by Paul to hold on to and teach the truth. Meditate especially on verse 16.

Quote "Christianity is not just a series of truths but truth – truth about all of reality" – Francis Schaeffer, *A Christian Manifesto* (Crossway Books, 1981).

Promise "Everything is possible for him who believes" (Mark 9.23).

DAY 19   And who also told us of your love in the spirit (1.8)

Good Morning, Disciple,

Sadly what people hear about the Church is often those petty squabbles which we all know can, and do, happen in the best of families. What an impact it would make on the world if believers were to gossip enthusiastically about all the good and heart-warming things which go on week by week in their churches: acts of generosity and spontaneous kindness; words of encouragement and sympathy; battles won over our fears and prejudices and the sweet spirit of forgiveness reconciling broken relationships. If half these stories were broadcast outside the Church the world would beat a path to our door.

I once worked with a youth club called T.U.F.F. (Teens United For Fellowship), and some of the lads were pretty tough. On one occasion when two boys were brawling, I waded in to separate them. Another youth shouted, "You can't stop them, Mr Vic, they're brothers." The London street code was that families should be left to get on with their private fights without outsiders interfering.

Now don't get me wrong, I would not advocate Christians fighting it out in the church family. On the contrary, because we have fellowship "with the Spirit" (Philippians 2.1), we can be "one in the Spirit" (Philippians 2.2), overcoming our problems without tittle-tattling to outsiders. If they must hear about our divisions it should always be in the context of healing, because "God has poured out his love into our hearts by the Holy Spirit" (Romans 5.5). "A Spirit of power, of love and self-discipline" (2 Timothy 1.7) enables us to fulfil Christ's command that we should "Love one another" (John 13.34).

The unity of God the Father with the Son and the Holy Spirit is always at work on our behalf. Notice, for instance, how Paul has focused first on God the Father (vs. 2-3), then on God the Son (vs. 3, 4 and 7), and now upon the Holy Spirit (v. 8).

John warns the fractious and divisive among us of God's perspective: "Whoever does not love does not know God, because God is love" (1 John 4.8). Love is the very first ingredient in Paul's list of the fruit of the Spirit (Galatians 5.22), just as it is the highest of all God's commands (Mark 12.28-31).

As you read 1 John 4, see if you can pick out the work of Father, Son and Spirit working in love for us.

Quote "Where the Spirit is, love must be" – Frederick Brook Westcott, *A Letter to Asia* (Klock & Klock, 1981 reprint).

Promise "Love covers over a multitude of sins" (1 Peter 4.8).

DAY 20 **For this reason, since the day we heard about you, we have not stopped praying for you (1.9a)**

Good Morning, Disciple,

On Cup Final day every true Brit is a soccer fan, but in 1988 the whole nation held its breath as underdogs, Wimbledon, beat the mighty giants, Liverpool, 1-0. The game could have gone the other way when the referee allowed a dubious penalty against Wimbledon. Never before in the history of the F.A. Cup had any penalty shot been saved.

As Aldridge blasted the ball toward the lower left-hand corner of the goal mouth, Dave Beasant, Wimbledon's goalkeeper, threw himself in the path of the ball as if he knew by premonition where the penalty would land.

After the euphoric victory the goalkeeper was asked at what point he knew the ball would be kicked to his left. "Last Christmas," he laughed, "well, not quite. But before the match anyway." He then revealed his secret. He had studied Aldridge on video and computed that the Liverpool kicker would most likely choose the left-hand corner. Gambling? No, strategy!

The apostle Paul was also a strategist. He knew from years of experience as an evangelist that Satan always goes for young blood. The embryonic church at Colosse was vulnerable to the attack of heretics, but he knew that the ultimate weapon is prayer. Knowledge of Satan's strategy was enough to convince Paul and his prison companions to pray, pray and keep on praying. Victory would depend on it.

Years ago I constructed a sentence to help me in my own praying: Thank you for giving yourself and others to me.

Thank you to God for His gifts – contentment grows only in proportion to the level of gratitude. *Forgiving* – here I confess my sins and forgive those who sin against me. *Yourself* – here I focus on the greatness and wonder of the Lord, and listen to Him. *And others* – I divide this part of my praying like this: Monday for missionaries; Tuesday for teenagers; Wednesday for world leaders; Thursday for the Third World; Friday for the larger family; Saturday for "saints and sinners" and Sundays for the services of the day. *To me* – my personal needs and aspirations.

Try it for yourself today. As you do, read the Shepherd Psalm 23 – it will restore your soul.

Quote "Anything large enough for a wish to light upon is large enough to hang a prayer upon: the thought of Him to whom that prayer goes will purify and correct the desire" – George MacDonald in C. S. Lewis, *George MacDonald, An Anthology* (Fount Paperbacks, 1948).

Promise "If you believe, you will receive whatever you ask for in prayer" (Matthew 21.22).

DAY 21 Asking God to fill you with the knowledge of his will (1.9b)

Good Morning, Disciple,

What better prayer could be prayed than this, that today you may be filled with the knowledge of God's will?

You may be sure that what fills your life will control your actions. A person filled with anger is as much controlled by it, as the alcoholic is controlled by drink. The mind filled with thoughts of sin will soon act them out. As Paul so eloquently reminds us, "The mind of sinful man is death, but the mind controlled by the Spirit is life and peace; the sinful mind is hostile to God. It does not submit to God's law, nor can it do so" (Romans 8.6-7).

The gnostics, whose name is derived from the Greek *gnosis* meaning "knowledge", believed they could manipulate the spirit world, and even God Himself, by the use of special knowledge. These heretics were apparently trying to persuade the young Christians at Colosse of other paths to fulness and knowledge, outside of Christ. Hence Paul's strong emphasis in this letter on fulness and knowledge, and this prayer that they be filled with the knowledge of God's will.

The highest ambition for the believer is to know and to do God's will. It may be known by reading His word in an attitude of openness to His Holy Spirit. Paul urges his readers in Romans 12.1-2: "Offer your bodies as living sacrifices, holy and pleasing to God – this is your spiritual act of worship. Do not conform any longer to the pattern of this world, but be transformed by the renewing of your mind. Then you will be able to test and approve what God's will is – his good, pleasing and perfect will."

In 1838 when a young missionary candidate preached his very first sermon while on probation, he managed only one sentence: "Friends, I have forgotten all I had to say." It was suggested that the young man had evidently missed his calling and mistaken God's will for his life.

Many years later that same young man, after trekking 29,000 uncharted miles and preaching to many thousands of African villagers, was found one morning on his knees in an attitude of prayer – dead. Well has it been said of David Livingstone that "nothing fitted his life so well as his departure of it".

At his mill-house home, now a museum in Blantyre, Scotland, you can see the wax seal he used on his last letter. Inscribed into it are the words "Christ in me the livingstone". There's the secret!

Read about your ministry in 2 Corinthians 4.1-18.

Quote "I shall place no value on any possession or on anything I do except in its relation to the kingdom of Christ" – David Livingstone.

Promise "All who follow his precepts have good understanding" (Psalm 111.10).

DAY 22 Through all spiritual wisdom and understanding (1.9c)

Good Morning, Disciple,

Have you ever wondered how you can know God's plan for your life? It's a question most Christians ask at some time. The short answer is given here in Paul's prayer – through all spiritual wisdom and understanding.

Knowledge, wisdom and understanding are, according to Aristotle, the three essentials of intellect. Knowledge is the practical know-how, wisdom is the grasp of general principles, and understanding is the critical faculty by which one may discern what is right or wrong in particular circumstances.

But the possession of all three is no guarantee of *spiritual* insight. In one of his own prayers to the Father, Jesus said, "You have hidden these things from the wise and learned, and revealed them to little children" (Matthew 11.25). Elsewhere, "I will destroy the wisdom of the wise; the intelligence of the intelligent I will frustrate" (1 Corinthians 1.19).

The key to knowing God's will is spiritual wisdom and spiritual understanding. "No one knows the thoughts of God except the Spirit of God" (1 Corinthians 2.11), says Paul. "We have not received the spirit of the world but the Spirit who is from God, that we may understand what God has freely given us. This is what we speak, not in words taught us by human wisdom but in words taught by the Spirit" (see 1 Corinthians 2.11-14).

Christopher Columbus said, "It was the Lord who put into my mind (I could feel his hand upon me) the fact that it would be possible to sail from here (Spain) to the Indies. All who heard about my project rejected it with laughter, ridiculing me. There is no question that the inspiration was from the Holy Spirit, the Holy Scriptures . . . For the execution of the journey to the Indies, I did not make use of intelligence, mathematics or maps. It is simply the fulfilment of what Isaiah prophesied."

Columbus made use of the Scriptures, which not only make one "wise for salvation" (2 Timothy 3.15), but wise in all the ways of God.

By reading the Scripture, by listening in prayer, by studying the circumstances and submitting to the Body, the Church, in dependence upon the Holy Spirit, we may all discern God's plan and purpose.

As you read Romans 12 this morning ask the Lord to baptise your intellect with His Holy Spirit so that you may know His will for your life.

Quote "God is not concerned with satisfying our speculative curiosity but with building his kingdom through making his will known" – Charles A. Trentham, *The Shepherd and the Stars* (Broadman Press).

Promise "If any of you lacks wisdom, he should ask God, who gives generously to all without finding fault, and it will be given to him" (James 1.5).

DAY 23 And we pray this in order that you may live a life worthy of the Lord and may please him in every way (1.10a)

Good Morning, Disciple,

The poet Samuel Taylor Coleridge was highly gifted but never used his skills to the full. He abandoned his course at Cambridge for an army career but was discharged soon after joining for refusing to groom his horse. After resuming his studies at Oxford, he left yet again before completing his degree, this time to establish a newspaper which lasted all of ten issues. His mind was full of books which never reached manuscript form. We shall never know what masterpieces were denied to the English language because of his lack of discipline.

It is one thing to have a gift, quite another to develop it for the pleasure of others. And this is equally true in the art of living. The Christian who has received spiritual wisdom and understanding to know God's will must translate that learning into living practice in order to give pleasure to His Lord. "Those controlled by the sinful nature cannot please God" (Romans 8.8), but we who are in Christ, "controlled by His Spirit", are urged to live a life worthy of our calling (Ephesians 4.1).

Dr Billy K. Simbo, principal of the Sierra Leone Bible College, once gave this devastating analysis of Western Christianity as viewed from an African context. "Western theology emphasises the intellectual and theoretical. People who accept a set of beliefs are called Christians, even though, in actual practice, these beliefs have no effect on their lifestyles. Secular culture shapes their lives and values. Third World people have often wondered where the theology and Christian principles of their Western brethren were when they needed answers to burning issues such as slavery, racism, apartheid, economic and social exploitation and oppression."

This may be an over-generalisation, but it's challenging, isn't it? We must never confuse human intellect with divine insight or mere comprehension of biblical truth with transformed conduct. We are to become like Enoch, who is said to have "walked with God" (Genesis 5.22), and "pleased God" (Hebrews 11.5). We should be like a child willing, wanting, working to please Daddy, for no other reason than the smile on his face and the sound of his "Well done, son", "Well done, daughter".

Meditate upon this changed lifestyle as you read 2 Peter 1.1-12, and pray that God will give you the power to live it.

Quote "May the outward and the inward man be one" – Socrates.

Promise "If you do these things, you will never fall, and you will receive a rich welcome into the eternal kingdom of our Lord and Saviour Jesus Christ" (2 Peter 1.10-11).

DAY 24   Bearing fruit in every good work (1.10b)

Good Morning, Disciple,

Whether you are growing corn, studying for a degree or manufacturing merchandise, the results are dependent on the amount of work you put in. Harvest demands work. But this is not true of salvation. People often assume that salvation must be a prize for doing good works, and are quite surprised when they hear for the first time that a person becomes a Christian by grace, through faith, as a gift from God, and not as a result of human effort or works (Ephesians 2.8-9). We cannot earn our way to heaven.

But the truth does not end there. That statement in Ephesians is followed by this one: "We are God's workmanship, created in Christ Jesus to do good works, which God prepared in advance for us to do" (Ephesians 2.10). We are not saved *by* good works, but we are saved *to do* good works, because this, too, is part of God's plan for our lives. If He has prepared them in advance for us to do, we must first discover what they are, then do them.

Some are clearly stated in Scripture as God's plan for every believer. We are all to love our neighbours, feed the hungry, obey the law of the land, maintain marital fidelity, speak the truth and tell others about Christ. Only when we are bearing fruit in these good works are we likely to discover His particular plan for our lives.

Good works, therefore, are not merely an optional extra to salvation, they are the very essence of new life in Christ. The law of the harvest comes back into operation. There is no harvest without cultivation. The applause dancing on the ears of a musician at the end of a spectacular performance is the prize for much practice far away from the public eye. Any great enterprise demands hard work before a satisfactory conclusion is reached. No less so for those whose end is to glorify God. A life of good works will bear a fruitful harvest giving pleasure to both God and man. "This is to my Father's glory," said Jesus, "that you bear much fruit, showing yourselves to be my disciples" (John 15.8).

Compare the two fruits in Matthew 7.15-29 and pray again for insight into God's plan for your life, and in particular, His plan for today.

Quote "Until we recognise that life is not just something to be enjoyed but rather is a task that each of us is assigned, we'll never find meaning in our lives and we'll never be truly happy" – Victor Frankl.

Promise "He rewards those who earnestly seek him" (Hebrews 11.6).

DAY 25 Growing in the knowledge of God 1.10c

Good Morning, Disciple,

If you cut down an apple tree, as we had to recently, you are able to tell by the number of rings on the stump how many years it has been bearing a crop. Each year the circumference is greater because, in the very process of bearing fruit, it is also growing and can sustain more fruit.

This should be the progress of every believer. Hearing and understanding God's plan of salvation plants a seed of hope. God breathes His Holy Spirit creating new life through belief and surrender. The first ring is formed. The new Christian listens again to God's word, this time to His plan of sanctification, and the same happens. Hearing and understanding give way to belief and action. Result? Fruit! Every time the believer acts upon what is revealed – more fruit, more growth, and best of all, more insight into God's will and God Himself.

Kiri Te Kanawa tells how one day the telephone rang and a request came: "Charlie wants you to sing at his wedding." "Charlie?" she replied. "I don't know a Charlie." It was then disclosed that it was none other than Prince Charles who was asking her to sing at his wedding. The world watched and listened as her beautiful soprano voice filled St Paul's Cathedral. By fulfilling the royal couple's wish, the door was opened to knowing them personally as friends.

My daughter Ruth, a budding soprano herself, had admired Kiri for years. All her pocket-money was spent on collecting Kiri's recordings. She wrote to the BBC's "Jim'll Fix It" programme to ask if she might play her harp to accompany the great opera star, and some two years later her dream came true. In front of the TV cameras Kiri sang as Ruth played. The remote virtuoso had become a warm, friendly, charming human being.

Friendship is one of life's most beautiful commodities, but to be maintained it has to be worked on. By continuous contact we get to know each other's likes and dislikes, and every time we act in a way that brings mutual pleasure, the bond of intimacy is strengthened.

"You are my friends," said the Lord Jesus, "if you do what I command you" (John 15.14). It is not a prince, nor an opera star, but God Himself who invites us to know Him in such a way.

Meditate on His love for you this morning as you read 1 John 5.1-21, and tell Him how much you love Him.

Quote "Zeal without knowledge is rank fanaticism. Knowledge without zeal is a Christian anomaly" – Morgan Patterson, *Professors in the Pulpit* (Broadman, 1963).

Promise "Then the King will say to those on his right, 'Come, you who are blessed by my Father; take your inheritance, the kingdom prepared for you since the creation of the world.'" (Matthew 25.34).

DAY 26 Being strengthened with all power according to his glorious might (1.11a)

Good Morning, Disciple,

When Mount St Helens erupted on 18th May, 1980, an explosion equal to 500 Hiroshima bombs or ten million tons of TNT was unleashed, giving the world an awesome display of volcanic power. It was as if all the fiery energy of the earth's core spewed out in one concentrated orgy of destruction.

But to the God who holds the universe in the palm of His hand, Mount St Helens was a mere fireworks display. At His word, "Be still", raging waves became a millpond (Mark 4.39).

When Paul prays for strength he is not seeking omnipotence. Alas, human history has shown only too vividly how we would use such power. As Lord Acton wrote, "Power tends to corrupt, and absolute power corrupts absolutely."

The apostle no doubt had in mind the confidence-tricksters who had wheedled their way into the Colossian church with promises of instant spiritual victory, not available to the ordinary Christian. For the weak, faltering, failing new believer, the offer of mysterious powers from a hidden source was irresistible.

But, you may say, isn't that precisely what God offers us? Yes! But only in Him. Beware of the counterfeit which invites you to tap into your own inner powers. The path to spiritual power never comes from resurrecting your own ego. That is dead and must remain buried. The only source of spiritual power for the Christian is God Himself. He cannot be ordered or manipulated into releasing His power or sharing it with anyone who simply wants to flex his spiritual muscles for self-glorification or authority over others.

The word used here for power, *kratos*, is only ever used in the New Testament for God's power and is inseparable from His glory. We are strengthened by this power, but the power and the glory still belong to God alone. If we are to live in a way that pleases the Lord, by the standards of the kingdom, we need this strength.

Have you ever had one of those frustrating moments when you think an electric appliance has gone on the blink, only to find later that it was not switched on? Sometimes we believers are like that – "plugged in" to Christ, but not "switched on" to His power. That's the point of this prayer.

Read Psalm 46, meditate especially on the first verse and remember throughout the day – His is the kingdom, the power and the glory.

Quote "God uses people who are weak and feeble enough to lean on Him" – Hudson Taylor.

Promise "I will strengthen you and help you; I will uphold you with my righteous right hand" (Isaiah 41.10).

DAY 27 So that you may have great endurance and patience (1.11b)

Good Morning, Disciple,

Many years ago the editor of a Kansas City provincial newspaper called a young lad from the art department into his office to talk about his prospects as a cartoonist. "You don't have the talent," he counselled. "Why don't you get out of the drawing business and into something where you can succeed?"

The fledgling artist was discouraged, but decided to persevere and improve on his undeveloped talent. It's as well he did or we might never have known the name of the man who went on to found his own great entertainment empire – Walt Disney.

Persistence in the face of discouragement often makes the difference between failure and success, in the area of spiritual advance as much as any other human venture. In a world of twenty-eight-minute programmes and thirty-second commercials, we do well to remember that through perseverance even the snail reached the ark.

The Greek word *hupomone* in this verse is even richer in meaning than the NIV translation "great endurance". It is the resolution to keep on keeping on, overcoming whatever obstacles are in the way, in order to reach the prize at the end of the struggle. Like an Olympic athlete who, through all the rigours of a gruelling training schedule, has his eye on the medal rostrum, the Christian has his eye on the heavenly reward. "One thing I do," says Paul. "Forgetting what is behind and straining toward what is ahead, I press on toward the goal to win the prize for which God has called me heavenward in Christ Jesus" (Philippians 3.13-14).

We fail most often, not because we lack ability, but because we lack stickability. Like the postage stamp, we need to stick to it until we reach our destination. It was that kind of *hupomone* endurance which enabled Paul, at the end of his life, to say, "I have fought the good fight, I have finished the race, I have kept the faith. Now there is in store for me the crown of righteousness" (2 Timothy 4.7).

The prayer of Sir Francis Drake, though Elizabethan in tone, is full of meaning even today: "O Lord, when thou givest to Thy servants to endeavour any great matter, grant us also to know that it is not the beginning, but the continuing of the same until it be thoroughly finished which yieldeth the true glory . . ."

Meditate on James 1.1-18, especially verse 12.

Quote "Perseverance is the queen of virtues" – Cryposteur.

Promise "Be faithful, even to the point of death, and I will give you the crown of life" (Revelation 2.10).

DAY 28   And joyfully giving thanks to the Father
(1.11c-12a)

Good Morning, Disciple,

When Christ broke into my prison cell at Winchester Prison I
received Him with an explosion of happiness. I did not know then
the promise of Isaiah the prophet, "With joy you will draw water
from the wells of salvation" (Isaiah 12.3). Had I known, I would
have proclaimed a hearty "Amen!" and gone on gladly to fulfil his
next injunction, "Give thanks to the Lord; call on his name; make
known among the nations what he has done, and proclaim that his
name is exalted" (Isaiah 12.4). Some would say that I've not stopped
doing it since, but that is because life is so wonderful. How right
J. B. Priestley was when he quipped, "We need long endurance but
not long faces."

The unbeliever finds it hard to understand how joy can exist in the
middle of calamity. Perhaps this is because joy is confused with
pleasure, which so often depends upon the right environment,
circumstance or stimulant. It's not hard to be happy when everything
is conducive to comfort and laughter. The real test is how we react
when our situation is difficult.

The unspiritual person would be baffled by James's advice:
"Consider it pure joy, my brothers, whenever you face trials of many
kinds" (James 1.2). He would be open-mouthed at our Lord's final
beatitude: "Rejoice and be glad" (Matthew 5.12) in the face of false
accusations, insults and persecution. One of those who listened to
that sermon on the Galilean hillside later told a persecuted church,
"Do not be surprised at the painful trial you are suffering, as though
something strange were happening to you. But rejoice that you
participate in the sufferings of Christ, so that you may be overjoyed
when his glory is revealed" (1 Peter 4.12-13). Perhaps he recalled the
last words of that beatitude: "Great is your reward in heaven"
(Matthew 5.12).

Giving thanks is the palette on which are blended the colours
of Christian experience to turn a landscape of shade and contrasting
brightness into a masterpiece of praise. When Adelaide Proctor's
health broke down she penned a famous hymn of joyful
thanksgiving:

> I thank Thee too that all our joy
> Is touched with pain;
> That shadows fall on brightest hours,
> That thorns remain:
> So that earth's bliss may be our guide,
> And not our chain.

What could be more appropriate this morning than to read Isaiah 12. Have a joyful day.

Quote "Joy is the serious business of heaven" – C. S. Lewis, *The Business of Heaven* (Fount Paperbacks, 1984).

Promise "With joy you will draw water from the wells of salvation" (Isaiah 12.3).

DAY 29 Who has qualified us to share in the inheritance of the saints (1.12b)

Good Morning, Disciple,

At Hollybrook Homes in Southampton, where I spent most of my childhood, each boy and girl was allocated a plot of land about the size of one space in a car-park. In this mini allotment we were permitted to grow our own flowers. In reality, of course, they were not ours in any legal sense. We had no rights of ownership. The privilege lasted only as long as our good behaviour, which meant that I suffered an occasional temporary confiscation of land. When eventually we left the orphanage, there was no right of transfer to a special buddy, it reverted to the owners.

Such was not the case in Canaan where each tribe of Israel was given a parcel of land as an inheritance (Joshua 14.2). It could be passed on to succeeding generations as a birthright, an inheritance.

The apostle has this piece of Jewish history in mind when he uses the word "inheritance" here. We are promised an inheritance with all the saints, the holy ones, the believers of every nation and generation, and even the holy angels of God. We, who were disqualified from the presence of God because of our sin, have been qualified, made fit, for the inheritance by the work of God in Christ upon the cross.

While the inheritance is a future hope, the qualification is a present reality. Compare those angel worshippers mentioned in chapter 2.18, who would be disqualified from their inheritance. We may confidently say, with the apostle Peter, "Praise be to the God and Father of our Lord Jesus Christ! In his great mercy he has given us new birth into a living hope through the resurrection of Jesus Christ from the dead, and into an inheritance that can never perish, spoil or fade – kept in heaven for you" (1 Peter 2.3-4).

In his book *Why I Am Not A Christian* Bertrand Russell lamented: "When I die I shall rot, and nothing of my ego shall survive. There is darkness without, and when I die there shall be darkness within. There is no splendour, no vastness anywhere; only triviality for the moment, and then nothing."

As you read Ephesians 2.11-22, give thanks for your "inheritance".

Quote "Death is the ultimate statistic: one out of every one dies" – George Bernard Shaw.

Promise "If we are (God's) children, then we are heirs – heirs of God and co-heirs with Christ" (Romans 8.17).

DAY 30   In the kingdom of light (1.12c)

Good Morning, Disciple,

Once in the wee hours of the morning during my first pastorate in London I received a telephone call inviting me to go immediately to a home in Wandsworth. No further explanation was given and, in my sleepy state, no questions were asked. Like a zombie, I drove to the house, where I was requested to remove my shoes and go into the front room. There, amid smouldering joss sticks and the sweet smell of incense, in front of a portrait of a bearded and orange-robed Indian guru, I was asked to consider enlightenment. Why they had chosen me I have no idea. I certainly didn't wait to find out. A hasty retreat was in order.

In every age there have been wizards and witches, gurus and guides, intent upon teaching about "hidden doors", occultic passages and mystical pathways into altered states of consciousness, divine enlightenment and mysterious powers.

But Paul asserts that the "kingdom of light" is the common inheritance of "all the saints", of every believer.

"God is light; in him there is no darkness at all" (1 John 1.5). He dwells in the kingdom of light, and in his presence there is no need for lesser lights (Revelation 22.5).

When Isaiah the prophet spoke of God's incarnation on earth it was as the coming of light (Isaiah 69.1); and John heralds Him as "the light of men" (John 1.4), shining and overcoming the darkness.

When Jesus said to His followers, "You are the light of the world" (Matthew 5.14), He was reminding them not of their special status but of their awesome responsibility to testify to the one true light. How could they do that? Were there special enlightenment seminars?

Fortunately, Paul's companion letter to the church at Ephesus contains the clue. There he reminds them in their day, and us today, "You were once in darkness." That darkness was typified by poor behaviour: immorality, impurity, greed, obscenity and deception. "But now," he goes on, "you are light in the Lord. Live as children of light." How? By goodness, righteousness, truthfulness and everything which pleases God (Ephesians 5.3-10). In other words, our habitual behaviour tells us whether we are walking in the light.

John's first letter has something important to add. Why don't you take five minutes extra today and read all the way from 1 John 1.5 right through to chapter 2.11. You won't regret it.

Quote "The fundamental thing is our attitude of walking in the light, rather than the act" – Roy Hession, *The Calvary Road* (Christian Literature Crusade, 1950).

Promise "The Lord your God will be with you wherever you go" (Joshua 1.9).

DAY 31 For he has rescued us from the dominion of darkness (1.13a)

Good Morning, Disciple,

The story is told of an experimental language project involving a chimpanzee called Washoe. Apparently, after many years of using sign language with simple recognition tasks, the animal had learned about

140 signs. The project director decided it was time for the chimp to say whatever it wanted to say. The animal had been well kept, even pampered. Even so, the first three words she put together and repeated many times over were, "Let Me Out!"

Only the prisoner knows the joy of release; the slave the exhilaration of freedom. The Israelites, as they looked back over the Red Sea towards Egypt, the land of bondage, again and again gave thanks to their God for deliverance.

Paul has in mind here yet another rescue mission, for which every heaven-bound Christian gives thanks: our release from the power of darkness into the Kingdom of Christ.

I imagine Pontius Pilate thought he was doing his duty when he sentenced the only truly innocent man to die on a cross. The priests and politicians probably believed that Jesus was a threat to religious orthodoxy. The people who cried out for His death were probably no more mindless than the average Saturday afternoon football crowd. No doubt they said, "There's no smoke without fire."

But Jesus prays for them all, "Father, forgive them, for they do not know what they are doing" (Luke 23:34).

Why were they so blind? Because "The god of this age has blinded (and still does blind) the minds of unbelievers, so that they cannot see the light of the gospel of the glory of Christ" (2 Corinthians 4.4). The irony is that, from the heart of this pitch black night, the unbeliever protests his enlightenment.

Hitler said in *Mein Kampf*, "By means of shrewd lies, unremittingly repeated, it is possible to make people believe that Heaven is Hell and Hell is Heaven . . . The greater the lie the more readily it will be believed."

Satan, the father of all liars, has darkened the soul of humanity by causing people to question God's word, deny God's judgment and declare their freedom to be anything they choose to be. But we who believe God's truth have been rescued. Free − free at last.

Watch out for the contrast between light and darkness as you read John 12:15-46. Meditate especially on verse 46.

Quote "The character of the dominion depends on the ruling power" − Frederick B. Westcott, *A Letter To Asia* (Klock & Klock, reprint, 1981).

Promise "I have come into the world as a light, so that no one who believes in me should stay in darkness" (John 12:46).

DAY 32   And brought us into the kingdom of the Son he loves (1.13b)

Good Morning, Disciple,

Donald Grey Barnhouse told the story of a farmer whose wheat field caught fire. To save his grain stored in the barn nearby he quickly lit a backfire to impede the progress of the flames.

When both fires had eventually burned themselves out and the barn had been saved, the farmer walked through the field of smouldering ashes. There he found the burned remains of a hen which had been caught between the two fires. Sorrowfully he turned over her corpse with his foot. To his amazement, four little chicks ran from underneath their mother. Her sacrifice had saved them. They had been "redeemed" from the flames.

We, too, have been rescued from the flames by Christ Jesus who died in our place. Unlike the hen, though, He proved His superior power over Satan and his dark forces by His resurrection from the dead. Like a conquering king He has snatched us from captivity and certain death and brought us home.

This exciting verse assures us that we who belong to Jesus are already in His kingdom! God has already transferred us from Satan's domain into the kingdom of His loved Son.

The Jewish believers at Colosse were familiar with the idea of transferring whole groups, even nations, lock, stock and barrel into captivity, as when Nebuchadnezzar deported much of the population of Jerusalem to Babylon. In the second century BC some of their own great-grandparents were probably among the 2,000 or more Jews transported from Babylon to Colosse by Antiochus the Great.

Deliverance from such captivity was the occasion for much rejoicing and thanksgiving to God, as is evidenced in many of the Psalms which celebrate the exodus from Egypt. Zechariah's song of praise, at the birth of his son John the Baptist, rejoices in "salvation from our enemies and from the hand of all who hate us" (Luke 1.71).

Little wonder then that Paul calls for thanksgiving (v.12) from those who have been rescued from darkness and belong to Christ.

This seems a good time go to the very last book of the Bible, Revelation 22, to catch a glimpse of our final transfer into the very presence of God.

Quote "We rejoice in the coming Kingdom, in the fact of eternal salvation . . . and yet long for our full deliverance, the full coming of the Kingdom, the completion of our salvation" – Bruce Milne, *The End of the World* (Kingsway, 1979).

Promise "Blessed are those who wash their robes, that they may have the right to the tree of life and may go through the gates into the city" (Revelation 22.14).

DAY 33 In whom we have redemption (1.14a)

Good Morning, Disciple,

I love the rather quaint old story of the little boy who made himself a model sailing boat. When the paint had dried he took it down to the lake for an afternoon of sailing pleasure, but a soft breeze took the boat out to the middle of the lake where it was there becalmed. Try as he might he could not retrieve his treasured creation. He returned home sad and misty-eyed.

Some days later, passing by a secondhand shop, he spied what was unmistakably his boat. He begged the owner of the shop to believe that he had made it and that it belonged to him. The man merely retorted that if the boy wanted it, he would have to buy it.

The boy saved his pocket money, did extra chores to earn more, and when he had saved enough went back to the shop to buy what was really his already.

As he left the shop he held the boat close to his heart and said, "You're my boat. I made you, so you're mine; but now I've bought you, so you're twice mine."

The boy would not have known the meaning of the word redemption, but that is what he had done. He had redeemed his boat – bought it back.

In the everyday language of New Testament times the term was used of a slave whose freedom had been bought. So it was natural to use it for one who was delivered from the bondage of Satan's dark realm.

Jesus said, "Everyone who sins is a slave to sin. Now a slave has no permanent place in the family, but a son belongs to it forever. So if the Son sets you free, you will be free indeed" (John 8.34-36).

Because "the wages of sin is death" (Romans 6.23), the cost of our freedom is death. Who can redeem us from this penalty? Not another man, even if he were willing to die in our place, for he is under the same condemnation. He would be paying his own penalty. No – only the sinless, completely innocent Son of God could "give his life as a ransom for many" (Matthew 29.28).

As you read Hebrews 9.11-28, stop at verses 14-15 to meditate on the cost, the great cost, of our salvation.

Quote "Only the man who is prepared to share in the guilt of the cross may claim his share in its grace" – Canon Peter Green, *Watchers by the Cross*.

Promise "In him we have redemption through his blood, the forgiveness of sins, in accordance with the riches of God's grace" (Ephesians 1.7).

DAY 34 The forgiveness of sins (1.14)

Good Morning, Disciple,

Suppose I were to break into your house and your neighbour's and steal a treasured possession from each of you. Some years later, having disposed of your treasure long ago, I return to confess and ask for forgiveness. I discover you have moved on, so I call on your neighbour to ask for his forgiveness, which he readily gives. Then I ask if he will also forgive me for stealing your property. He is likely to answer, "No! I can forgive you for what you did to me, but it's not in my power to forgive you for what you did to my neighbour."

Only the person who has been offended has the right to forgive.

King David realised this truth when the prophet, Nathan, confronted him with his adultery and murder. Yet he prays to God, "Against you, you only, have I sinned and done what is evil in your sight" (Psalm 51). All sin is falling short of the standard God has set, therefore all sin is against God.

But few of us are as sinful as David – are we? Imagine that we are standing on one side of a ravine with a sheer drop in front of us. Behind us a fire is raging, coming closer and closer to the cliff's edge. We are trapped. Our only way of escape is to jump across the ravine to the opposite cliff 20ft away. You run, jump and get three quarters of the way across. I jump and only get half way across. Which of us is the better off?

Neither, for we have both fallen short. The Scripture tells us, "All have sinned and fall short of the glory of God" (Romans 3.23).

Like King David, we have to confess our sin. "If we confess our sins, He is faithful and just and will forgive our sins and purify us from all unrighteousness" (1 John 1.9).

What a rich word is forgiveness. It means "released from the debt", pardoned and sent away. As King David put it, "As far as the East is from the West, so far has He removed our transgressions from us" (Psalm 103.12). The removal of our sin is also the removal of our guilt.

As you read Luke 5.17-26 this morning, meditate upon the theme of God's forgiveness. You may want to pray about anything which is pricking your conscience – knowing that He can and will forgive you.

Quote "Forgiveness shatters the shackles which enslave the soul" – Charles A. Trentham, *Shepherd of the Stars*, (Broadman Press, 1962).

Promise "Look, the Lamb of God, who takes away the sin of the world!" (John 1.29b).

DAY 35   He is the image of the invisible God (1.15a)

Good Morning, Disciple,

Hallelujah! We are forgiven. What a relief. Did you think yesterday's reading was the summit? No, there's more to come.

I remember an occasion on a family holiday when my daughter, Christy, and I tried one evening to climb Catbells Hill overlooking Derwent Water, near Keswick. The darkness beat us. Even though we were just below the summit we turned back.

The next morning my wife, Sue, and my other daughter, Ruth, joined us. We came to the point which Christy and I had reached the night before. "Not far now," I said, as we raced up the slope together. Imagine the mixture of laughter and embarrassment as we climbed over the last few rocks only to be confronted with a view of the real summit some distance away. As long as we were beneath the first summit we could not see, beyond it, the long dip downward before it rose again to a much loftier height.

That's where we are this morning. Having climbed the first summit, we can look back in appreciation at all Christ has done for us, but we can also look up to greater heights.

Until Jesus came on the scene, no man had ever seen God (John 1.18). Man had been made in the image of God (Genesis 1.26-27), but had lost the true likeness by sinning. God had shown His power and His nature in the created order (Romans 1.20) and had revealed Himself to individual prophets. But now, in Christ, we would see not just a vision, not a shattered reflection or a facet, but the real thing.

The Greek word for image is *eikon*. It was used in the time of Paul in place of a signature. If I were to enter into a contract with you, I would write in the document a full description of myself: 5ft 6in tall, brown-greying hair, blue eyes, stocky build, chipped front tooth, scar right forearm . . . You would write your description. If at a later date anyone wanted to be sure who had made the agreement, they would simply look at you, look at me, and tick off these items. That description was called an *eikon*.

Paul is saying: Jesus is the *eikon* of God. Look at Him – and you see God.

Keep this in mind as you meditate on John 1.1-18. Just one helpful hint: "the Word" in verse one is Jesus. This is made clear in v. 14. God grant you a rich and rewarding day.

Quote "The creature views the unbegotten beauty in the only begotten" – St Basil.

Promise "For to us a child is born, to us a son is given, and the government will be on his shoulders. And he will be called Wonderful Counsellor, Mighty God, Everlasting Father, Prince of Peace" (Isaiah 9.6).

DAY 36   He is the image of the invisible God (1.15a)

Good Morning, Disciple,

There have always been "spiritual gurus" who believe that they are more enlightened than the masses. Such were the gnostics whose influence was being felt in Paul's day, and whose later heresies are still with us today in the wardrobe of the New Age Movement. The word "gnostic" means the "knowing ones" – we might say the "know-it-alls", for they love to pose as knowledgeable about the secrets of the spiritual realm.

Here's an example of their warped thinking. They assumed God, who is spirit, to be good, and the world, which is eternal matter, to be evil. Therefore God could not have created the world. Rather, He sent out from Himself emanations (angelic beings), the lowest of which ceased to be spirit, and therefore ceased to be good.

Imagine a series of Russian Babushka dolls – the kind which break in half and reveal inside a smaller replica. The big doll is God, the smallest is demi-god, like Him but not like Him, if you see what I mean. The small doll created a bad world, hostile to God.

Where did Jesus fit into this gnostic nightmare? He was not unique, they decided. He was merely one of those emanations. He may have been the next to largest doll, therefore more spirit than material, but He was limited in His power.

Could He deliver man from the world of evil to the spiritual world of God and good? No, for this, they said, you need the "little dolls", starting with the material emanations which look like human beings, who can teach you the hidden secrets which are the passport to the next level of consciousness, which will, eventually, lead to God.

If all that sounds confusing, believe me, I haven't told the half. But this is why Paul is so clear in his statement that Jesus is the image of the invisible God. He is saying, in effect, "Forget your theories. There is only one; one 'only begotten of the Father'; one 'mediator'; one God; His name is Jesus." He is "the radiance of God's glory", as it says in Hebrews 1.3, "the exact representation of His being." As Jesus said, "Anyone who has seen me has seen the Father" (John 14.9).

As you read Hebrews 1 this morning, jot down what it teaches you about Jesus, then meditate on those themes.

Quote "God dwells in Light inaccessible, and may not be seen by human eye, but in the Son we may see His true likeness" – H. M. Carson, *Tyndale New Testament Commentary* (Tyndale, 1960).

Promise "Therefore God exalted him to the highest place and gave him the name that is above every name, that at the name of Jesus every knee should bow, in heaven and on earth and under the earth, and every tongue confess that Jesus Christ is Lord, to the glory of God the Father" (Philippians 2.9-11).

DAY 37 The firstborn over all creation (1.15b)

Good Morning, Disciple,

What glorious vistas are spread before us this morning. We have climbed the mountain in the last two days and found the summit in King Jesus. From this vantage point everything else fits into place. We may take our binoculars to zoom in on some distant feature, but from here we see it in relation to the whole.

But before we look away to what is below we must view the summit itself, for here we discover more great truths about the King of kings and Lord of lords.

At first sight the designation "firstborn" may seem odd. Surely Adam was the firstborn of creation. Yes, but Paul uses it as a title of honour or rank to describe Christ. He is the firstborn over all creation.

Usually the honour would go to the true firstborn son, but there are instances in the Old Testament where a later born son receives the title. Isaac, for instance, was born later than Ishmael but took the title of preference. Jacob tricked Esau out of his birthright, and Joseph became head over his eldest brother Reuben.

Paul repeats here the messianic title of Psalm 89.27: "I will appoint him my firstborn, the most exalted of the kings of the earth." Jesus has the right to the throne as heir of all things.

Just as "image" shows the relationship of Jesus to the Father, so "firstborn" shows the relationship of Jesus to the creation. He who was before all things is the one who brought all things into being.

This fourth century carol by Aurelius Prudentius expresses profoundly some of the truths of this chapter of Colossians.

> Of the Father's love begotten
> Ere the worlds began to be,
> He is alpha and omega,
> He the source, the ending He,
> Of the things that are, that have been,
> And that future years shall see:
> Evermore and evermore.
>
> By His word was all created;
> He commanded and 'twas done;
> Earth and sky and boundless ocean,
> Universe of three in one;
> All that sees the moon's soft radiance,
> All that breathes beneath the sun.
> Evermore and evermore.

As you read John 3.1-31 you will no doubt get excited about the first half of the passage, but it is the last part I want you to meditate on, most especially verse 31.

Quote "A Saviour not quite God is like a bridge broken at the further end" – Bishop Moule.

Promise "The one who comes from above is above all; the one who is from the earth belongs to the earth, and speaks as one from the earth. The one who comes from heaven is above all" (John 3.31).

DAY 38 For by him all things were created (1.16a)

Good Morning, Disciple,

Today's subject makes me want to sing that great old Satchmo song, "I think to myself, What a wonderful world!"

All this, says Paul, is the creative work of Christ: in Him, by Him and for Him. It has the very stamp of God upon it. As it says in Romans 1.20, "Since the creation of the world God's invisible qualities

. . . have been clearly seen, being understood from what has been made." That's why nature is so beautiful. It didn't create itself. It wasn't a cosmic accident. As the astronautical engineer Eugene Mallove reports in *The Universe as Happy Conspiracy*, "Some cosmologists are proposing that the Universe has been 'perfectly' designed for life in a way that could not have happened by chance."

The French mathematician, Le Compte de Nouy, used the science of probabilities to look into the possibility of a single high dissymmetry molecule being formed by chance. Do you know what the odds are? Wait for it! Ten to the 243 power billions of years. He goes on, somewhat tongue-in-cheek: "Let us admit that no matter how small the chance that it could happen, one molecule could be created by such astronomical odds of one chance. However, one molecule is of no use. Hundreds of millions of identical ones are necessary. Thus we either admit the miracle or doubt the absolute truth of science."

As science advances it comes more and more to the inevitable conclusion that there are just too many coincidences for life to have begun by a mere cosmic accident.

James Watson, the co-discoverer of DNA, would often repeat his conviction that once the code was broken it would prove to be beautiful. On the night he finished his research he looked at the double helix and exclaimed, "It's so beautiful, you see, so beautiful!"

I'm not surprised, are you? When God Himself, through the agency of King Jesus, looked at each unfolding drama of His creation, He looked at it and said, "It is good."

Now, here's a good chapter for you to read today: Genesis one. And I think to myself, "What a wonderful world!"

Quote "God is not greater if you reverence Him but you are greater if you serve Him" – St Augustine.

Promise "Do you not know? Have you not heard? The Lord is the everlasting God, the Creator of the ends of the earth. He will not grow tired or weary, and his understanding no one can fathom" (Isaiah 40.28).

DAY 39   Things in heaven and on earth, visible and invisible (1.16b)

Good Morning, Disciple,

What Christmas present would you buy for a man who has everything?

Patrick Lichfield, the photographer, niggled over just that question as he thought about what to get for his brother-in-law, Gerald Cavendish Grosvenor, 15th Baronet of Eaton, 9th Baron of Grosvenor, 9th Baron of Belgrave, 9th Earl of Grosvenor, 8th Marquis of Westminster and (whew!) 6th Duke of Westminster. You see, the Duke of Westminster is reckoned to be the richest man in England and one of the richest in the world.

Lichfield's novel answer was a Monopoly game, specially marked with all the properties from which the Duke collected rents. Mayfair and Park Lane remained because he had houses and probably hotels there already, and for this reason, Belgravia and Grosvenor Square were added. Railway stations were a problem as these are held in national ownership, so they hit on the fun idea of putting in their place the airports the Duke most frequently flew from to check on his foreign investments.

The gift no doubt acted as a good reminder to the family of the transitory nature of earthly wealth. If you've played Monopoly you know what I mean. One minute you can be buying hotels, the next you're broke.

Now I can hear you saying, "What on earth has this to do with Jesus creating the heavens and the earth, the visible and the invisible?" Just this: we have inherited, in Christ, more than all the wealth of the Duke of Westminster. Everything you can see in the world, and even what you can't see in the realm of the Spirit, was created by King Jesus. One day the wealth of the nations will return to its rightful owner – the One who made it.

In the meantime, let us be content with and enjoy what we have, without becoming attached to, or covetous of, those things which perish. Let us "fix our eyes not on what is seen, but on what is unseen. For what is seen is temporary, but what is unseen is eternal" (2 Corinthians 4.18).

When you open your Bible this morning at Proverbs 8 you'll be in a veritable King Solomon's Mine of treasures. As you look at each of them from verse 11, ask yourself in what ways Jesus is the very substance of this old vision of Wisdom. Happy treasure hunt!

Quote "Either this man (Jesus) was, and is, the Son of God; or else a mad man or something worse" – C. S. Lewis, *Mere Christianity* (Fount Paperbacks, 1956).

Promise "He gives strength to the weary and increases the power of the weak" (Isaiah 40.29).

DAY 40   Whether thrones or powers or rulers or authorities (1.16c)

Good Morning, Disciple,

All the conflicting views about evolution and creation are mind-boggling, but that's mere child's play compared with the supernatural. Everybody seems to have their own ideas. Beliefs are two-a-penny. Unscrupulous charlatans take advantage of the confusion and lead many astray into even deeper pits of confusion.

It has never been any different. As we shall see in chapter two, spiritual kidnappers were causing havoc in the little Colossian church in the name of philosophy and mysticism.

Paul begins to address that problem here by showing Christ's supremacy over the various unseen spiritual powers. Some folk call these "angels", but I am inclined to call them simply "unseen spirits". "Angel" comes from the Greek word *angelos* meaning messenger – so when I get up to preach I am an angel telling the Good Message. That is why the gospel is called the "ev-angel", from which we get our word "ev-angelism".

All these unseen spirits were created by God, including the greatest one, Lucifer, who through his treason became Satan. The thrones and powers and rulers and authorities mentioned here are all lower than Satan, but Satan is not an equal with Jesus. He is limited in his power and his end is sealed.

Read Ezekiel 28.11-19, bearing in mind these points: when the prophet speaks to the King of Tyre, he is talking about Lucifer (Satan); all the precious stones and gold are symbols of his position, and the fact that he was a guardian cherub shows that he was allowed next to the throne of God Himself. When in verse 17 it says, "I threw you to the Earth", and thereafter the prophet speaks in the past tense, it is, in fact, still to happen. This is called a "prophetic past". Because God dwells in a timeless eternity, that which He has decreed shall happen is as if it has already happened.

As you meditate on this passage, compare it with the fall of man in Genesis 3.1-7 to see what similarities there are.

My friend Dick Lucas reminds us: "For the loyal Christian it is enough to know that these 'powers' have neither treasures to give, nor 'terrors' with which to frighten the one who lives under the sovereign rule of Christ."

He who has the power to create all things has the power to keep you in His love.

Quote "You know His identity only if your description is 'totally awesome!'" – Charles Swindoll, *Growing Deep In The Christian Life* (Multnomah Press).

Promise "I give them eternal life, and they shall never perish; no one can snatch them out of my hand" (John 19.28).

DAY 41   All things were created by him and for him (1.16d)

Good Morning, Disciple,

When I was at school one of the most popular hymns in assembly was: "All things bright and beautiful, All creatures great and small, All things wise and wonderful, The Lord God made them all." Then, verse by verse, it finds different ways of saying the same thing.

That is pretty much what Paul is doing here. He affirms that Jesus is the agent of creation, then illustrates the point, then reaffirms it in case we miss the point.

John does the same thing when he says, "Through him all things were made" (John 1.3), then he adds, as though to underline it, "Without him nothing was made that has been made."

The story goes that a Swedish guy called Wilhelm Bergling was travelling in a train with a scientist who was pooh-poohing the idea that God in Christ had created the world. As they rumbled over a viaduct, Bergling pointed to the balustrade and asked, "Do you believe this bridge made itself?"

"No, of course it didn't."

"Well," said the Christian, "when one believes that a bridge made itself, one is counted a fool; but when one believes the world created itself, one is a scientist! Is not the name for such science, perhaps, 'foolishness'?"

I think he was right, don't you? There is, after all, more design and intricacy in one human cell than in the most elaborately constructed bridge.

Design is one evidence of intelligence. The construction of an object, whether for aesthetic beauty or utilitarian function, is proof of purpose. This is why Paul rightly concludes that Jesus is not only the one through whom creation came into being, but also the one for whom it was created. He is, Himself, the very object of creation.

In saying this, Paul is not denying the truth that "In the beginning God created", for Jesus is the only begotten Son of the Father within the Godhead.

On day 38, you read about the creation in Genesis chapter one, with a wide angled lens. Today you can use the zoom lens to focus in on one very important detail of the creation of man and woman. You'll find it in Genesis 2.4-25. Meditate this morning on verse 15 and ask yourself what you are doing to "take care" of God's beautiful world.

Quote "We are all moving, not toward extinction, but toward Christ" – Charles A. Trentham, *The Shepherd and the Stars*.

Promise "He chose to give us birth through the word of truth, that we might be a kind of firstfruits of all he created" (James 1.18).

DAY 42   He is before all things (1.17a)

Good Morning, Disciple,

Welcome to a new day of amazing opportunity. If you will let Him, God can use your life to be a blessing and help to others. By now, I hope you are more aware of who Jesus really is. This is crucial, not only for your own growth in understanding God's word, but also as a foundation for witnessing to others.

One day a Jehovah's Witness came to my door selling *Watchtower*. Usually I am far too busy to stop what I am doing to chat so I courteously decline. However, on this occasion I was drawn into conversation about the deity of Christ.

I steered our conversation quite deliberately to Colossians 1.15-18, but when I quoted from verse 15 "the firstborn over all creation", he showed me his Bible where it said "the firstborn of creation", and argued that Jesus was merely made in the image of God as we are in Adam. I must confess he had me stumped! The Greek would certainly allow either "of creation" or "over creation". Which was true?

The answer is in the context of all four verses. Verse 17 especially is a statement of deity. It makes a grammatical choice nonsense. The New International Version has plumped for the only possibility – "over creation" – because Jesus is God.

Permit me to explain. The "He" at the beginning of this verse is emphatic, and is surely meant to remind the reader of the great "I AM" statement of the Old Testament. When Moses asked God's name, "God said to Moses, 'I am who I am. This is what you are to say to the Israelites: "I AM has sent me to you"'" (Exodus 3.14).

I AM is the name of God. The Lord God says, "I am the Alpha and Omega . . . who is, and who was, and who is to come, the Almighty" (Revelation 1.8). This same name is used by Jesus, "I am the Alpha and the Omega, the First and the Last, the Beginning and the End" (Revelation 22.13).

The Jews were scandalised when Jesus claimed, "Before Abraham was born, I am!" (John 8.58). Notice in the very next verse how they "picked up stones to stone him". Why? Because He had claimed to be God.

As you read John 17 meditate on verse 5 and look for what unites Jesus to the Father.

Quote "Begotten of the Father before all worlds" – Nicene Creed.

Promise "Jesus Christ is the same yesterday and today and forever" (Hebrews 13.8).

DAY 43   In him all things hold together (1.17b)

Good Morning, Disciple,

How did you get on with your study of John 17 yesterday? Did you notice that one of the unifying factors among believers is their knowledge of God the Father and the Son (John 17.3)? I would add to that, God the Spirit, for Jesus said, "The world cannot accept him (the Holy Spirit), because it neither sees him nor knows him. But you know him" (John 14.17).

When we remain in harmony with all that we know of God we are able to live as one within the Church. The world is unable to live at harmony with Him because it does not know Him (John 17.25).

Did you know that there are one hundred trillion individual cells in your body? Each one of them is coded with your unique DNA, a veritable library of information ready to respond to the messages sent from your brain. Unless you have some cancerous parasites, all these cells live in perfect symbiotic harmony.

Wherever you look there is evidence of a cosmic order. To the naturalist it is the law of nature. To the scientist, cause and effect. To the ecologist, an eco-system. To the Jungian psychologist it is a universal mind. To the mystic, "Cosmic Consciousness". To this and all human observation, Paul boldly asserts Christ. In Him all things hold together. He not only made it, He sustains it.

The whole is always greater than the sum of its parts. If you could observe two atoms independently you would come to some altogether different conclusions than if you put them together. I rather like the novel way in which Sir Arthur Eddington explained this. "We often think when we have completed our study of 'one' we know all about two, because two is one and one. We forget that we still have to make a study of 'and'."

If I might coin a phrase, Jesus is the "and" behind every "one", because He made every "one". He is the "prime mover" of the universe, who set in motion every law of the natural order which He sustains for the duration of time itself. He is to the universe what the architect and the cornerstone are to a cathedral. He is the composer of a great symphony and its conductor.

Take a peek into Isaiah 11.1-10 and see what it will be like when all come under the banner of King Jesus.

Quote "God does not play dice with the cosmos"- Albert
Einstein.

Promise "I will be exalted in the earth" (Psalm 46.10).

DAY 44 He is the head of the body, the church (1.18a)

Good Morning, Disciple,
   Today we launch into a new dimension in our exploration of Christ.
We have already observed with Paul His position and power as King
over the natural order. He bears no equal except God who has given
Him "the name that is above every name, that at the name of Jesus
every knee should bow" (Philippians 2.10).
   But He is not only the King of creation, He is also the Lord of the
new creation, the Church. The Greek word used here for Church is
ecclesia, the "called-out ones". Jesus talks of His followers as the ones
whom God has given Him "out of the world". They are, He said,
"not of the world", any more than He is of the world (John 17.6
and 16).
   Now here is the mind-boggling thing, Jesus is not just the captain
of our *ecclesia* team, He is the head of His *ecclesia* body. We are a part
of Him and He is a part of us. By coming to earth Christ identified
Himself with mankind, but not to the extent that mankind and Christ
are one. He could be "in the world" but the world was never "in
Him".
   In this He differed from the speculations of philosophers who
thought of the cosmos as a living entity, the "world soul". In other
words, all nature is God and God is all nature. No, says Paul, that
is to worship and serve created things rather than the creator (see
Romans 1.25).
   Christ identified Himself with His disciples when He said, "He who
receives you, receives me" (Matthew 10.40); "Whoever accepts
anyone I send accepts me" (John 13.20); and, most significantly, to
Paul on the road to Damascus, "Why do you persecute me?" (Acts
9.4). Paul, of course, had never met Jesus but did persecute His
followers.
   What an awesome privilege – to be part of the very body of Christ.
Please note though that only those who "have Christ as head" can

be an arm or a hand, a leg or a toe in His body. Not all who are in the institutional church, or house group, or Christian Union are "in Christ".

Meditate this morning on what it means to be "one body and many parts" in Paul's earlier letter, 1 Corinthians 12.12-27.

Quote "Where Christ rules human wills, He is Himself present" – Dietrich Bonhoeffer, *Sanctorum Communio* (Collins, 1963).

Promise "Now the dwelling of God is with men and he will live with them. They will be his people, and God himself will be with them and be their God" (Revelation 21.3).

DAY 45 The beginning and the firstborn from among the dead (1.18b)

Good Morning, Disciple,

I am so glad you have managed to win that battle of "mind over mattress"! I do hope you have a really good day.

Two young men came up to Oxford as undergraduates in the early 18th century, Lord Lyttleton and Gilbert West. They were sceptical of Christianity and decided together to do humanity a favour by debunking its truths.

West rightly concluded that the resurrection of Christ was the foundation. If he could disprove it then Christ would be merely a wise, good, noble teacher. His friend said he would prove that the apostle Paul had not been converted to Christ.

They failed in their quest. In 1747 West published a book called *Observation on the History and Evidences of the Resurrection of Jesus Christ*. The quotation on the fly leaf, taken from Ecclesiasticus, read, "Blame not before thou hast examined the truth." Both became staunch defenders of the faith – as have many others since who undertook to disprove the resurrection.

I well remember another kind of scepticism being expressed years ago when I worked for a company called Cementation, which was bidding to dig a tunnel between England and France. Some on the payroll said it was an impossible pipe dream. It could not be done. The rest, as they say, is history.

Did you see the pictures of that huge and powerful drill which bored its way through, foot by foot, and metre by metre? That was the beginning. The machine has made it possible for others to follow from one side to the other.

Jesus, in an infinitely more powerful way (the power of an indestructible life, Hebrews 7.16) has broken through the barrier of death to become the "beginning" of the new creation. He has destroyed him who holds the power of death so that we too may be born from among the dead.

The tunnel only provides an easier option to sea and air. Our resurrection could come no other way. As Paul said, "If Christ has not been raised, your faith is futile and you are still in your sins" (1 Corinthians 15.17).

Meditate on the difference between what you were without Christ and what He promises you will be as you read 1 Corinthians 15.12-32.

Quote "His resurrection has led me, as often as I have tried to examine the evidence, to believe it as a fact beyond dispute " – Lord Chaldecote, quoted in Linton H. Irwin, *A Lawyer Examines the Bible* (Baker Book House, 1943).

Promise "Before long, the world will not see me any more, but you will see me. Because I live, you also will live" (John 14.19).

DAY 46 So that in everything he might have the supremacy (1.18c)

Good Morning, Disciple,

I do not know whether you are into art. It has taken me almost fifty years to discover the delights of the great masters with the help of my younger daughter, Ruth.

It can be like that with Jesus. Some come to a real faith very early. Others come in their adult years, even in old age, to the realisation that Jesus is Lord and wonder how they could have missed knowing Him for so long.

Napoleon might have proved a different kind of leader had he discovered Christ earlier. Exiled from power to the island of Saint Helena, he said: "I know men, and Christ was no man. Charlemagne,

Alexander the Great and I founded great empires upon force, and here is one founded on an empire of love; and I am now alone and forsaken, and there are millions who would die for Him.''

Paul has painted for us an exquisitely rich masterpiece – a study of Christ – in which every stroke, every nuance, every colour states boldly: He is God. He has a right to the throne.

Charles Ernest Butler's painting "King of Kings" depicts Jesus, not on the throne, but standing at the foot of the cross. There, 158 of history's greatest rulers bow in homage. Satan cowers in the darkness as Edward the Confessor kisses his Saviour's pierced hand. Constantine kneels alongside King Athelstan. The Zulu King Cetewayo stands with Queen Victoria. Well has it been said that at the foot of the cross the ground is levelled. Richard the Lionheart, Julius Caesar, Washington, Cromwell – every knee will bow, every tongue will, one day, declare His supremacy.

If I were an artist the one painting in my exhibition would be of Jesus on that awful night of His betrayal, with His hands tied behind His back, standing in silence in front of Herod for his judgment. The true King before the pretender.

Here lies our greatest challenge – to push aside every allegiance in favour of the eternal one, so that in everything He might have the supremacy.

Because I am not an artist you will have to paint your own picture. Meditate this morning on that grim scene (Luke 23.8-12). Then picture yourself, on a day to come, kneeling alongside Herod as you bow before Jesus.

Quote "In all Christians Christ is present. In some Christians Christ is prominent. In tragically few Christians Christ is pre-eminent" – F. B. Meyer.

Promise "Of the increase of his government and peace there will be no end. He will reign for ever" (Isaiah 9.7).

DAY 47   For God was pleased to have all his fulness dwell in him (1.19)

Good Morning, Disciple,

Have you read Melville's *Moby Dick*? If you have you will remember how, when Captain Ahab set out on his lunatic quest after the great white whale, he nailed a gold doubloon to the mainmast. The first sailor to spot Moby Dick would receive the coin as a prize. Each sailor contemplated the gold reward from his own viewpoint. One thought it would be proof of his superior seamanship. Another considered how many cigars it would buy. Pip, the crew's simpleton, made the astute observation, "I see, you see – we all see."

So it is with Christ. Each person sees Jesus through the filter of faith or doubt, religious background or lack of it. To the Muslim He is but a prophet. To the Hindu, yet another god. To the atheist, no god at all.

Rabbi Klausner, late President of the University of Jerusalem, remarked, "His parables are matchless; His ethics are not surpassed by anything in the Old Testament: He is the supreme fruit of the tree of Judaism."

Mahatma Gandhi could never go that far. He said, "I could not assign to Jesus of Nazareth a solitary throne above the universe, for there have been many incarnations of God."

Each sees through his own eyes. Into the confusion of subjectivity booms the outrageously confident assertion of the man who met Him on the Damascus road – "He is God." If I were to risk a paraphrase of today's verse it would go something like this: All that makes God fully and uniquely God the Father willed to live fully and uniquely in Jesus Christ incarnate.

In effect Paul was underlining everything he had already said about Christ. He is the image of the invisible God. He is over all. He is creator. He is the object of creation. He is eternal. He is head. He is risen. He is God.

The deity lives in Him permanently. That which He had before the foundation of the earth was in Him as a man – on the cross, at the ascension, at the right hand of the Father.

Now use your own eyes. Go back to where you left off yesterday and meditate on Luke 23.13-49.

Quote "Only God could provide in Himself, that is, within the Godhead, the solution to the tragedy of a lost and estranged creation" – Everett F. Harrison, *Christ All Sufficient* (Moody Press, 1971).

Promise "All that belongs to the Father is mine. That is why I said the Spirit will take from what is mine and make it known to you" (John 16.15).

DAY 48 And through him to reconcile to himself all things, whether things on earth or in heaven (1.20a)

Good Morning, Disciple,

If you occasionally come across a Bible verse which makes you scratch your head and say, "Phew! I don't understand that" – you're in excellent company. Simon Peter said of Paul, "His letters contain some things that are hard to understand, which ignorant and unstable people distort, as they do other Scriptures, to their own destruction" (2 Peter 3.16).

Alexander Maclaren, a godly theologian of a former age, said of today's verse, "On no subject is it more necessary to remember the limitations of our own knowledge than on this great theme. On none is confident assertion more out of place."

Origen, flying in the face of other Scriptures, distorted the verse to mean that Satan, all his fallen angel followers and unbelievers alike were saved.

So how shall we understand the verse? We must walk humbly and admit, "The secret things belong to the Lord our God, but the things revealed belong to us" (Deuteronomy 29.29). Let's look at what is revealed.

Firstly, the Jesus who is the agent of creation (v.16) is also the one whom God uses to reconcile all things in heaven to Himself. Note the order of creation – heaven, then earth. But the order of reconciliation is earth, then heaven. As you compare verses 16 and 20 do you see what is not included in the reconciliation? Thrones, powers, rulers and authorities. Though created by Christ Jesus, led by Lucifer (Satan) these revolted against God's authority. Their doom was sealed, as indeed is the fate of those who refuse to obey the gospel.

You may well ask then, who and what are covered by the "all things"? One clue may be in Romans 8.20-23, which reminds us that mankind's sin has had a devastating effect upon the whole of God's creation, but one day it too will be made new (Revelation 21.1).

We can conclude that all things in heaven and earth will be reconciled to God because of what Christ did upon the cross. Those in rebellion, whether human or spirit beings, will be pacified by His conquest and subjected to His judgment. But those who willingly accept what He has done, human, angelic, and the physical universe, all are brought back into a right relationship with God.

You will thoroughly enjoy your meditation this morning in Romans 8.

Quote "When a man is one with God, what should he do but live for ever" – George MacDonald.

Promise "He who did not spare his own Son, but gave him up for us all – how will he not also, along with him, graciously give us all things?" (Romans 8.32).

DAY 49 By making peace through his blood shed on the cross (1.20b)

Good Morning, Disciple,

So you are still with me after yesterday's session. Great! Today we look at the heart of Christianity – the cross.

Dr Paul Brand in his book *In His Image* sheds light on the relationship between the inherent properties of blood and what Christ did for us on the cross. Let me share with you just the headlines.

Blood gives life. It feeds and sustains 100 trillion cells in the body with its precious nutrients and an endless supply of oxygen, nitrogen, sodium, potassium, magnesium, sugars, cholesterol and everything needed to sustain life. Jesus said, "Unless you eat the flesh of the Son of Man and drink His blood, you have no life in you . . . The one who feeds on me will live" (John 6.53-57). When you take communion in church you are enacting this spiritual truth, that Jesus is your only hope of eternal life.

Blood cleanses. These same red blood cells act as internal garbage collectors. The blood carries waste products such as carbon dioxide to the lungs for expulsion, and urea and uric acid to the organs which dump them outside the body.

Jesus said, "This is my blood of the covenant, which is poured out for many for the forgiveness of sins" (Matthew 26.28). Or, as John put it, "The blood of Jesus, His Son, purifies us from all sin" (1 John 1.7).

Blood heals. Platelets, delicate flower-shaped cells, act as a sort of mobile first aid box. When your skin is punctured by a cut they do a plugging-up job by spinning out a gossamer web of fibrogen into which red blood cells crash in their millions to form a clot to staunch the flow of blood. "By His wounds you have been healed" (1 Peter 2.24).

Blood protects. But prevention is better than cure. White blood cells lie in ambush to attack intruders such as unwelcome bacteria or viruses, using billions of antibodies as artillery.

When a really strong invader comes in, though, a transfusion of clean powerful blood may be the only answer.

Spiritually this was the only answer for sin-diseased mankind. Jesus gave His blood for us on the cross, which is why we are referred to as those who overcame Satan "by the blood of the Lamb" (Revelation 12.11).

Meditate on Christ's words about His precious blood given for you – John 6.53-71.

Quote There is a fountain filled with blood
            Drawn from Emmanuel's veins
            And sinners, plunged beneath that flood,
            Lose all their guilty stains.

                                         – William Cowper

Promise "In this world you will have trouble. But take heart! I have overcome the world" (John 16.33).

DAY 50 Once you were alienated from God and were enemies in your minds because of your evil behaviour (1.21)

Good Morning, Disciple,

Well, it was a good day until you read our text for today – unless you spotted that little word "once" and remembered that it is sandwiched between two great verses about reconciliation.

Many years ago I visited two elderly sisters. One of these dear ladies, referring to my sermon on the previous Sunday, asked why I preached so much about being saved from sin. "I am quite sure," she said, "that I have never committed any sin." I gently but ineffectively tried to explain that we have all sinned.

I was just about to give up when her sister spoke up. Five minutes of remembered examples were worth a hundred sermons.

The trouble is, we tend to compare ourselves with others who are more sinful than we are, rather than comparing ourselves with God's standards.

Human law never counts a man guilty until he has been proven to have done something to break the law. A man found by the police in the garden of a private house may be suspected of committing a crime, but if he has no loot and the house appears to be secure he is guilty only of trespass. A man is not a thief until he has stolen. He is not a murderer until he has killed someone.

But God says, "You stole because you are a thief; you killed because you had murder in your heart." As Jesus put it, "Any one who looks at a woman lustfully has already committed adultery with her in his heart" (Matthew 5.28). By this standard we have all sinned.

Paul reminds believers that we were once like this, estranged from God, because we were enemies with Him in our inward thinking and evil in our outward behaviour.

Our minds were hostile towards God because they were darkened by ignorance (Ephesians 4.18), in slavery to our sinful nature (Romans 7.5) and proud (Luke 1.51). Our deeds, immorality, idolatry, adultery, homosexuality, stealing, greed, drunkenness, slander and swindling (1 Corinthians 6.9-11), and many more, were all included in that little word "once".

"That is what some of you were. But you were washed, you were sanctified, you were justified in the name of the Lord Jesus Christ and by the Spirit of our God'' (1 Corinthians 6.11).

Now meditate on Romans 5.1-11, which will cheer your soul.

Quote ''It is the mind of man, not the mind of God, which must undergo a change'' – J. B. Lightfoot, *Colossians* (Macmillan, 1869).

Promise ''But seek first his kingdom and his righteousness, and all these things will be given to you as well'' (Matthew 6.33).

DAY 51 But now he has reconciled you by Christ's physical body through death 1.22a

Good Morning, Disciple,

Two days ago we were reminded that the price of our freedom was not silver or gold but the ''precious blood of Christ'', represented at the communion service by the wine. Today, the focal point is His body, recalling the haunting words of our Saviour, ''Take and eat; this is my body'' (Matthew 26.26), represented by the loaf of bread.

Paul asks, ''Is not the cup of thanksgiving for which we give thanks a participation in the blood of Christ? And is not the bread we break a participation in the body of Christ?'' (1 Corinthians 10.16). Yes, but our participation is only possible because God took the initiative. Gentiles were ''separate from Christ, excluded from citizenship in Israel and foreigners to the covenants of the promise, without hope and without God'' (Ephesians 2.12). But now, by Christ's physical death on the cross, Jew and Gentile alike are reconciled to God ''in this one body'' (Ephesians 2.16).

Why such an emphasis on Christ's physical body? It is possible that one of the early heresies denied the physical death of Christ, claiming that He was only a spirit, a phantasm, or that somehow His spirit left His body before He died.

But if Christ was not really human He could not be our Saviour. The cross would be a huge confidence trick. Only the sinless Son of God in the flesh could save us. The litmus test of the spirits and false prophets is their denial of the deity or the humanity of Christ (1 John 4.2).

When Jesus said, "This is my body . . . this is my blood of the covenant, which is poured out for many for the forgiveness of sins," He meant body, not phantasm. He was pointing to a real death awaiting Him (Hebrews 2.14-15).

The devil will do all in his power to destroy Christ's work and what better way to do it than to undermine our confidence in the cross. Therefore, we say with Peter, as a statement of faith, "He himself bore our sins in his body on the tree, so that we might die to sins and live for righteousness" (1 Peter 2.24).

As you turn to Luke 22.7-23, meditate deeply on the words of Jesus, "This is my body given for you."

Quote "The peace of God is first and foremost peace with God; it is a state of affairs in which God, instead of being against us, is for us" – J. I. Packer, *Knowing God*, (Hodder & Stoughton, 1973).

Promise "I am the resurrection and the life. He who believes in me will live, even though he dies" (John 11.25).

DAY 52   To present you holy in his sight, without blemish and free from accusation (1.22b)

Good Morning, Disciple,

It is many days since we climbed this spiritual mountain and viewed together the heights of God's work in Christ. We have been awestruck at the towering pinnacles of His love and power, creating, recreating, redeeming, forgiving, reconciling. Before we start our descent, we must take in one more peak – this time a peek into heaven itself.

The promise set before us is the object of all that God has been doing in Christ, the culmination of His divine acts of love and justice. On a day already fixed (Acts 17.31) we shall be presented at the tribunal of heaven "in the presence of God and of Christ Jesus, who will judge" (2 Timothy 4.1).

Listen to the poetry of this promise: "Christ loved the church and gave himself up for her to make her holy . . . and to present her to himself as a radiant church, without stain or wrinkle or any other blemish, but holy and blameless" (Ephesians 5.25-27).

Holy – "Not because of righteous things we had done, but because of His mercy" (Titus 3.5).

Without blemish – "And this not from yourselves, it is the gift of God – not by works, so that no one can boast" (Ephesians 2.8-9).

Free from accusation – because "A man is not justified by observing the law, but by faith in Jesus Christ" (Galatians 2.16).

But, you might say, if I am already pronounced clean, justified – what is to stop me sinning?

Wherever the gospel is preached that question automatically arises, just as it did for the apostle Paul (Romans 6.1). Read that chapter, and meditate on his answer. Your faith is secure, you are declared just, he explains. But justification carries with it a moral imperative to be holy. It is in view of what God has done for us that we willingly offer our "bodies as living sacrifices, holy and pleasing to God" (Romans 12.1).

Catch this. He presents us holy, *fait accompli!* Yet, though it take a lifetime to achieve the ambition, we must seek to present ourselves holy before Him (2 Corinthians 7.1). This ambition springs from a thankful heart, to "please Him in every way" (Colossians 1.10).

Romans 7.7-25 is not an easy passage so you may want to take time to take it in. Make sure you also read Romans 8.1.

Quote "The tree must be first, then the fruit. For the apples make not the tree, but the tree makes the apples" – Martin Luther, *Epistle to the Galatians*.

Promise "And so Jesus also suffered outside the city gate to make the people holy through his own blood" (Hebrews 13.12).

DAY 53 If you continue in your faith established and firm (1.23a)

Good Morning, Disciple,

Tell-tale cracks in the brickwork of a house can send the owner into a panic and severely affect the value of a property, as several of my close neighbours know. When the houses were built, insufficient attention was given to the nature of the clay soil. It tends to expand and contract and shift and slide in accordance with the amount of water it absorbs. Current building regulations would never allow for their mere nine-inch foundation. One neighbour has had to have new foundations pile-driven under the house to make it secure.

The words used here, "established" and "firm", would have been common language among the builders of the day. One refers to standing on a solid foundation, the other concerns the built-in strength of a building.

Our confidence is in a reliable foundation. Jesus Christ is thoroughly trustworthy because of who He is and what He has done. We may confidently establish our lives on Him. The alternatives to Christ are all mere quicksand, however attractive, novel, intelligent, popular or established they may appear.

The edifice of our faith is strong enough to withstand the attacks of the world, the flesh and the devil, only so long as it is established in the person of Christ and in all the Father accomplished for us in His life, death and resurrection. Therefore, hold firm.

We are reminded of what the Master said about building a house upon the rock which will withstand the assault of wind and water. The foolish man whose home came crashing down around him is likened to the one who hears the words of Jesus but does not put them into practice.

What would you think of a person who built a superb house to the highest specifications, then left it empty year after year and gave it no attention, never painted it, never pointed the brickwork, never unclogged the drains? Such is the man or woman who puts his or her faith in Christ Jesus for an eternal home, but refuses to live in it now – by faith.

To continue in the faith demands courage and consistency. You will be inspired this morning as you read in Hebrews 11 about some of the Old Testament figures who kept the faith even without the benefit of knowing Christ as we do.

Quote "The God who has ordained the end, has also ordained the means" – H. M. Carson, *Tyndale New Testament Commentary*, 1960.

Promise "I write these things to you who believe in the name of the Son of God so that you may know that you have eternal life" (1 John 5.13).

DAY 54 Not moved from the hope held out in the gospel (1.23b)

Good Morning, Disciple,

I have just experienced one of life's little frustrations. The camera was set up on its tripod, focused on a rock in the shallow river bed of the Windrush. My long wait was just at the crucial point of being worthwhile. The grey wagtail which I had seen feeding there on previous days had returned and was preening itself right at the anticipated spot. Stealthily I moved toward the camera. But before my finger could reach the shutter a dog barked behind me and the bird was gone. Five minutes later I gathered my photographic equipment and returned to my desk – hope dashed. There will, of course, be another day and I have every hope of catching my bird on film.

That is a reasonable hope – but not a certainty. The little boy who goes to school having skived off his homework may hope to get away with it, but his hope is probably misplaced. The child who dashes downstairs on Christmas morning hoping to see a bicycle may have indulged in wishful thinking – unless Daddy has actually promised a bike, for then it would be a virtual certainty. What we have in the gospel is the promise of our heavenly Father. We only call it "hope" because we do not possess it all now. But one day we shall have, not just a down payment, but all the fulness of our inheritance in Christ.

Sincere Christians disagree as to whether, once a person is saved, he or she is always saved. This doctrine, called "the perseverance of the saints", has enough biblical evidence on both sides of the divide to caution against dogmatism. Suffice to say, on a practical level, that if we hold on to the hope of the gospel and are not moved away from it into error or back into the world, we need not even ask the question for ourselves.

The surest way to hold on is to have something to hold on to. Paul gives us confidence both in what we have and in what we have to hold on to when he says, "By this gospel you are saved, if you hold firmly to the word I have preached to you" (1 Corinthians 15.2).

Catch a flavour of this tension as you meditate this morning in Hebrews 10.19-39. Keep your eye fixed on what Christ has done, then *you* will know what to do.

Quote "God demands active faith; we seek irrefutable certainty"
– John Sennett, *The Wittenburg Door*, August 1986.

Promise "All men will hate you because of me, but he who
stands firm to the end will be saved" (Matthew 10.22).

DAY 55 This is the gospel that you heard (1.23c)

Good Morning, Disciple,

I wonder how you first heard the gospel, the good news about Jesus
Christ. Perhaps you went to hear someone preach. Maybe a Christian
friend witnessed to you. You may have learnt it from a book or read
it in the Bible. Wherever or however – hearing was the starting point.

How you heard is of little importance, though there are some quite
amazing stories to be told. A workman was doing some repairs high
up in the old Crystal Palace building, long before the days of
microphones, when a loud voice boomed out from nowhere, "Behold
the Lamb of God, which taketh away the sin of the world." Thinking
the voice had come from the very courts of heaven itself, the man
then and there repented of his sin and became a Christian. Nor did
he change his mind when he discovered the voice was not an angel's
but Charles Haddon Spurgeon's. The great preacher was testing the
acoustics for an evangelistic rally the following day.

It is not how you hear or who you hear from that matters. It is
what you hear that is of vital importance.

Hear the wrong message, even one which claims to be based on the
Bible, and you may be left on the outside. For instance, somebody
might preach universalism – all roads lead to heaven – by quoting
John 12.32: "I, when I am lifted up from the earth, will draw all
men to myself." But, clearly, Jesus was not saying "all without
exception", but "all without distinction" – Jew and Gentile, rich
and poor, Iraqi, Russian, Brit and Aussie.

Many people in the United States who buy a dictionary plump for
a Websters, believing it to be from the pen of Noah Webster who
published a standard work early in the nineteenth century. They may
not realise that a book title is not copyright. Anyone can publish a
dictionary called Websters and put what they like on the inside.

What Paul has done is to endorse the gospel preached by Epaphras by restating it. In effect he is saying, "If this is what you heard, then it is reliable – a gospel worthy of your trust."

Consider this morning the warnings contained in Galatians 1, and thank God our Father for the true gospel.

Quote "'Hear', in its full biblical sense, implies attention, assent, and application . . . with a firm purpose to obey" – J. I. Packer, *God Has Spoken* (Hodder & Stoughton, 1979).

Promise "Heaven and earth will pass away, but my words will never pass away" (Luke 21.33).

DAY 56 That has been proclaimed to every creature under heaven (1.23d)

Good Morning, Disciple,

I wonder what was going through Paul's mind as he wrote these words. Imprisoned as he was, his thoughts must have turned to past travels. He had, after all, preached the gospel throughout the Mediterranean. Sights; people, hostile and friendly; smells of various foods – all would come flooding back.

Perhaps he thought of Athens, that city with its host of gods. Epimenides had been called there from his Cretan home to advise the city council during a time of unremitting plague. The superstitious population had sacrificed to all the known hundreds of gods – all to no avail. As the plague devastated family after family a pagan priestess warned that there must still be yet another, unidentified god which had not been appeased.

Epimenides hit on a grand scheme. "Gather together some hungry sheep," he said, "and do not feed them until the morning. Then, when they are at their hungriest, release them on to the pasture. Have stone-masons ready to build altars whenever you see a sheep that lies down without grazing. Sacrifice those sheep on the altars consecrated *agnosto theo* – to an unknown god."

Years later when Paul arrived in Athens and saw hundreds of idols and an altar inscribed "to the unknown god", he stood in the Areopagus and proclaimed Christ Jesus as that god of whom they were ignorant.

To those like the Athenians who have many gods, Paul preaches one all-embracing God, who is sufficient for all. To others, bent on excluding the masses by an elitist movement of enlightenment, he proclaims a gospel so all-inclusive that it is a saving message to "every creature under heaven" who will believe and surrender.

Read what happened in Athens – you will find it described in Acts 17.16-34. As you meditate on this remember that the gospel which has been preached to all mankind is unique. As Jesus said, "No one comes to the Father except through me" (John 14.6).

Quote "He who marries the spirit of the age, soon finds himself a widower" – Dean Inge, quoted in *Gravedigger File*, Os Guiness (Hodder & Stoughton).

Promise "But you will receive power when the Holy Spirit comes on you; and you will be my witnesses in Jerusalem, and in all Judea and Samaria, and to the ends of the earth" (Acts 1.8).

DAY 57 I, Paul have become a servant (1.23e)

Good Morning, Disciple,

By now, I hope, you are well and truly settled into the life of your local church and have begun to develop some in-depth fellowship with other believers.

I have fond memories of my days at Chatsworth Baptist Church in West Norwood, though it is now well over thirty years ago. I was really fortunate, as a young man just out of prison, to be given a home with two church members. It was overwhelming to experience strong love and acceptance after years of living by my own destructive philosophy of "do unto others what you think they are going to do to you". Such acts of kindness as I received from Alfie and Jennie Weekes and many others in the church taught me the Christlike value of service.

I am not thinking here about do-goodery, or the kind of person C. S. Lewis was talking about when he said, "She lived only for others, and you could tell who those others were by the haunted look upon their faces." There are always some who merely want to look good in the eyes of others, or use service as a means of jockeying for position or power or prestige. Pride is a deceptive animal which stalks our best motives and mauls our highest deeds.

The ultimate test of sanctification is whether our humanity has been transformed from its egotistical self-serving mode into the Christlike servant model. He who is King of kings is also the suffering servant. As He Himself put it, "Even the Son of Man did not come to be served, but to serve, and to give his life as a ransom for many" (Mark 10.45).

Paul opened his letter affirming his apostleship, but now he lays aside his leadership credentials and accepts Christ's "Order of the Towel".

Notice how the apostle's spiritual progression is mapped in his letters. To the Corinthians he is "the least of the apostles" (1 Corinthians 15.9). To the Ephesians, written at the same time as Colossians, he is "less than the least of all God's people" (Ephesians 3.8). Later, to Timothy, he would write, "Jesus came into the world to save sinners – of whom I am the worst" (1 Timothy 1.15). Progress? Yes, progress!

Look at Jesus again, and as you read Luke 22.24-38 jot down in two columns the ways of the world, and the way of Christ.

Quote "Religion is not inherently virtuous; it is merely the battlefield between God and man's self-esteem" – Reinhold Niebuhr.

Promise "Because he himself suffered when he was tempted, he is able to help those who are being tempted" (Hebrews 2.18).

DAY 58   Now I rejoice in what was suffered for you (1.24a)

Good Morning, Disciple,

All of us at some time face life's darker shades of grief and suffering. Like the tea-bag, we are not sure of our strength until we've been through hot water. Christians are not sheltered from the common experiences of life. They suffer colds, are attacked by viruses and cancers. They have accidents. The consequences of wrong choices and bad actions rebound upon their heads too – for the rain falls on the just and the unjust.

The suffering in which Paul rejoices is not that which is common to humanity, but that which is indispensable to mission. Forget the publicity given to a few modern day Elmer Gantrys who have descredited the name "evangelist" by their extravagant and self-centred lifestyles. The model for any preacher must be the Lord Jesus Christ. Isaiah prophesied that He would be the "suffering servant" – despised, rejected, a man of sorrows, stricken, smitten, afflicted, pierced, led like a lamb to the slaughter (Isaiah 53).

"Unless a kernel of wheat falls to the ground and dies, it remains only a single seed. But if it dies, it produces many seeds . . . Whoever serves me must follow me" (John 12.24, 26). The Roman historian Tacitus wrote of Christian gladiators: "Mockery of every sort was added to their deaths. Covered with the skins of beasts, they were torn by dogs and perished, or were nailed to crosses, or were doomed to flames and burnt to serve as nightly illuminations." But the seed of these martyrs became the fruit of a Christendom which encircled the globe.

This was their joy. As another historian put it: "The Christians marched from the prison to the arena as if they were marching to heaven with joyous countenances, agitated by gladness rather than fear."

From Rome to Stalin's Gulags, from Jerusalem to every place where people today suffer deprivation and loss of jobs, homes, families and even their lives, Paul's words have been a comfort and a challenge to endure. "I consider that our present sufferings are not worth comparing with the glory that will be revealed in us" (Romans 8.18).

You will experience your own level of suffering. "In fact, everyone who wants to live a godly life in Christ Jesus will be persecuted" (2 Timothy 3.12). Get prepared for this by reading 1 Peter 4.12 to 5.11, and pray that when it comes we may count it all joy.

Quote "Better is he that suffereth evil, than the jollity of him that doeth evil" – St Augustine.

Promise "But rejoice that you participate in the sufferings of Christ, so that you may be overjoyed when his glory is revealed" (1 Peter 4.13).

DAY 59 **I fill up in my flesh what is still lacking in Christ's afflictions, for the sake of his body, which is the church (1.24b)**

Good Morning, Disciple,

I did warn you that we would have to come down from the mountain tops into the valley some time! Down here too we need to keep our eyes fixed on Jesus.

What are we to make of this – Paul, filling up what is lacking in Christ's afflictions? Can anything be added to what Christ has done on the cross for our salvation? To that we may confidently answer no. We need go no further than Colossians 2 to be convinced of the apostle's teaching, that Christ plus anything equals nothing, and Christ plus nothing equals everything. When He cried from the cross, "It is finished," He meant it is finished. There is no additional sacrifice that can have any bearing on our salvation. "We have been made holy through the sacrifice of the body of Jesus Christ once for all" (Hebrews 10.10).

In what way, then, does Paul fill up what is lacking? Here are three possible answers.

1. He believed that the followers of Christ were in some mystical sense the continuation of Christ's work as the suffering servant, not adding to the efficacy of the cross but suffering for the spread of the gospel.

2. Whenever Christ's followers suffer, He Himself suffers. So when Paul was persecuting the Church the risen Lord asked him, "Why do you persecute me?" (Acts 26.14). When one member of the "body" is hurt, the head is hurt too. "Just as the sufferings of Christ flow over into our lives, so also through Christ our comfort overflows" (2 Corinthians 1.5).

3. Jewish apocalyptic writings anticipated a time of intense suffering – disease, earthquakes, famine, wars, etc. – just as the New Testament itself predicts for the return of Christ. The Jews believed that God had set a limit to these sufferings, that once the cup was full the Messiah would come.

Take your choice of these viewpoints. All three are true to the testimony of Scripture: "We must go through many hardships to enter the Kingdom of God" (Acts 14.22).

Read Mark 13. It will blow your mind but it will also prepare you for what is to come. Keep your eyes on the peak!

Quote "Mission sooner or later leads into passion" – Douglas Webster, *Yes to Mission*.

Promise "And the God of all grace, who called you to his eternal glory in Christ, after you have suffered a little while, will himself restore you and make you strong, firm and steadfast" (1 Peter 5.10).

DAY 60   I have become its servant by the commission God gave me (1.25a)

Good Morning, Disciple,

Over the past few days we have viewed snapshots from the battle zone. Our war correspondent has assured us of certain victory. The major and decisive confrontation is over. The command structure of the enemy is in disarray, but there are still objectives to be achieved in winning the hearts and minds of those held by the enemy. God's army is not yet the Church triumphant but the Church militant.

In this army Paul is a commissioned officer with specific responsibilities for his troops. He will not stand on the dignity of his office for two reasons. The Lord, his King, has forewarned him of how much he will suffer for the privilege of leadership (Acts 9.16). He also remembers the day of his appointment on which he received his orders from King Jesus Himself: "I have appeared to you to appoint you as a servant and as a witness of what you have seen of me" (Acts 26.16). He knows that the servant is not greater than his master.

I love John Stott's way of putting it. "The symbol of an authentic Christian leadership is not the purple robe of an emperor, but the coarse apron of a slave; not a throne of ivory and gold, but a basin of water for the washing of feet." The company crest of New Testament ministry displays the heraldic symbols of nails and a crown of thorns, a scourging whip and a cross.

Even our church leadership terms reflect this teaching. Minister means servant, pastor means shepherd, vicar (from the Latin *vicarius*) means underservant.

The real test of whether we are truly servants of Christ and His church comes when people treat us as servants. It is so easy to accept the title without the function, and even to use it as a means of manipulation and power in which the sheep are fleeced instead of fed.

As you read this morning about Christ's Grand Order of the Towel (John 13.1-17), take a special note of the last eight words, then meditate on verses 34 and 35 as you think of practical ways to implement His command.

Quote "The society of the crucified must neither be surprised nor dismayed, if it finds itself perennially called to bear the cross" – Stephen Neill, *The Christian Society* (Nisbet, 1952).

Promise "If you obey my commands, you will remain in my love, just as I have obeyed my Father's commands and remain in his love" (John 15.10).

DAY 61 To present to you the word of God in its fulness (1.25b)

Good Morning, Disciple,

Don Richardson's book *Eternity in Their Hearts* contains some pretty amazing missionary stories, but none more so than that of the Lahu tribe of north-east Burma.

One day as William Marcus Young was preaching in the market place of Kentung, a small group of Lahu people, in town to do some trading, watched him wide-eyed as he held his Bible aloft. With great emotion they pleaded with Young to return with them to their mountain homes. "We, as a people, have been waiting for you for centuries," they explained, "we even have meeting houses built in some of our villages in readiness for your coming."

They showed the rope bracelets hanging from their wrists. "We Lahu have worn ropes like these since time immemorial. They symbolise our bondage to evil spirits. You alone, as the messenger of Gwisha, may cut these manacles from our wrists – but only after you have brought the lost book of Gwisha to our very hearths!" (Gwisha was apparently their name for God.)

Through the teaching of God's word tens of thousands of Lahu were converted to Christ. Their appetite for the Scriptures was insatiable.

Wherever the Bible is faithfully preached, wherever the gospel is taught in its fulness, there is a succession reaching right back to the apostle, who said, "The Lord stood at my side and gave me strength, so that through me the message might be fully proclaimed and all the Gentiles might hear it" (2 Timothy 4.17). He found nothing as satisfying as preaching the gospel.

A half-baked message will not do for Paul, nor for us. We are stewards, held accountable, to present the Word of God in its fulness.

Donald Barnhouse said that if he knew the Lord was coming in three years' time, he would spend two of them studying God's Word and one preaching. Billy Graham said, "I wish I had studied more and preached less. People have pressured me into speaking when I should have been studying and preparing."

How about you? How are your studies going? Here is a good passage for you to meditate on: Romans 15. See how many tools for spreading the gospel you can count – then ask God to give them to you.

Quote "Without a satisfactory ministry of the Word, the Church must either wither and die or assume more or less grotesque forms" – Preb. Dick Lucas, *The Bible Speaks Today – Colossians* (Inter-Varsity Press, 1980).

Promise "So is my word that goes out from my mouth: it will not return to me empty, but will accomplish what I desire and achieve the purpose for which I sent it" (Isaiah 55.11).

DAY 62   The mystery that has been kept hidden for ages and generations, but is now disclosed (1.26)

Good Morning, Disciple,

I was privileged recently to travel in Czechoslovakia with the late Col. James Irwin, the Apollo 15 astronaut who has viewed earth from the unique vantage point of the moon's surface. It was fascinating to sit in the Prague Palace and hear him tell President Vaclav Havel what it felt like to be a man on the moon.

From the beginning of time, earthlings have looked up to the starry heavens and wondered about the moon. Was it a lump of cheese? Was it inhabited? Why did it make them feel romantic?

Now we know. The secret is out. It is a bunch of rocks and dust which makes a day at the seaside more interesting as we watch the tide come in.

Every scientific discovery about our planet was there all the time just waiting to be revealed. A mystery to our forefathers but knowledge to us. Beyond human comprehension in one age and a matter of fact today.

There is a sense in which God's mystery of the gospel to the Gentiles was like this. Though there were clues in the Old Testament, to all intents and purposes it was as much a spiritual mystery as the splitting of the atom was in the scientific realm.

But there is one basic difference between these two examples. The one could be discovered by human reasoning, the other could come only as a result of revelation.

The ancient mystery religions and later gnosticism (not fully developed until the second century AD but apparently in its infancy in Asia Minor a century earlier) took advantage of man's ignorance and introduced doctrines based on human imagination and sorcery.

Entry into these cults was through secret rites of initiation much as you would find today in movements of "enlightenment", witchcraft, New Age and Freemasonry. These secrets were called mysteries, the word Paul uses here.

The Holy Spirit, through Paul, says to the Colossian Christians and believers of every age: The gospel is not exclusive but inclusive. What was once hidden is now an open secret.

Jesus said that "the knowledge of the secrets of the kingdom of heaven" had been given to those who follow Him, but those who refuse to listen will never understand (Matthew 13.11). You will find the same truth expressed in your meditation today (1 Corinthians 2). Ask God to give you discernment.

Quote He wakes desires you never may forget,
He shows you stars you never saw before.
– Alfred, Lord Tennyson

Promise "Listen, I tell you a mystery: We will not all sleep, but we will all be changed" (1 Corinthians 15.51).

DAY 63   To them God has chosen to make known among the Gentiles the glorious riches of this mystery (1.27a)

Good Morning, Disciple,

And what is the mystery? "This mystery is that, through the gospel, the Gentiles are heirs together with Israel, members together of one body, and sharers together in the promise in Christ Jesus" (Ephesians 3.6).

This is hardly news to you and me. But the Jews did not understand it at all, even though it had been in the public domain for almost 2,000 years before Christ.

God had made a promise to Abraham: "I will make you a great nation and I will bless you . . . and all peoples on earth will be blessed through you" (Genesis 12.2-3). But throughout the Old Testament period the nation of Israel misread God's intention and accepted their special favour status while ignoring their responsibility to other nations. The full meaning of the covenant remained a mystery.

In the birth, ministry and death of Christ the mystery begins, like a tight winter bud, to fill out and blossom into the full flower of God's plan.

Simeon took the baby Jesus in his arms and said he would be "a light for revelation to the Gentiles" (Luke 2.32). Jesus had come not as a Jewish Messiah, but as a worldwide Saviour. Though He came primarily to minister to Jews (Matthew 10.5), He showed His wider concern by serving individual Gentiles – a concern which would eventually blossom into the open secret of the gospel to the Gentiles.

This is why Jesus was so indignant at those who had set up shop in the part of the Temple where Gentile converts were allowed to worship (Mark 11.15-18).

Some have reacted negatively to the Jews. But remember this: when Jesus was on the cross He had one arm outstretched to His "blood brothers" in Israel and the other stretched out to you and me, His "blood-bought brothers" from among the nations. He who has broken down the dividing wall of hostility between Jew and non-Jew does not expect us to pick up the bricks to throw at one another, but to start building with Him a new temple, a new people in whom His glory shines.

Meditate on that vision this morning as you read Ephesians 2.19

to 3.13 and give thanks that 4,000 years ago God told Abraham about your blessing.

Quote "Jews will go on praying for a Messiah, not knowing his name, and Christians will continue to pray to the Messiah, confessing "no other name" than Jesus Christ" – Carl E. Braaten, *The Resurrection of Jesus, by Pinchas Lapide* (Augsbury 1983).

Promise "And so all Israel will be saved, as it is written: 'The deliverer will come from Zion; he will turn godlessness away from Jacob. And this is my covenant with them when I take away their sins' " (Romans 11.26-27).

DAY 64 Which is Christ in you the hope of glory (1.27b)

Good Morning, Disciple,

The mystery at last is made known. The Messiah of the Jews is the Christ of the Gentiles. In the past converts to Judaism had to become Jews; now the God of the Jews was, in effect, saying, "Both come to me." Jesus put it like this: "I, when I am lifted up from the earth, will draw all men to myself" (John 12.32).

As I have said in previous letters, the "all" is not a kind of universalism which says all will be saved, for many people reject Christ. The "all" is Jew and Gentile, male and female, rich and poor, high IQ and low. There is no distinction.

In C. S. Lewis's book of *Letters to Children* he writes to Kathy: "Congratulations on keeping house! By the way, I also would say, 'I got a book'. But your teacher and I are not 'English teachers' in the same sense. She has to put across an idea of what the English language ought to be; I am concerned entirely with what is and however it came to be what it is. In fact, she is a gardener distinguishing 'flowers' from 'weeds'; I am a botanist and am interested in both as vegetable organisms. All good wishes. Yours, C. S. Lewis."

How like our Father! God has not changed His affections – "out with the Jews, bring on the Gentiles". He still has a plan for the Jews, but He is "interested in both".

Christ is now in you – Jew or Gentile – and is your hope of glory.

Do you see the span of this statement? It points back to Christ's work on the cross and points forward to His coming again for all eternity.

Here we are, "in the gap". The mount of Calvary on one side – the place where the Lord provided for Abraham a ram for sacrifice and for us a Saviour; on the other side, a higher mountain, the mount of our Lord's return in glory, where the children of Abraham, "in the flesh" and "in the faith", will at last be as one.

You probably will not find Romans 11 an easy chapter, but it is well worth concentrated effort this morning.

Quote "Other men see only a hopeless end, but the Christian rejoices in an endless hope" – Gilbert Beenker.

Promise "And if the Spirit of him who raised Jesus from the dead is living in you, he who raised Christ from the dead will also give life to your mortal bodies through his Spirit, who lives in you" (Romans 8.11).

DAY 65   We proclaim him (1.28a)

Good Morning, Disciple,

Put yourself in the disciples' shoes. If you had spent three years with Jesus and his final instructions to you were to preach the gospel to all nations, to go into all the world starting at Jerusalem, what would you have done?

It was relatively easy for the disciples at first, because the Lord arranged for Pentecost to take place in Jerusalem. Just in case they might have second thoughts about preaching to the thousands of foreigners who were in town, the Holy Spirit came upon them in special power. He gave them a miraculous ability to speak in various languages so that the visitors would understand their message. Not surprisingly, about 3,000 people were converted. No problem. They were all Jews.

This was exciting stuff. Every day more and more Jews were coming to Jesus. The church was growing and, of course, all these new Christians needed to be taught. Most especially they would need teaching that the message was not only for Jews.

They seem to have done a good job. Certainly, when persecution broke out in Jerusalem, not only did the converts cause a stir among their own folk. They also went out into Gentile territory and preached the gospel. Except the disciples – they stayed in Jerusalem. Were the disciples chickening out on the worldwide nature of the gospel?

We do not have to go on very far in the Acts of the Apostles to find the answer. Take a look right now at Acts 10. I think you'll see what I mean when you get to verse 34 . . .

Now do you see why the Lord needed a Paul? Little wonder that the Lord said to Ananias, "This man (Saul) is my chosen instrument to carry my name before the Gentiles and their kings and before the people of Israel" (Acts 9.15). Even after the Cornelius episode, Peter and the other disciples felt for years that new converts needed to come fully into the Jewish fold. They had apparently fallen right back into the old trap.

Saul changed his Jewish name to the gentile equivalent, Paul, and he spent his life declaring to Jew and Gentile alike the open secret that the gospel is not limited to any race or confined to any elite group. Will you?

Quote "Too many Christians are no longer fishers of men, but have become keepers of the aquarium" – Paul Harvey.

Promise "Come follow me," Jesus said, "and I will make you fishers of men" (Matthew 4.19).

DAY 66 Admonishing and teaching everyone with all wisdom (1.28b)

Good Morning, Disciple,

I once heard someone state: "All Bible teachers are just played-out evangelists."

If that were truly the case they would be poor teachers and poorer evangelists. The proclamation of the gospel, with its promise of forgiveness through the death and resurrection of Christ, was inseparable from the admonishing and teaching ministry of the Church.

Admonishment is what I should have done to the one who made

that silly statement. The word means correcting with warning, setting the mind right. Picture a sheepdog turning sheep away from danger and back to the shepherd. It may appear to be worrying the sheep but, in fact, it's a friend of both the sheep and the shepherd.

It is a necessary part of evangelism to warn people of the consequences of sin and unbelief, not as a bully, for that would surely frighten them away, but boldly and without favouritism. As Paul says, "I have declared to both Jews and Greeks that they must turn to God in repentance and have faith in our Lord Jesus" (Acts 20.21).

Tough action is sometimes needed in the household of faith. For instance, we are to "Warn (admonish) a divisive person once, and then warn him a second time. After that, have nothing to do with him" (Titus 3.10). Incidentally, that needs to be read in context or it can become simply a licence for further division.

In the same way, instruction is for everyone because it is the responsibility of church leaders to "prepare God's people for works of service" (Ephesians 4.12). There is no room here for the kind of elitist pseudo-spirituality of the mystery religions. The teaching is functional. Every disciple is to be taught how to be a useful servant and fulfil God's master plan.

Pray for your leaders. As the Scripture says, "Obey your leaders and submit to their authority. They keep watch over you as men who must give an account" (Hebrews 13.17). If they are in tune with God, they will not abuse that trust. They will teach you how to become a shepherd/leader.

As you read Acts 20.13-28 this morning have a go at listing the qualities of the shepherd/leaders. Then after you have meditated on the theme, pray for those who are teaching you.

Quote "There are no heights in Christian attainment which are not within the reach of all, by the power of heavenly grace" – F. F. Bruce, *New International Commentary on the New Testament, Colossians* (William B. Eerdmans, 1984).

Promise "All Scripture is God-breathed and is useful for teaching, rebuking, correcting and training in righteousness" (2 Timothy 3.16-17).

DAY 67   So that we may present everyone perfect in Christ (1.28c)

Good Morning, Disciple,

What an ambition! It's one thing to strive for personal perfection – but to aim for it in others seems an impossible dream.

Clearly we need to unwrap what Paul means by perfection. Possibly he was contrasting his desire for "everyone" to be perfect with the elitism of the gnostics and legalists at Colosse who considered themselves perfect in knowledge while others were unenlightened. Be that as it may, we do better to stay with God's word than speculate from history.

The word *teleion*, translated here as perfect, can equally well mean complete or mature, or even "at the last". Any one of these alternatives makes as much sense and fills out our understanding of the verse.

We have already seen (day 52) how Christ's death upon the cross cleanses the sinner: "By one sacrifice he has made perfect forever those who are being made holy" (Hebrews 10.14). Yet Paul says his goal is to present, at the last, everyone perfect in Christ. Is he simply seeking to close the gap between promise and practice? Maybe. He does say, "Stop thinking like children . . . Be adults" (1 Corinthians 14.20). James says that the person who is able to control his tongue is "a perfect man, able to keep his whole body in check" (James 3.2).

Maturity in behaviour and maturity in understanding are dependent one upon the other. Consider, for instance, these verses: "Anyone who lives on milk, being still an infant, is not acquainted with the teaching about righteousness. But solid food is for the mature, who by constant use have trained themselves to distinguish good from evil" (Hebrews 5.13-14). Constant use of what? God's word! (v.12). John Brown, a nineteenth-century theologian, hit the nail on the head: "Holiness does not consist in mystic speculations, enthusiastic fervour or uncommanded austerities. It consists in thinking as God thinks and willing as God wills."

Perhaps Paul's real meaning is explained in another letter when he spells out the function of apostles, prophets, evangelists and pastor-teachers: "To prepare God's people for works of service, so that the body of Christ may be built up until we all reach unity in the faith and in the knowledge of the Son of God and become mature (perfect), attaining to the whole measure of the fulness of Christ" (Ephesians 4.12-13).

As you read Hebrews 5.11 to 6.12 meditate especially on 5.14. I pray that it will have a profound effect upon your day.

Quote "It may be hard for an egg to turn into a bird; it would be a jolly sight harder for it to learn to fly while remaining an egg" – C. S. Lewis, *The Business of Heaven*.

Promise "Nevertheless, the righteous will hold to their ways, and those with clean hands will grow stronger" (Job 17.9).

DAY 68 To this end I labour, struggling with all his energy, which so powerfully works within me (1.29)

Good Morning, Disciple,

I'm sure you've heard the legend of St Christopher whose image of an old man carrying a child is found on so much popular jewellery.

The pagan giant lived by a river where he acted as a human ferry carrying travellers across, hoping these acts of kindness would please God.

One night a young lad asked to be carried across the river. Unperturbed the giant shouldered the boy and began to wade across. The current was stronger than usual and the boy seemed to get heavier and heavier. Eventually he made it to the other side and fell exhausted on the bank, wondering what on earth had happened.

As he lay there the boy spoke. "Christopher, your name means Christ-bearer. You are well named, for, though you think you have just carried the weight of the world on your shoulders, you have borne the one who created it. I am the Christ whom you seek."

I am not sure about the theology in the legend but Paul would certainly have understood the struggle.

There is rich meaning behind these two words, "labour" and "struggling". In the Greek, the former means "working to the point of exhaustion" – the kind of work that leaves you "dead beat". The latter is used of an athlete getting the last ounce of effort out of an already tired body to the peak of exertion – *agonizomai* – agonising!

Paul is not advocating that we should work "in the flesh". Far from it. He is all too aware of slipping back into a religion of works. He says, in effect, I could not do this without the Holy Spirit within me. To make the point he uses two equally strong words for God's powerful work. The first, *energeia* from which we get our word energy, is only used in the New Testament to designate supernatural effort. The other word is *dunamis* from which we get "dynamite". Wow! That's powerful!

Arthur Gossip, one-time pastor in downtown Glasgow, was visiting some poor tenement parishioners. The last family on his list lived on the fifth floor. Tired and footsore he decided to call it a day but as he turned to go home he heard a voice say, "Then I'll have to go alone." Gossip received a burst of new energy as he returned to his task praying, "No, Lord. We'll go together."

You will want to pray for that inner resource as you start a new day. Read 2 Timothy 2, and meditate on what you need to be a workman approved by God.

Quote Do not pray for tasks equal to your powers.
Pray for powers equal to your tasks.

– Philip Brooks

Promise "I can do everything through him who gives me strength" (Philippians 4.13).

DAY 69 I want you to know how much I am struggling for you and for those at Laodicea, and for all who have not met me personally (2.1)

Good Morning, Disciple,

I thought you would like to know that patience pays off. This afternoon I photographed the grey wagtail feeding in the shallow bed of the Windrush. Since my episode with the dog (day 54), I have daily awaited the bird's return. Now I wait again – this time to see whether I captured it without camera shake.

Patience must have been just part of Paul's struggle for the two congregations. Writing to people he had only heard about must have been another. But undoubtedly his greatest struggle came from his

deep love for the Lord and for those to whom he had been called
to minister and to save from false teaching. Such a love will drive a
man to prayer.

I am reminded of a moving story about Rees Howells, a Welsh coal
miner. Every night, after twelve hours down the pit, he would walk
two miles to a village in the valley to minister God's love to an eager
congregation. Late one night he returned home through the rain to
his little miner's cottage. "Rees, my boy," said his father, "I wouldn't
have gone over there tonight for twenty pounds."

"Neither would I for twenty pounds, dad," answered Rees.

Godly men and women are not motivated by personal gain. They
count the cost, then pay it with every deed of service. Their only
reward, at last, is to hear God's "Well done – good and faithful
servant".

Such were the pressures of being monarch that the eleventh-century
King Henry of Bavaria applied to a monastery to adopt a life of quiet
contemplation and prayer. The wise prior warned the King that he
would be expected to take a pledge of obedience. The King agreed.

"Then I will tell you what to do, your Majesty. Go back to your
throne and continue your service to the people of Bavaria, for that
is where God has placed you." When eventually the King died, this
was the summary of his life: "The King learned to rule by being
obedient."

A throne, a coal pit, a prison cell – wherever God has placed you
will not be without its ups and downs, pains and pleasures. The
important thing is to serve obediently.

Take a look at Revelation 3.14-22 to see what happened to the
church at Laodicea, just down the road from Colosse. Hot, cold,
lukewarm – which are you? Agonise for Jesus!

Quote "Men will never cast away their dearest pleasures upon
the drowsy request of someone who does not even appear to
mean what he says" – Richard Baxter.

Promise "For it is God who works in you to will and to act
according to his good purpose" (Philippians 2.13).

DAY 70 My purpose is that they may be encouraged in heart (2.2a)

Good Morning, Disciple,

I do hope you are, encouraged as you read God's Word each day.

Encouragement is like a honey sandwich. It is sweet, tasty and holds the bread together but, as we shall see in the days ahead of us, for Paul, its sweetness does not detract from its strength. Sometimes real encouragement comes from exposing our weaknesses, at other times from revealing our strengths.

F. E. Herzberger put into doggerel an event in the life of Martin Luther. Apparently the great reformer was feeling depressed by the constant opposition to his teaching and had begun to doubt the providence of God.

> One day when skies loomed the blackest
> This greatest and bravest of men
> Lost heart and in oversad spirit
> Refused to take courage again.
>
> Neither eating nor drinking nor speaking
> To an anxious wife, children or friends,
> Till Katherine dons widow's garments
> And deepest of mourning pretends.
>
> Surprised, Luther asked why she sorrowed.
> "Dear Doctor," his Katie replied,
> "I have cause for the saddest of weeping,
> For God in His heaven has died!"
>
> Her gentle rebuke did not fail him,
> He laughingly kissed his wise spouse,
> Took courage, and banished his sorrow,
> And joy again reigned in his house.

My younger daughter, Ruth, like her father, experienced considerable difficulty in learning to read due to dyslexia. At her first school she would come home distraught day after day because of the teacher's insistence that every child should read aloud in front of the class every day. Ruth's confidence was destroyed. She became more and more withdrawn until all her work suffered.

In desperation we moved her to another school where dyslexia was recognised as a learning difficulty. It was there that the art master, Mr Sackley, spotted her talent for painting. What fun she had trying out different techniques. School became a place of laughter and excitement. Eventually her confidence was restored. Her work improved and she went on to take A-levels with the likelihood of a useful career ahead – because an art teacher encouraged her talent.

Is there someone you can encourage today? Meditate on this theme in Acts 11.19-30 and pray about what you should do. Note the very special ministry of Barnabas.

Quote "Correction does much, but encouragement does more. Encouragement after censure is as the sun after a shower" – Goethe.

Promise "As a mother comforts her child, so will I comfort you; and you will be comforted over Jerusalem" (Isaiah 66.13).

DAY 71 United in love (2.2b)

Good Morning, Disciple,

The giant Californian redwoods have stood for hundreds of years. The largest trees are over 300ft tall, yet for all their height they have a very shallow root system – far too shallow to hold a tree that size in a storm. So what is their secret of long life? The answer lies underground. The root systems are so intertwined that what they could not achieve alone, they do by being knitted together.

That's one of the meanings behind the Greek word translated here as united, knit together in love.

In Roman fighting formation the soldiers interlocked their shields so that they could move forward against the enemy covered on all sides and above their heads: a solid wall of defence.

The apostle knew that if this little church was going to withstand the attack of destructive forces, it needed to be functioning just like those soldiers and redwoods. Error destroys, even truth may divide, but love unites.

When the Church is united it is not only able to withstand the winds of false doctrine, but it also fulfils the vision of Jesus. He said, "A new command I give you: Love one another. As I have loved you, so you must love one another. By this all men will know that you are my disciples, if you love one another" (John 13.34-35).

Another possible meaning of the word is "teach": "being taught together in love". This would certainly fit the context, for Paul is clearly anxious that love should be discerning and that truth should not be cold hard dogma. Discerning love and courteous truth need to be taught or else, left to ourselves, we are inclined to have so much love that we degrade truth, or so much truth that we abandon love.

I came across a true story in *Leadership* magazine of two ladies in a nursing home. Margaret was paralysed down her left side and Ruth down her right. Both had been accomplished pianists but, of course, could play no longer – until the director of the home sat them down at a piano and encouraged them to play solo pieces together. The two became one in a very beautiful way, as they learned the art of complementing each other's strengths and weaknesses.

I trust you are getting to know the folk in your church. Meditate on the clues to fellowship in Ephesians 3.14-4.16.

Quote True love in this differs from gold and clay,
that to divide is not to take away.
– Percy Bysshe Shelley, *Epipsychidion*

Promise "All men will know that you are my disciples, if you love one another" (John 13.35).

DAY 72 So that they may have the full riches of complete understanding, in order that they may know the mystery of God, namely Christ (2.2c)

Good Morning, Disciple,

Whenever Paul speaks of Christ Jesus he can hardly help the superlatives falling off his pen. "Full riches" and "complete understanding" of the open secret – nothing short of this will confound the pretentious claims of the wreckers, whose pseudo-intellectualism threatened the faith of ordinary believers.

You have it all, in Christ, says the apostle. You are not spiritual paupers. When it comes to spiritual insight you are overflowing with riches. These pretenders offer only shallow human insights. But "Oh the depth of the riches of the wisdom and knowledge of God!" (Romans 11.33).

All this is no less relevant to our own day. Only this morning I was reading how Whitley Strieber, an author of horror books, says he was lifted up by aliens on Boxing Day night in 1985 into another world dimension. There he was subjected to experiences more horrendous than anything his imagination had concocted in his novels. Real event, a delusion or hoax, we must take seriously the fascination such stories have for our contemporaries. Disillusioned by the emptiness of materialism, many fall hook, line and sinker for any spiritual counterfeit.

Tal Brooke says in *When the World Will Be as One*, "They claim the whole human race is being prepared for the New Age, but that only the worthy will make it all the way. And this depends on the ability of individuals to absorb the new teachings and the new models of reality, and to abandon the old negative programming."

Such concepts are the very stuff of Colossians 2. We must heed the Scriptures' warnings if we are not to be led astray or press-ganged into error by media hype and popular opinion.

I come back to Paul's superlatives. The Greek word for "complete" is unique to the New Testament and even there it is used only three times. Hebrews 6.11 talks about making your hope "sure" and Hebrews 10.22 about "full assurance" of faith. We could use this idea of certainty to translate it "fully assured understanding". The King James version has "all riches of the full assurance of understanding". That's what we have in Christ!

I hope that, as you read 1 Corinthians 1.18-31, you will gain an even fuller insight from God's own perspective.

Quote "The major reason for so much mental, emotional and spiritual immaturity in our world, is that we have deserted the only soil in which we may grow" – Charles A. Trentham, *Shepherd of the Stars* (Broadman, 1962).

Promise "For there is no difference between Jew and Gentile – the same Lord is Lord of all and richly blesses all who call on him" (Romans 10.12).

DAY 73 Christ, in whom are hidden all the treasures of wisdom and knowledge (2.3)

Good Morning, Disciple,

Once again we have ascended to the high peak of Paul's teaching. To those who take their stand on mysteries whispered in the shadows, to the worldly wise who boast the achievements of science without gratitude to God, to philosophers, whether humanist or religious, the word is out – it is not in "it" but in "Him" that we are called to put our trust.

A follower of the Christian Science cult once visited a simple Christian friend to convince her of the teachings of Mary Baker Eddy. After listening to several hours of sophisticated theorising about mind and matter this Christian lady said, "I don't understand what it is you're driving at. Can't you put it in simpler terms?"

"Well," replied the other, "in the first place you must get hold of this: God is a principle, not a person. You see, my dear, we worship a principle."

"Enough," exclaimed the Christian, "that would never do for me! I worship a personal God revealed in Christ, my blessed, adorable Saviour."

I am reminded of how the apostle warned his spiritual son Timothy, "Guard what has been entrusted to your care. Turn away from godless chatter and the opposing ideas of what is falsely called knowledge" (1 Timothy 6.20).

Such knowledge there at Ephesus, and possibly here at Colosse, was the kind passed around by Jewish ascetics who built great mystical schemes out of the wisdom literature and the law. The "in group" glorified this "hidden knowledge".

Now, says Paul, the only wisdom and knowledge you need are in Christ. Hidden in Him. Not hidden from the believers, but hidden from the arrogant (Matthew 11.25).

Hidden like treasures in a home safe, protected from burglars but available to the owner. Hidden, as ammunition might be by an army, camouflaged to avoid capture by the enemy but available to replenish supplies. All that you need is available to you in Christ.

As you read Proverbs 2 replace the word wisdom with the name of Jesus. You will then be able to meditate on how Christ fulfils what is promised. And remember – the wise still seek Him!

Quote "Jesus is the great Book. He who can indeed study Him in the Word of God will know all he ought to know. Humility opens this divine book, faith reads in it, love learns from it" – Quesnel, quoted in *The Cambridge Bible* (Cambridge University Press, 1893).

Promise "He holds victory in store for the upright, he is a shield to those whose walk is blameless" (Proverbs 2.7).

DAY 74 I tell you this so that no one may deceive you by fine-sounding arguments (2.4)

Good Morning, Disciple,

Browsing through a New Age book store in Dallas, Texas, to see what was new in the world of paganism, I came across the almost unbelievable title, *Myths to Live By*. It was a salutary reminder that there are some people gullible enough to believe anything.

Early nineteenth-century settlers in New York State and Ohio found huge burial mounds. Local legend had it that the mound builders were a lost race, an advanced civilisation overrun by barbaric invaders. The mounds, according to this theory, were evidence of a catastrophic war resulting in the burial of a whole civilisation.

Though it was later proved that the mound builders were actually upper Mississippi Indian tribes who made a practice of gathering the remains of the dead into common graves, this did not stop a certain smooth-talking charlatan from duping even Christians away from their faith in the gospel to follow him.

Joseph Smith claimed an angel led him to gold plates on which the history of the "lost race" and the Saviour's visit to America were inscribed. Smith "miraculously" translated the gold plates which were, with equal good fortune, "miraculously" taken from the earth before they could be seen by anyone else except the founder of Mormonism – the so-called Church of Jesus Christ, Latter Day Saints.

It was his own mother who exposed the lie when she wrote that he was spinning yarns like those found in the Book of Mormon years before the golden plates were thought of.

Someone once asked a farmer how a cow gets lost. "Oh," said the dairyman, "as it grazes with its head down, it spies another, more delicious turf, then another and another until it has strayed."

Paul, aware of the many ideas and philosophies prevalent in the Lycus Valley, warns the believers of his day and our own against fast-talking spiritual conmen who by plausible argument, psychic phenomena and deceptive reasoning divert faith into a blind alley. Though the matter be false, the manner of persuasion is so beguiling that the unwary are carried away by its eloquence.

Deception and self-deception are countered, as you will find in James 1.19-27, by putting into practice daily what God shows you in His word.

Quote "Nothing is so dangerous as feeble reasoning allied to fast talking" – Dick Lucas, *The Message of Colossians* (Inter-Varsity Press, 1980).

Promise "But the man who looks intently into the perfect law that gives freedom, and continues to do this, not forgetting what he has heard, but doing it – he will be blessed in what he does" (James 1.25).

DAY 75 For though I am absent from you in body I am present with you in spirit (2.5a)

Good Morning, Disciple,

Relationship is based upon personal knowledge. For example, though I am speaking to you every morning through these letters I can love you only in a rather abstract sense. If, on the other hand, we were meeting together on a daily basis the true depth of Christian fellowship would flourish the more we got to know each other.

Paul was between these two extremes. He was unable to be with the little congregation at Colosse, which he had never met personally, because of his imprisonment. Yet he had heard so much about them from Epaphras and from Onesimus, the slave who ran away from the very house where the church met, that he felt as if he knew them intimately.

As the two of them talked about the personalities and problems of their home church Paul was stirred, as we have already seen, to pray. This would breed deeper affection, so much so that the apostle could almost have been with those whom he had never met and seen those whom he had never set eyes on.

True Christian fellowship is not severed by distance or separation. We have an unbreakable fellowship if we are one in Christ. The real problem is not how to love at a distance, but how to maintain our affection for one another when we are thrown together. You may know the old ditty:

> Oh, to live above with the saints I love
> Will all be heaven and glory!
> But to live below with the saints I know –
> That's a very diff'rent story!

The key, whether together or apart, is to meditate on our oneness.

> We are one in receiving God's grace.
> One in faith and faithfulness.
> We are one in prayer before God our Father.
> One in thanksgiving for His mercy.
> We are one in the gift of the Holy Spirit.
> One in the family. Brothers, sisters,
> We are one in serving each other.
> One in sharing the good news.
> We are one, separated from the world.
> One in spiritual warfare.
> One, and only one, in Christ.

As you read Philippians 1 see if you can detect other areas of oneness. Though we have never met, I am glad that you and I are one.

Quote "Love finds a way. Indifference finds an excuse" – Anon.

Promise "Now that you know these things, you will be blessed if you do them" (John 13.17).

DAY 76　I . . . delight to see how orderly you are (2.5b)

Good Morning, Disciple,

Are you ready to face whatever comes your way today? Tuesday 19th February, 1991, was like any other day to David Corner, until he reached Victoria Station where he was due to change trains. At 7.45 a.m. his day – his life – was brought to an abrupt end as he took the full blast of an IRA bomb planted in a waste bin.

That same evening his widow, Jane, was interviewed on BBC television. "I don't feel any hatred," she said, "I just feel very sad that he's gone."

Asked by a reporter whether her husband would have been as forgiving she answered, without hesitation, "Absolutely. No question. He was a very forgiving man."

Jane and David Corner, parents of sixteen-month-old Adam, were practising Christians. At their church in Thornton Heath David was serving as a church warden and Jane as a Sunday School teacher. When tragedy struck they were not ready for it but neither were they unprepared for it. The orderly faith at work in the home, where the night before his murder David had bathed and put his son to bed, was a daily preparation for the events of life.

The word Paul uses for orderly is a military term used of a formation or rank of soldiers ready for battle. How appropriate! The Corners' study of God's word, fellowship with other believers, church responsibilities, Christian lifestyle, prayers and faithfulness to their duties were all like so many soldiers ready in formation for 7.45 a.m., Tuesday 19th February.

On that same news bulletin Brigadier Patrick Cordingly, commander of the 7th Armoured Brigade, was seen gathering together his troops in the desert of Saudi Arabia to prepare them for combat. Years of training, months of logistical preparation and marshalling of supplies enabled him to stand on top of an armoured vehicle and assure them, "We are the best trained brigade in the British Army." Battle orders are only an extension of the daily orders of barrack life.

Let me ask you that question again. Are you ready to face whatever comes your way today? Build order into your world, then you will be prepared for any event.

Psalm 91 is a reassuring meditation which will give you new confidence, as you read it and live it.

Quote "To bring order into one's life is to invite His control over every segment" – Gordon MacDonald, *Ordering Your Private World* (Oliver Nelson, 1984).

Promise "He who dwells in the shelter of the Most High will rest in the shadow of the Almighty" (Psalm 91.1).

DAY 77   And how firm your faith in Christ is (2.5c)

Good Morning, Disciple,

Yesterday we looked at one military term and today we have another. *Taxis*, the Greek word for order as in a formation of soldiers, I like to see as being ready for the battle. Today's word, *stereoma*, has to do with a rock and means a bulwark, a place of security. King David sang, "The Lord is my rock, my fortress and my deliverer; my God is my rock, in whom I take refuge . . ." (Psalm 18.2). Elsewhere he says, "In the day of trouble he will keep me safe in his dwelling; he will hide me in the shelter of his tabernacle, and set me high upon a rock" (Psalm 27.5).

In other words, the firmness of our faith in Christ is the solid ground on which we stand. It is like a fortress when we come under attack. It is like a strong defensive wall which protects the land from a raging sea. It is the Patriot missile which downs the incoming Scud.

A group of jealous architects once criticised Sir Christopher Wren's designs for a new London church. Despite his success with St Paul's Cathedral the church officials would not believe Wren's insistence that the columns he proposed were sufficient to hold the roof. Instead they listened to his critics and ordered two extra supporting columns. Fifty years after the building had been completed some painters working high up in the church discovered that these two supporting columns were two feet short of the roof. Wren's faith in the original number of columns had been vindicated. They stood firm for centuries. The other supports were mere show.

So it is with Christ. He is able to hold us up when we come under attack. We have a whole spiritual armoury placed at our disposal, as you will see when you read Ephesians 6.10-20. Notice that all but one piece is defensive armour. Meditate on the weapon and how you might use it.

Quote   On Christ the solid rock I stand;
         All other ground is sinking sand.
                  – Edward Mote (1797-1874) and others.

Promise "Trust in the Lord forever, for the Lord, the Lord, is the Rock eternal" (Isaiah 26.4).

DAY 78   So then just as you received (2.6a)

Good Morning, Disciple,
   You might think I have bitten off a mouse-sized morsel this morning. But in reality each phrase in this one sentence is pivotal to our understanding of the whole letter to the Colossians.
   This word "received" is, in the Greek language, an almost technical term denoting the reception of a specific tradition. Jewish traditions had been safeguarded from one generation to the next by careful transmission, right down from Moses to the leaders of the synagogue. The process was intended to preserve and protect the law, but it was fundamentally flawed. Jesus warned, "You have let go of the commands of God and are holding on to the traditions of men" (Mark 7.8).
   In contrast Paul is always at pains to show that the gospel is God speaking directly through Jesus. Therefore, he can say, "When you received the word of God, which you heard from us, you accepted it not as the word of men, but as it actually is, the word of God" (1 Thessalonians 2.13).
   Initially the teaching of Christ was passed on in the same way as the rabbinical teaching of Judaism. So, for instance, Paul exhorts his protégé, Timothy, "What you have heard from me, keep as a pattern of sound teaching, with faith and love in Christ Jesus. Guard the good deposit which was entrusted to you – guard it with the help of the Holy Spirit who lives in us" (2 Timothy 1.13-14). And Paul had clearly instructed Pastor Epaphras in the same way, so that the Colossian church might receive the word of truth.

So here Paul endorses the teaching of faithful Epaphras and contrasts it with the "traditions of men", which were threatening to do the same with the gospel as they had done with the Law. In so doing, of course, he passed on to us in written form this letter which the Holy Spirit has preserved in the Scripture for us.

It is these very Scriptures which are able to "make you wise for salvation through faith in Christ Jesus. All Scripture is God-breathed and is useful for teaching, rebuking, correcting and training in righteousness" (2 Timothy 3.15-16).

I urge you to continue receiving and building your understanding with me, day by day. Turn to 1 Corinthians 15.1-11 and see how the gospel was given, and give thanks to God for its preservation.

Quote "All growth and progress in the Christian life must be entirely consistent with its beginnings" – Dick Lucas, *The Message of Colossians* (Inter-Varsity Press, 1980).

Promise "Everyone who listens to the Father and learns from him comes to me" (John 6.45b).

DAY 79 Christ Jesus as Lord (2.6b)

Good Morning, Disciple,

Have you noticed something? We are back on the summit again. There is no peak higher than this one in which Paul uses three descriptive titles for the one whom we have received.

He is "the Christ" – the expected Messiah of the Old Testament, the one who will come again in unmistakable glory and power. Beware of any who comes saying that Christ Jesus is only one of many gods. He is the only God. He is not a Hindu "avatar" come to "point the way". He is The Only Way. He is not a mystical guru come to "introduce the truth". He is The Truth.

Mystics love to tell the story of four blind men describing an elephant. The first felt its trunk and said, "The elephant is like a huge snake."

Another felt its tail and said, "No. It is like a length of rope."

"Surely not," said the third who had pulled on his ear, "he is like a canvas tent."

The last blind man, putting his arms around the elephant's leg, declared it to be like a tree.

The "christ" spirit, they conclude, is whatever you want it to be – Krishna, Sun Myung Moon, Rama, Shiva or the personal "christ" of your own intuition.

My answer to their illustration is, let the man who is not blind give the description, for as Jesus said, "If a blind man leads a blind man, both will fall into a pit" (Matthew 15.14).

To make his point absolutely clear Paul defines "the Christ" by His earthly title, "Jesus". Jesus the Christ ties down our belief to an historic person at a point in time.

The title "Lord" is that which sealed the death of Paul and, if tradition is correct, all but John in the disciple band and many of the early believers. To call Him "Jesus the Christ" might displease the Jews. But to call Him "Christ Jesus the Lord" – that was to challenge the very authority of Rome. The Caesars had for many years claimed divinity, but with Nero it became a test of loyal allegiance to bow and declare, "Caesar is Lord."

Christians could "give to Caesar what is Caesar's", but they could not give him the title that belongs to God alone.

As you read Romans 10 meditate on verse 9 and ask yourself, "What does this name mean to me?"

Quote "You cannot believe on a half-christ. We take Him for what he is – the anointed Saviour and Lord who is King of Kings and Lord of Lords!" – A. W. Tozer, *I Call It Heresy* (Christian Publications, 1974).

Promise "If you confess with your mouth, "Jesus is Lord," and believe in your heart that God raised him from the dead, you will be saved" (Romans 10.9).

DAY 80 Continue to live in him (2.6c)

Good Morning, Disciple,

Now this, as they say, is where the rubber meets the road – where the nitty gets gritty. Receiving Christ Jesus as Lord is not only the starting point of Christian faith, it is the day-by-day, hour-by-hour exercise of that faith. For faith is not just mental assent to a set of truths. Unapplied dogma has about it the stench of death.

So Paul urges us to "continue to live in him". We might translate it, "Keep on walking in a Christ-centred lifestyle."

As we have already seen, we were not saved "by good works" but "unto good works". Do you remember your meditation on day five, in Titus 3? He reminds us of our old sinful nature, of God's mercy which brought us salvation, of our rebirth through the Holy Spirit. Then he stresses that those who have trusted God should be "careful to devote themselves to doing what is good". Do you see the progression?

Guideposts magazine carried the story of a psychology student at Washington State University who received head injuries in a motor accident. Doctors warned that he had complete memory loss and would probably never walk again.

By sheer grit he learned painfully how to walk and talk, but then, with no recall of any previous experience or education, he began the much harder job of relearning everything from scratch. A new life at twenty-three. One day, when struggling from one room to another, he stopped in front of a picture of a bearded man kneeling in agony beside a huge rock. He asked his mother who this man was. She introduced him to the Jesus who could "make all things new".

As a young Christian he read Paul's words: "Forgetting what is behind and straining to what is ahead, I press toward the goal to win the prize for which God has called me heavenward in Christ Jesus" (Philippians 3.13-14). For Stan Peterson that meant going on to become a PhD in Psychology, now heading his own clinic with brain-injured patients and stroke victims. When they are tempted to look back with regret he points them forward to a new life.

Read 1 Thessalonians 4, and meditate on what lies ahead as you surrender every part of your life to Jesus as Lord.

Quote "The more I considered Christianity, the more I found that while it had established rule and order, the chief aim of that order was to give room for good things to run wild" – G. K. Chesterton, *Orthodoxy* (Doubleday & Co., 1959).

Promise "After that, we who are still alive and are left will be caught up with them in the clouds to meet the Lord in the air. And so we will be with the Lord forever" (1 Thessalonians 4.17).

DAY 81 Rooted (2.7a)

Good Morning, Disciple,

Here is a riddle to start your day. When is a Christian not a Christian?

At the end of a one-day evangelism training seminar for Christian leaders in Surrey, a middle-aged Scotsman asked if I would stay behind and chat to him.

"From what you have said today," he started, "though I have been a minister in the Church of Scotland for these past twenty-five years, I do not qualify to call myself a Christian."

I asked him a question. "Suppose you were to stand before God and He were to say to you, 'Why should I let you in to my heaven?' What would you say?"

"Well," says he, "I think, until today, I would have said that I am a caring person, on the side of the poor and disadvantaged, and hope that as I was on His side He would be on my side. But clearly that is wrong! I should be trusting in Him, in what He has done for me." He then asked me to lead him in a prayer of faith and acceptance.

About 250 years before that encounter, an Oxford don and Anglican missionary wrote of the faith he had found earlier that evening: "I felt I did trust in Christ, Christ alone, for salvation, and an assurance was given to me that He had taken away my sins, even mine, and saved me from the law of sin and death." His name? John Wesley.

Here's my point: as the root is, so is the branch. As Paul puts it, "If the root is holy, so are the branches" (Romans 11.16). But "the love of money is the root of all kinds of evil" (1 Timothy 6.10). A "bitter root" (Hebrews 12.15) will have disastrous results in the life of a congregation. What is planted will be harvested.

Some people go to great lengths to research their family trees. Why? Because of roots.

Paul says (notice the tense), "You, having been rooted." Where? In Christ! You cannot grow up into Christ unless you have been rooted "in Christ". You cannot "bear fruit" (1.10) unless you are, first of all, firmly planted.

Take your choice of meditation passages this morning. Read again
the parable of the sower in Mark 4, or go to Psalm 1 and drink in
its message.

Quote "The meaning of 'new birth' is that we know God by a
vital relationship, not only by our intellect" – Oswald
Chambers, *The Psychology of Redemption* (Christian Literature
Crusade, 1930).

Promise "He is like a tree planted by streams of water, which
yields its fruit in season and whose leaf does not wither.
Whatever he does prospers" (Psalm 1.3).

DAY 82   And built up in him (2.7b)

Good Morning, Disciple,
   Today the metaphor changes. We move from the garden to the
building site. I have a sneaking suspicion that in his "quiet time" that
morning the great apostle came across God's promise to His rebellious
nation Israel: "My eyes will watch over them for their good and I
will bring them back to this land. I will build them up and not tear
them down; I will plant them and not uproot them" (Jeremiah 24.6).
   Be that as it may, we are this morning faced with one of Paul's
favourite themes, for though he was a tent-maker by trade, I think
he must also have dabbled in a stretch of bricklaying. He does, after
all, call himself "an expert builder".
   Not only does he mix his metaphors; he also mixes his tenses. Having
"been rooted", we are now "being built up". Like our "walking"
it is a continuous process.
   The image is that of the individual Christian and the corporate body
of believers being built into a spiritual temple.
   Physically it took a lifetime, forty-six years (John 2.20), to build
the temple in Jerusalem. There is a sense in which a building needs
a builder as long as it stands. The foundation stone of Salisbury
Cathedral was laid in 1220. As I write to you today its famous spire
is wearing a collar of scaffolding as stonemasons take eight years to
restore the ancient structure.
   Stonemasons of old could spend a whole lifetime working on one

building. I recall the story of when two of them were asked how they viewed their work. "It's a job," said the first, "I just muddle along from one day to the next." "Ah! to me," said the second, "it's my life and my joy. For when I am long gone this edifice will stand to the glory of God."

If we are in partnership with the master-builder, we will not just muddle along, but consider it our life and joy to build and be built to the glory of God. In Christ the whole building is joined together and rises to become a holy temple in the Lord (Ephesians 2.22).

You can read more in 1 Corinthians 3, and as you do, meditate on which you would rather be part of – the construction gang or the demolishers. What a choice!

Quote "The disciple is one who in every area of life determines from the Bible what is right and lives it consistently, rather than allowing circumstances to shape his conduct" – Walter A. Hendrichsen, *Disciples Are Made Not Born* (Victor Books, 1976).

Promise "And in him you too are being built together to become a dwelling in which God lives by his Spirit" (Ephesians 2.22).

DAY 83   Strengthened in the faith as you were taught (2.7c)

Good Morning, Disciple,

As one brick said to the other brick, "We may be under construction today but I'll see you at the top tomorrow."

The word "strengthened" in the Greek can be used as a legal term meaning to guarantee a contract. Our standing before Christ is guaranteed by the content of "the faith", that is, the body of teaching which is called "the gospel of truth". More straightforwardly the word fits the context of a building being strengthened.

You may have spotted already how Paul is deliberately echoing his prayer in chapter one. "Live a life worthy of the Lord" and "continue to live (walk) in Him"; "bearing fruit" and "rooted"; "growing" and "built up"; "strengthened with all power according to his glorious might" and "strengthened in the faith". And tomorrow we shall see "giving thanks to the Father" become "overflowing with thankfulness".

What Paul has prayed for he now instructs, so that we may be ready for the attack which comes from the "faith-wreckers".

In C. S. Lewis's book *The Screwtape Letters*, Screwtape, the Devil, writes to Wormwood, a junior demon. In one of the letters he tells him: "What we want, if men become Christians at all, is to keep them in a state of mind I call 'Christianity And'. You know – Christianity and the Crisis, Christianity and the New Psychology, Christianity and the New Order, Christianity and Faith Healing, Christianity and Psychical Research, Christianity and Vegetarianism . . . Substitute for the faith itself some fashion with a Christian colouring. Work on their horror of the same old thing."

Nothing changes! Oh, we may have different names – Christianity and Yoga, Christianity and New Age, Christianity and Ecology. Even better for old Screwtape if it is something apparently good, just so long as it takes our attention off "the faith".

Hebrews has a good summary of the warning in this chapter: "Do not be carried away by all kinds of strange teaching. It is good for your hearts to be strengthened by grace" (Hebrews 13.9).

I wonder if, as you meditate on 1 Timothy 4, you can see some of the special qualifications required for those who aspire to teach God's word.

Quote "Conformity. This, not true religion, is the opiate of the masses, leaving us easy victims to the seductions of the consumer culture" – Dick Keyes, *Christianity Today*, May 1988.

Promise "He will keep you strong to the end, so that you will be blameless on the day of our Lord Jesus Christ" (1 Corinthians 1.8).

DAY 84 And overflowing with thankfulness (2.7d)

Good Morning, Disciple,

I wonder if you have ever thought of yourself as a turtle? – a spiritual turtle, of course! Let me explain what I mean.

Alex Haley, the much-admired author of *Roots*, has hanging in his office a drawing of a turtle sitting on a fence. He delights to explain to visitors that the picture is there to remind him that, just as the turtle which cannot climb must have had the help of someone, so he is grateful to the folk who helped him in his career.

In a world of self-assertive pomposity such humility of spirit is refreshing. Thankfulness can only grow in the soil of humility, but it bears a harvest of exuberant content.

I think this is what Paul has in mind here. Look at the context. God has rooted us in Christ. He is building us up in Christ. We are being strengthened in our faith as we learn to hold on to ''the faith'', the gospel. What is the result? We overflow, like a river bursting its banks, with thankfulness.

The contrast is with the false teachers who promised spiritual fulfilment by an egotistical dependence on their own ideas, good works and asceticism. Who on earth would they say thank you to? To themselves! At best they could only pat each other on the back.

Gratitude is the overflow of what God has graciously been pouring into our lives. It is the bubbling over of praise from the heart overwhelmed by the goodness of God. Without it we would become insufferably self-righteous. If spiritual growth is not constantly accompanied by such thanksgiving, we develop a self-centred superiority which focuses the attention of others on us rather than on Christ. To keep up this facade of spirituality we begin, before long, to neglect the resources available to us in Christ, and wander off into myths and fables.

Alexander Maclaren, a Scottish expositor of a former generation, put it well when he said, ''The highest nobleness of which man is capable is reached when, moved by the mercies of God, we yield ourselves living sacrifices, thank-offerings to Him who yielded Himself the sin-offering for us.''

Meditate this morning on Psalm 107. It is a great hymn of thankfulness. Then compose your own personal hymn for what God has done in your life.

Quote ''Gratitude is that which completes the circle whereby blessings, that drop down into our hearts and lives, return to the Giver in the form of unending, loving and spontaneous adoration'' – William Hendriksen, *N. T. C. Colossians* (Baker Book House, 1979).

Promise "Give thanks to the Lord, for he is good. His love endures forever" (Pslam 136.1).

DAY 85 See to it that no one takes you captive through hollow and deceptive philosophy (2.8a)

Good Morning, Disciple,

I have a hunch that, while the apostle Paul was chained to his Roman soldier guard, he must have talked over battle strategies. The shift at this point in his letter is into an all-out land offensive on those who would seek to destroy the young Church by taking it back into the very slavery from which it was freed (1.13-14). The plundering parasites will not kidnap the believers, if he can forewarn them of the enemy's tactics. They will not be taken as prisoners of war if they will heed his warnings. There is a minefield of deception, but he has the map.

In the sixth century BC Pythagoras was to be honoured with the title *sophos* (wise), but in a spirit of true humility he declined the title in preference for *philosophos* (lover of wisdom). So was born the first philosopher. Not all who have since sported the name have been as modest.

Paul is not against philosophy of itself, just those who flaunt their "superior" wisdom as confidence tricksters to devalue the faith of believers.

Who were these philosophers? They may have been converted "pagans" who had slipped back into a primitive gnosticism. More likely they were Jews who wanted to drag the young Church back into the ritual, Law and ceremonies of Judaism. Evidently a group of converted Jews was trying, in Galatia and later in Ephesus, to bind the Gentiles to circumcision and ceremonial Judaism, and it is quite likely that the problem surfaced in Colosse, too.

Paul's word to the Galatians was relevant for Colosse and is even more so today: "It is for freedom that Christ has set us free. Stand firm, then, and do not let yourselves be burdened again by a yoke" (Galatians 5.1).

You may be sure that anything which seeks to add to what Christ has already done is sham. It promises what it cannot deliver. Its hollow emptiness must not be traded for "the glorious riches" of Christ. "The serpent deceived me," pleaded Eve (Genesis 3.13). Don't let him deceive you! He wears many disguises, some of them respectable, many religious. Beware! – Christ plus anything equals nothing. Rejoice! – Christ plus nothing equals everything.

See how Paul had to fight for this in Galatians 5.1-12 and meditate on the "fulness of Christ".

Quote "Christians conquered the pagan world because the Christian outlived, out-thought and out-died the pagan" – T. R. Glover, in *Treasury of Sermon Illustrations* by C. L. Wallis (Abingdon Press, 1950).

Promise "But if you are led by the Spirit, you are not under the law" (Galatians 5.18).

DAY 86 Which depends on human tradition (2.8b)

Good Morning, Disciple,

How time flies. It must be all of twenty years ago that I took my young bride to see *Fiddler on the Roof*. Set in Russia, it tells the story of a Jewish ghetto community torn apart by the generation war between the young who were tempted to take up new ideas, and their elders who held on tenaciously to their traditions. The opening song, "Tradition", shows the depth of feeling aroused when traditions are threatened.

Paul's argument is not with Christ-centred philosophy or tradition. He knows full well that if the teaching of the gospel is to be preserved, we must keep the "pattern of sound teaching" – just as you and I are seeking to do together each morning – and take every opportunity to study and hear God's word.

The tradition the apostle had in mind was probably derived from a dogmatic Judaism or, even more likely, a Jewish asceticism. The most cursory reading of the Old Testament shows that the nation of Israel in general kept no closer to the faith as delivered by the partiarchs, than their modern-day counterparts.

A form of Jewish gnosticism called Merkabah was being practised at the time, as witnessed in the Dead Sea Scrolls. It advocated the strictest observance of the Law and an ascetic disciplining of the body which made it possible, with the help of angels, to enter into the heavenlies. An "out of the body" experience, whether by mysticism or LSD, has always been an enticement to a minority of spiritual adventurers.

The Jewish philosophers were a thorn in the side of Jesus (Mark 7.8). And their successors are with us today – not Jewish myths but pseudo-Christian myths and church traditions that are just as dangerous. Tradition dogged our master to the cross, and its pernicious influence persists. As one wag has put it, "Come weal or woe; our status is quo."

Which would you have? The traditions of men or the word of truth, the gospel? The dark secrets whispered by a guru or the open secret of Christ? "You know that it was not with perishable things such as silver and gold that you were redeemed from the empty way of life handed down to you from your forefathers, but with the precious blood of Christ" (1 Peter 1.18-19).

As you meditate on 1 Timothy 1.1-20 give particular thought to verse 19.

Quote "Folly indeed it is, to establish a science wholly divine on foundations wholly human" – Pere Quesnel, *Cambridge Bible – Colossians* (Cambridge University Press, 1893).

Promise "Let us hold unswervingly to the hope we profess, for he who promised is faithful" (Hebrews 10.23).

DAY 87 And the basic principles of this world rather than on Christ (2.8c)

Good Morning, Disciple,

As you know, I try not to use Greek words unless it is really necessary. Today it is necessary. *Stoicheia*, basic principles, originally meant anything in sequence such as 1, 2, 3, 4, or A, B, C. It came eventually to mean "elementary teachings" in the same way as we might say "elementary maths" or the ABC of language.

You will see immediately how attractive such a word would be to the mystics who taught the necessity of progressing ever upward in secret knowledge from novice to master.

It became even more attractive to them when *stoicheia* in popular

Greek came to be used for the four elements, earth, water, air and fire. Philo said, "Some have deified the four *stoicheia* – whilst others have deified the sun and moon and the other planets and fixed stars; others again the heaven alone and others the whole world."

The First Poimandres Tract has an eerily modern, New Age ring to it, when it promises that human beings can escape matter (the body) and by special knowledge liberate the soul to go at will into the celestial sphere. Sounds like astral planing? There is nothing new under the sun!

Bondage to planetary gods (fate, *karma*) or human traditions meant submitting to those powers. This is what the new Christians at Colosse had been rescued from. Why go back into bondage?

Once again, just as with philosophy and tradition, Paul is not pooh-poohing progressive teaching. On the contrary, he urges the believers to move on from elementary teaching of the gospel to knowing God and His word that will combat deceptive philosophies, human traditions and alien spiritual powers. They cannot co-exist, for there are only two alternatives. Either submit to the elementary powers, the "basic principles of this world", or submit to Christ. Go back into bondage or forward into Christ.

Galatians 4 is quite a difficult passage but by now you are ready for solid food. Do not worry too much if you do not understand everything. The heart of the matter is in verses 3 and 4 so you can meditate on these with great benefit.

Quote "If we are not governed by God we shall be governed by tyrants" – William Penn.

Promise "So you are no longer a slave, but a son; and since you are a son, God has made you also an heir" (Galatians 4.7).

DAY 88 For in Christ all the fulness of the Deity lives in bodily form (2.9)

Good Morning, Disciple,

You are not going to believe this, but when I was a student at Spurgeon's College in London I had a decided antipathy towards the study of Greek, in spite of an admirable tutor. So why am I, two days on the trot, falling back on the Greek?

The answer is quite simple. If I do not you will miss the full impact of what the Scripture is teaching.

Consider this then. The word that Paul uses for divinity, *theotes*, is used only this once in the whole New Testament. Why? Because in this ground offensive the teacher of the Gentiles must use his biggest guns.

To understand fully its meaning we must look at another word for divinity, *theiotis*, used in Romans 1.20 to say that God has revealed Himself in nature. But note, He is not nature. Nature reveals divine qualities, not deity.

Jesus reveals divine qualities and characteristics because He is God and is to be worshipped as God. The word divinity is too elastic. Jesus was not a god, sharing with other "divinities" the divine nature, but "The God" in whom all the fulness of God dwells.

This is bad news for Jehovah's Witnesses, and all who would deny His divinity. It is equally unacceptable to those, such as Hindus and New Agers, who would give Him a place as a mere divinity among others. Jesus is uniquely and absolutely God.

This is why the Jews picked up rocks to stone Him when He said, "I and the Father are one" (John 10.30). It was the scandalous "blasphemy" which took Him to the cross.

At the cross it was God in Christ, the perfect righteous Judge of all, fully God, accepting His own self-sacrifice for and on behalf of all mankind, as the perfect man made to be sin. There are not three actors on this stage, only two – God and man. Christ plays both parts at once. If He is not man, He cannot represent man. If He is not God He cannot reconcile man. As John Stott has put it, "Divine self-satisfaction through divine self-substitution."

Christ's humanity and deity are both at work in your meditation this morning, in Luke 8.19-56. As you read, jot down His divine qualities and His human qualities.

Quote "Faith knows its Lord as Divine equally in value and in fact – not a higher angelic visitor, not a man sainted or deified, but a historic incarnation of the only God there is" – H. R. Mackintosh, *The Person of Jesus Christ* (T. & T. Clark, 1912).

Promise "He will proclaim peace to the nations. His rule will extend from sea to sea" (Zechariah 9.10).

DAY 89   And you have been given fulness in Christ (2.10a)

Good Morning, Disciple,

No Greek today – just a marvellous promise! We who are in Christ have His fulness in us. Wow! As we live in the air around us, we breathe and live by that air in us. Not that we are ourselves gods, for the promise is the fulness of Christ, not the deity of Christ. We renounce the pantheism which says that God is all and all is god.

The promise of fulness in Christ contrasts dramatically with the futility of those who promised fulfilment by adding to Christ other doctrines, taboos and rituals. To do so would be to fall into the two sins of Jeremiah 2.13 where God says, "My people have committed two sins: They have forsaken me, the spring of living water, and have dug their own cisterns, broken cisterns that cannot hold water."

How crazy! To hear one say, "If anyone is thirsty, let him come to me and drink", then to turn instead to a polluted stream, would surely be madness. Will a man who is not only offered bread but given the bakery say, "I am still hungry", and go rummaging in the waste bins?

I can hardly contain my excitement as I share with you such a treasure. Take any one of the 365 names attributed to God. Each one belongs to Jesus. He is the great "I AM". He is the rock of ages, the Good Shepherd, the King of Kings, the Prince of Peace, the bright morning star, the pearl of great price – the goal of all your aspirations, until you attain "the whole measure of the fulness of Christ" (Ephesians 4.13).

But amid all this euphoria there is an important point to note: "From the fulness of his grace have we all received one blessing after another" (John 1.16), but all blessings are to flow through us to others.

The one who receives the water of life must become "streams of living water", flowing out to others (John 7.38). He who is a branch of the Vine must prove his discipleship by bearing fruit (John 15.8). Christianity does not exist as a bubble of plenty in a world of need.

So back to basics. As you read the story of the Good Samaritan (Luke 10.25-37) meditate on this question – who was he?

Quote "We are not as barges, having to be towed by others on the bank, nor are we sailing ships, depending on the favourable winds of comfortable circumstances for our progress, but we are as liners, that have the power of their engines within to triumph over waves and storms" – Guy King, *Crossing the Border* (Marshall, Morgan & Scott, 1957).

Promise "He who did not spare his own Son, but gave him up for us all – how will he not also, along with him, graciously give us all things?" (Romans 8.32).

DAY 90   Who is the Head over every power and authority (2.10b)

Good Morning, Disciple,

What has Christ to do with politics? Everything, the Scripture answers.

At the American Constitutional Convention in 1787 delegates from the thirteen States of the Union had spent two months trying to thrash out an agreement. Independence had been won from the English, but the peace was proving to be difficult as each state vied for its own interests.

Benjamin Franklin, then in his eighties, looked at the chaos in the assembly and asked permission to speak. The scientist, rationalist and philosopher leaned on his cane, peered through the spectacles pinched on the end of his nose and addressed the assembly.

"How has it happened, sir, that we have not hitherto once thought of humbly applying to the Father of Lights to illuminate our understanding? In the beginning of the contest with Britain, when we were sensible of danger, we had daily prayers in this room for Divine protection. Our prayers, sir, were heard, and they were graciously answered . . . Do we imagine we no longer need His assistance?

"I have lived, sir, a long time, and the longer I live, the more convincing proofs I see of this truth: 'that God governs in the affairs of men', and if a sparrow cannot fall to the ground without His notice, is it probable that an empire can rise without His aid?"

"We have been assured, sir, in the sacred writings that except the Lord build the house, they labour in vain that build it. I firmly believe this. I also believe that, without His concurring aid, we shall succeed in this political building no better than the builders of Babel: we shall be divided by our little, partial, local interests; our projects will be confounded; and we ourselves shall become a reproach and a by-word down to future ages."

He then went on to move a motion that prayers should precede each day's deliberations. Not one of the delegates was prepared to second the motion. The Convention went on prayerlessly to enact a constitution which would fudge the issue of slavery and thereby ensure a bloody Civil War.

Franklin had, like Nebuchadnezzar of Babylon, learned that "The Most High God is sovereign over the kingdoms of men and gives them to anyone he wishes" (Daniel 4.32).

Because we do not see His hand, that does not alter His headship of powers on earth or in the heavenlies. Whether president or poltergeist, senate or spirit, government or ghost, minister or medium, all come under one authority but not all are part of His body, the Church.

Nebuchadnezzar's testimony in Daniel 4 is a long story but well worth the meditation.

Quote "Live on The Fountain, not in its streams" – H. C. G. Moule, *The Cambridge Bible* (Cambridge University Press, 1893).

Promise "For I am convinced that neither death nor life, neither angels nor demons, neither the present nor the future, nor any powers, neither height nor depth, nor anything else in all creation, will be able to separate us from the love of God that is in Christ Jesus our Lord" (Romans 8.38-39).

DAY 91 In him you were also circumcised, in the putting off of the sinful nature, not with the circumcision done by the hands of men but with the circumcision done by (or to) Christ (2.11)

Good Morning, Disciple,

God gave instructions to Abraham that "Every male among you who is eight days old must be circumcised". To be uncircumcised was a breach of the covenant (Genesis 17.12-14).

God pointed forward to a time when He would achieve what human hands could never do. "The Lord your God will circumcise your hearts . . . so that you may love him with all your heart and with all your soul, and live" (Deuteronomy 30.6). God's covenant to Abraham and the act of circumcision throughout the Old Testament pointed forward to Christ and His fulfilment of both (Galatians 3.16).

What many, even among the believing Jews, could not comprehend was the opening of salvation to the uncircumcised Gentiles. They stumbled at the gospel which proclaimed, "To all who received him (Jesus), to those who believed in his name, he gave the right to become the children of God – children not born of natural descent (the blood line of Abraham) . . . but born of God" (John 1.12-13).

So Paul, a "Hebrew of Hebrews", puts no confidence in his blood relationship, but says, "Neither circumcision nor uncircumcision mean anything; what counts is a new creation" (Galatians 6.15). A man is not a Jew (child of the covenant) if he is only one outwardly (circumcised), nor is circumcision merely outward and physical (minor surgery). No, a man is a Jew (child of the covenant) if he is one inwardly; and circumcision is of the heart, by the Spirit (without hands), not by the written code (legalism) (Romans 2.28).

Jesus has been circumcised for us, not just on the eighth day, but mysteriously on the cross. "In Him you were also circumcised (you died as He died on the cross), in the putting off (stripping away) of the sinful nature (that guilt which God took upon Himself in Christ), not with a circumcision done by the hands of men but with a (heart) circumcision done by (and to) Christ." "It is we who are the circumcision, we who worship by the Spirit of God, who glory in Christ Jesus, and who put no confidence in the flesh" (Philippians 3.3).

As you read Galatians 3 meditate on what it cost for God to deal with your sin – but rejoice!

Quote "What was done to Christ on the cross was done by Christ in the believer" – David Pawson, *The Normal Christian Birth* (Hodder & Stoughton, 1989).

Promise "For we know that our old self was crucified with him so that the body of sin might be done away with, that we should no longer be slaves to sin – because anyone who has died has been freed from sin" (Romans 6.6-7).

DAY 92   Having been buried with him in baptism and raised with him through your faith in the power of God, who raised him from the dead (2.12)

Good Morning, Disciple,

Perhaps yesterday you had a surprise. You discovered you were circumcised. But have you been baptised?

In this one sentence there are three activities of Christ in which we have a share: death, burial, resurrection.

G. K. Chesterton challenged communicators never to present anything which cannot be pictured in colour. So let me present you with some pictures which may be helpful in understanding Christian baptism.

My first picture would be a cross. This is to symbolise step one of being identified with Christ. "If anyone would come after me, he must deny himself and take up his cross and follow me" (Mark 8.34-35).

Five pictures depict the second step, that of baptism. The dove represents God's Holy Spirit which came upon Jesus at His water baptism (Matthew 3.16). Listen to Peter's words at the birth of the Church at Pentecost: "Repent and be baptised . . . And you will receive the gift of the Holy Spirit" (Acts 2.38).

A bath symbolises, as baptism does, the process of washing away our sin. Ananias told Paul, "Get up, be baptised and wash your sins away" (Acts 22.16).

As you are submerged in the waters of baptism it symbolises a burial; as you rise up from the water, a resurrection. But between the act and meeting the Master face to face, we are engaged to be "The Bride of Christ" (Revelation 21.2). A ring symbolises our pledge of love and loyalty to Him. "This water symbolises baptism that now saves you also – not the removal of dirt from the body but the pledge of a good conscience toward God" (1 Peter 3.21).

We shall see the symbolism of the wardrobe when we get to chapter 3. "You who were baptised into Christ have clothed yourselves with Christ" (Galatians 3.27).

Our fifth picture would have to be a body. "For we were all baptised by one Spirit into one body" (1 Corinthians 12.13).

To picture the resurrection I would use a spaceship. Notice the tense here, "raised with him". When Christ was raised and returned to the Godhead, in a mysterious but magnificent way, we were raised with Him. Yes, "God raised us up with Christ and seated us with him in heavenly places" (Ephesians 2.6).

Meditate on our Lord's own baptism in Matthew 3.1-17 which anticipates His later burial.

Quote "The experience of Jesus at His Baptism is as foreign to us as His Incarnation" – Oswald Chambers, *Bringing Sons to Glory* (Christian Literature Crusade, 1943).

Promise "If we have been united with him like this in his death, we will certainly also be united with him in his resurrection" (Romans 6.5).

DAY 93   When you were dead in your sins and in the uncircumcision of your sinful nature, God made you alive with Christ (2.13a)

Good Morning, Disciple,

Leonard Griffiths tells the story of when Cecil B. de Mille went fishing. As the film producer lay reading a book, a big black beetle came crawling out of the water over the gunwale, and fell on to the floor of his canoe. He noticed later that it had died and he thought, "Poor beetle, if only it had stayed down there in the murky depths it would still be living."

As evening drew in, he noticed the brittle black corpse begin to move. It split open to reveal two bulbous eyes, and after a few more erratic shakes out came a gorgeous dragonfly which began to dart over the surface of the lake. Now de Mille viewed those still grubbing in the mud with a new thought. "If only you knew the life and adventure awaiting you, you would leave your grubbing around in the gloom and mud, come into my canoe and die."

God has matched His design of metamorphosis in nature – no, surpassed it – with the gospel. We, who were grubbing around in the darkness of our sinful nature, were walking dead. But we have been raised with Christ to a new life. The God who made the sunlight to dance on the wings of a dragonfly has said to us, "Wake up, O sleeper, rise from the dead, and Christ will shine on you" (Ephesians 5.14).

Here's a riddle for you: what was dead, that died and put death to death? The Christian! That is the process that every believer has gone through. We, who were dead in our trespasses and sin, died to the old sinful nature in Christ our substitute on the cross, thereby putting death to death and receiving life – eternal life.

Here, the ground between Jew and Gentile is level. Both are called uncircumcised, regardless. When it came to passing from death to life both are in the same boat. The new life is not dependent on nationality, status or works but entirely upon God, who made us alive with Christ.

As you meditate on this great theme in Romans 5.12 to 6.11, think how you would express to another what God has done for you. Then pray for an opportunity to share it lovingly, carefully and sensitively.

Quote   I did not think, I did not strive,
                 The deep peace burnt my "me" alive;
                 The bolted door had broken in,
                 I knew that I had done with sin.
                             – John Masefield,
                         "The Everlasting Mercy"

Promise "I tell you the truth, whoever hears my word and believes him who sent me has eternal life and will not be condemned" (John 5.24).

DAY 94 He forgave us all our sins (2.13b)

Good Morning, Disciple,

I recently received a letter from a friend in Alabama, Bob McLeod, who has been visiting a group of men on "death row" in a local prison. He quotes one of the men as saying, "Bob, those of us here who are sentenced to death in the electric chair have an advantage over most people. We are forced to face our inevitable death and have time to get right with God. When I turn the corner heading for that electric chair, I'll know where I'm going because I've accepted and received the forgiveness of God."

Here is a man who has understood the full impact of this verse. He is not pleading to be released from the judgment American law has passed on his crime. But in his imprisonment he has found a God-given pardon, not just for a particular crime, but for all sin. The death penalty for that has already been carried out, not in an electric chair, but on a cross. Perhaps criminals find the gospel so much easier to understand. I sum it up like this. I did something wrong but God, in Christ, took the rap for me. He paid my debt!

It is now more than thirty years since I sat in a prison cell awaiting trial for my criminal activities. The verdict could be none other than "guilty". I had for many years engaged in housebreaking and other forms of petty crime. Like the man in Bob's letter, I had a debt to pay and pay it I did.

Before the great assize of God we all have a debt to pay, a penalty for our sin: "For the wages of sin is death" (Romans 6.23). That judgment has already been made, and if it were the end of the story we would be spiritually on "death row". But the verse goes on to tell us that "the (free) gift of God is eternal life in Christ Jesus our Lord".

Here is yet another gift, the gift of forgiveness: "He forgave us all our sins." Literally translated the word means "having made us a present of our debts". What a beautiful picture of God's grace. It's like presenting your charge sheet of sin to Christ and He in turn giving it back to you with the words, "It is already paid in full." In fact, that is just what He did say from the cross – "It is finished" (John 19.30).

Read Luke 7.36-50 and see a demonstration of one person's thankfulness. How would you express yours?

Quote "The cross of the Lord was the Devil's mousetrap" – St Augustine.

Promise "I have swept away your offences like a cloud, your sins like the morning mist" (Isaiah 44.22).

DAY 95   Having cancelled the written code, with its regulations that was against us and that stood opposed to us (2.14a)

Good Morning, Disciple,

Imagine for a moment that every sin you ever committed were entered into a little black book. This ledger is a record of your indebtedness – rather like running up a slate or a signed IOU There is nothing you can do to repay the debt. You are bankrupt and helpless. If you were to stand before God in this state your judgment would be sure.

Now for the good news! Christ has cancelled your debt. As we saw yesterday, when He dealt with your sins it was as if He had paid the overdraft. He cancelled the IOU; wiped the slate clean; balanced the ledger. Your sins have been crossed out by the cross. They have been washed away (Acts 22.16).

Do you still doubt your forgiveness? Paul has not finished yet. He has one more picture. For this we must go to the foot of the cross. As we look up we see above the head of our dying Saviour a sign written in Aramaic, Latin and Greek: "Jesus of Nazareth, The King of the Jews" (John 19.19). Look again: "Look, the Lamb of God, who takes away the sin of the world" (John 1.29). This time in place of the sign we see with the eyes of faith the cancelled bond, the debt of sin, nailed to the cross.

In his book *Miracle on the River Kwai*, Ernest Gordon tells the story of a group of British prisoners of war forced to labour on a jungle railway. As they passed through a checkpoint one day, the guards counted their shovels and found that one was missing. The Commanding Officer, brandishing a gun, threatened to shoot the whole squad if the culprit did not step forward. After a long silence one of the men confessed. The C.O. picked up a shovel and beat the man across the head until he fell dead.

At the next checkpoint the shovels were counted yet again. But this time the number was correct. The guards at the first check had miscounted. An innocent man had died for his innocent comrades.

"God demonstrates his own love for us in this: while we were still sinners, Christ died for us" (Romans 5.8).

Share with King David as you read Psalm 51, then meditate upon the cross and see there your charge sheet nailed above the head of Jesus.

Quote   Jesus for thee a body takes,
                   Thy guilt assumes, thy fetters breaks,
                   Discharging all thy dreadful debt,
                   And canst thou then such love forget?
                                        – Krishna Pal.

Promise "I, even I, am he who blots out your transgressions, for my own sake, and remembers your sins no more" (Isaiah 43.25).

DAY 96   And having disarmed the powers and authorities, he made a public spectacle of them, triumphing over them by the cross (2.15)

Good Morning, Disciple,

Today we must put on our thinking caps to grapple with a problem in this text. The difficulty focuses on that word "disarmed" which, if translated literally, would read "having stripped himself".

Stripped Himself of the powers and authorities? It is one thing to take upon Himself our sinful nature (v. 11) and to strip it off, but quite another to take upon Himself the very powers of darkness to strip them off. What are we to make of this?

The problem is eased slightly if we take God to be the subject of the sentence; that would have God doing the stripping or disarming, which is what the translators have plumped for.

I prefer to see the logical progression of Paul's arguments here. (a) Sinful nature taken on to be cast off. (b) The debt of our sin taken on only to be washed off. (c) The powers of darkness taken on only to be stripped off.

When speaking of His death Jesus predicted that "the prince of this world is coming," but that "he has no hold on me" (John 14.30). Was He saying that in that final hour Satan would have his full sway, only there to be defeated? Did He not say to the religious mob in the Garden of Gethsemane, "This is your hour – when darkness reigns"?

It would also add weight to the pictorial flow of this verse. Jesus, who created the powers and authorities, draws them to Himself on the cross, to disarm them, "so that by death He might destroy him who holds the power of death" (Hebrews 2.14). Then having stripped them of their power He makes a spectacle of them, much as general might lead the captured enemy in a victory parade. Today the Geneva Convention would prevent us from humiliating the defeated enemy so.

But God has no such qualms. Satan and his followers must be seen to be defeated; the powers stripped of their power. For then we have no need to fear. The devil may still prowl around (1 Peter 5.8), but for the Christian he is a toothless wonder. He has no authority over us and no power to harm us so long as we are in Christ.

Paul may well have had Zechariah 3 in mind as he wrote this verse. As you meditate on it remember that Joshua is the Hebrew for Jesus (Jeshua).

Quote "From the instant of his departure from God, Satan was doomed to win little battles but to lose all wars" – Donald Grey Barnhouse, *The Invisible War* (Zondervan, 1965).

Promise "(Jesus) has gone into heaven and is at God's right hand – with angels, authorities and powers in submission to him" (1 Peter 3.22).

DAY 97 Therefore do not let anyone judge you by what you eat or drink (2.16a)

Good Morning, Disciple,

I must remember this verse the next time my wife looks at me sideways for eating a second helping of apple pie! She's in league with my doctor in trying to reduce my ever-expanding midriff.

But today's verse is neither advocating poor dietary control nor denying our freedom for personal preferences. It is simply warning us of those who would place pseudo-religious controls on what we eat.

Possibly the Jewish Christians at Colosse wanted to retain Old Testament practices of eating kosher foods and ceremonial washings. More likely it was a combination of this Jewishness and pagan mysticism which Paul had in mind. Hence that all-important introductory word, "therefore". Remember the rule? Whenever you see a "therefore" look to see what it's there for.

It refers to verse 8, "See to it that no one takes you captive." All that God has done for you in Christ has given you freedom. Do not squander this freedom by allowing cranks to put restrictions on your diet. As Paul said elsewhere, "It is for freedom that Christ has set us free. Stand firm, then, and do not let yourselves be burdened again by a yoke of slavery" (Galatians 5.1).

The gnostics, believing all matter to be evil, either inclined to over-indulgence because it did not matter what you did to the body, or they moved in the direction of asceticism, denying the body in order to be released from its limitations. Prolonged fasting and abstinence of certain food and drink, in particular meat and wine, were promoted as necessary, in addition to the work of Christ.

No, says Paul. "Food does not bring us near to God; we are no worse off if we do not eat, and no better off if we do" (1 Corinthians 8.8). Jesus Himself ate meat and drank wine. This gnostic heresy threatened, by its dogmatic vegetarianism and teetotalism, the "communion" and the gospel itself.

We have been warned that some will abandon the faith and fall into the trap of asceticism (1 Timothy 4.1-2). This does not mean that if you are a vegetarian out of personal preference, you should eat meat. The key is found in 1 Corinthians 10.31: "Whether you eat or drink or whatever you do, do it all for the glory of God."

I think you will enjoy what the Master has to say in Mark 7.1-23. What a great meditation!

Quote "Conformity to rules is often a rationalisation for allowing self to remain on the throne" – Charles A. Trentham, *The Shepherd of the Stars* (Broadman Press, 1962).

Promise "If we live, we live to the Lord; and if we die, we die to the Lord. So, whether we live or die, we belong to the Lord" (Romans 14.8).

DAY 98   Or with regard to a religious festival, a New Moon celebration or a Sabbath day (2.16b)

Good Morning, Disciple,

At first glance you may see nothing in today's subject which touches you very deeply, but hold on, there may be more here than meets the eye.

Remember the context. Do not let anyone drag you back into bondage since Christ has set you free. It would appear that some in the Colossian church were wanting to hold on to annual feasts, monthly celebrations and weekly Sabbaths – in other words, to reinstitute the requirements of the Law.

It is only when you look at what went with these days that you can begin to understand Paul's concern. At the special feasts, New Moons and Sabbaths, "burnt offerings were presented to the Lord . . . regularly in the proper manner and in the way prescribed" (1 Chronicles 23.31).

The danger was not only a return to special days but to sacrifice and all the trimmings of the old order which Christ had fulfilled and abolished. "How is it," questions Paul, "that you are turning back to those weak and miserable principles? Do you wish to be enslaved by them all over again? You are observing special days and months and seasons of the year."

This does not mean a prohibition of celebration. Oliver Cromwell made that mistake when he banned the celebration of Christmas during the years of the Commonwealth. The voluntary setting apart of high days and holidays is to be encouraged just so long as they do not dishonour or devalue the work of Christ. A voluntary day of prayer and fasting is quite different from a fast imposed by the church calendar. Lenten abstinence will only be a blessing if it is a voluntary focusing on the finished work of Christ.

The same is true even for Sunday observance. The Lord Himself said concerning the Sabbath that it was "made for man, not man for the Sabbath" (Mark 2.27). In this He reflected its original meaning as a gift or a blessing to be received by all mankind (Genesis 2.3). There can be no doubt that, from a physical, emotional, spiritual and family point of view, Sunday observance is a blessing, but we must not turn it into a curse by hedging it about with petty restrictions and tiresome legalism. It is to be enjoyed as an opportunity for the free association of believers.

Meditate further on this theme in Romans 14. Your life will be enriched as you understand these things.

Quote "Was there a feast? Was there a New Moon? Was there a Sabbath? It was all fulfilled in Christ" – Frederick Brook Westcott (Klock & Klock, 1981 reprint).

Promise "Now the Lord is the Spirit, and where the Spirit of the Lord is, there is freedom" (2 Corinthians 3.17).

DAY 99 These are a shadow of the things that were to come; the reality, however, is found in Christ (2.17)

Good Morning, Disciple,

Have you seen the weather forecast today? I do hope it will be fine for you and that you will have some time to enjoy it. What do I mean by "it"? Well, the weather, of course, not the forecast! It would be a strange kind of stupidity to look forward to a sunny afternoon, then waste it by staying indoors watching a video recording of the weather forecast over and over again.

Such was the mentality of the Judaisers. Instead of enjoying the reality of all that Christ had accomplished, they wanted to go back into the shadow-lands of ritual.

Now don't get me wrong. I'm not saying that there was anything wrong with the Law. It came from God for a purpose and a period, to point us to Christ and to heaven. Hebrews, which is really an extended commentary on this verse, states boldly, "The law is only a shadow of the good things that are coming – not the realities themselves." To this extent the law was good, but it should be given a decent burial.

Unless you understand this you will be easy prey for those inside and outside the Church whose confidence is in religiosity.

We see it, for example, in the institutional church where much store is placed on form and order, where only the "priest" may officiate at "holy communion" – notwithstanding the clear statement of Scripture that all who belong to Christ are a "holy priesthood, offering spiritual sacrifices acceptable to God". Ceremonial which has become the exclusive reserve of a professional or "ordered" elite ought to set the alarm bells ringing throughout the Church. Christianity should never seek to be a reflection of the Judaism of which it became the substance in Christ. We have what the prophets looked forward to.

Beware then of those who promise life on a higher religious plane by means which are not taught plainly and unmistakably in the Scriptures. Their formulas and prescriptions are not to be trusted. Their presumed holiness is a cloak for spiritual pride and worse. Your security is in what Christ has done, not in what they tell you to do!

As you read Hebrews 8 you may like to meditate on verse two.

Quote "The death of Christ is the central point of history: here all the roads of the past converge; hence all the roads of the future diverge" – Bishop Stephen Neill, *The Truth of God Incarnate*, ed. E. M. B. Green.

Promise "Therefore he is able to save completely those who come to God through him, because he always lives to intercede for them" (Hebrews 7.25).

DAY 100 Do not let anyone who delights in false humility and the worship of angels disqualify you for the prize (2.18a)

Good Morning, Disciple,

Would you agree with me that there is nothing quite so obnoxious as religious humbug? We anticipate and, to some degree, excuse it in the worldling. "Of inference all are capable: of judgment only a few," is the kind of arrogance we expect from a Schopenhauer. His bedfellow, Nietzsche, said in effect: You will never understand me because I exist on a higher plane.

That is precisely the kind of superiority which the religious pretenders at Colosse displayed, though hedged about by a display of humility. Not a sickly Uriah Heep humility, still less the conniving pretence of Barchester's Mr. Slope. This humility was designed to impress God by the ascetic religious observance of fasting and ceremonial.

These early gnostics thought they could not come directly into the presence of God because they were of the material world which was evil. They worshipped the spirit beings (angels) in the hope that they would mediate between God and themselves in much the same way as even to this day some pray to Mary or their chosen saint. By doing so they violate the Lord who said, "No one comes to the Father except through me" (John 14.6), and disobey the Scripture which states expressly that there is but "one mediator between God and men, the man Christ Jesus" (1 Timothy 2.5). Even the angels forbid us to worship them (Revelation 19.10).

Dissatisfied with their own mundane worship, it seems, they tried to mimic the angels in the hope that it would give them an edge with the Almighty.

This may be why Paul emphasises so strongly the necessity of thanksgiving. Gratitude breeds both contentment and true humility.

These men are like athletes who take steroids and then try to disqualify runners who compete according to the rules (2 Timothy 2.5). They are still with us. Beware of those who by feigning ''special insight'' and by adopting supra-normal techniques invite you to take a higher road to spirituality. You cannot be disqualified from that which God has given you.

Now, if you would really like an insight into how angels worship, join in the worship of heaven as you read Revelation 5.

Quote ''Angels will always win the day over Jesus Christ despised and crucified; if the choice of a mediator between us and God is left to the vanity of the human mind'' – Pere Quesnel, H. C. G. Moule, *The Cambridge Bible* (Cambridge University Press, 1893).

Promise ''Blessed is the man who perseveres under trial, because when he has stood the test, he will receive the crown of life that God has promised to those who love him'' (James 1.12).

DAY 101 Such a person goes into great detail about what he has seen, and his unspiritual mind puffs him up with idle notions (2.18b)

Good Morning, Disciple,

Henry Kissinger once said, ''Power is not an aphrodisiac; it is a toxin.'' Spiritual power, no less so! It is a poison, like arsenic, which can build up in small doses until it has done its deadly work.

Few men set out to be charlatans or false prophets, but the taste of adulation, unchecked by the debunking influence of real friends and the antidote of submission to God and His word, can beguile any one of us.

In Dr Paul Brand's fascinating book *Fearfully and Wonderfully Made* he says, ''A lipoma is a low grade, benign tumour. It derives from a single fat cell, skilled in its lazy role of storing fat, that rebels against the leadership of the body and refuses to give up its reserves. It accepts deposits but ignores withdrawal slips. As the cell multiplies, daughter cells follow its lead and a tumour grows like a fungus, filling in crevices, pressing against muscle and organs. Occasionally a lipoma crowds a vital organ like the eye, pushing it out of alignment or pinching a sensitive nerve, and surgery is required.''

This is an almost perfect illustration of what Paul was warning the Colossians about. A rebel cell in the body getting fatter and fatter, puffing itself up at the expense of the whole body. Unchecked, it may threaten its very life. Such were these alien spiritualists, taking their stand on visions which can never be verified and which are open to no objective test of authenticity. Give me one secure word of Scripture over ten thousand words of knowledge. Not that I deny spiritual insight and understanding, but as we have seen already, we have this completely in Christ.

When the apostle Paul had one such ''real'' experience, akin to John's vision in the Revelation, he would not even speak of what he called ''inexpressible things'', things that man is not permitted to tell (2 Corinthians 12.4). We do not know for sure what Paul's ''thorn in the flesh'' was (2 Corinthians 12.7) but we do know, because he has told us, that it was to stop him becoming conceited. He did not want to be like Jude's ''shepherds who feed only themselves. Clouds without rain . . .'' (Jude 12).

As you read God's specific warning against false prophets in Jeremiah 23.15-40, meditate upon what He there tells us to listen to.

Quote ''The enemy is always out to obscure or depreciate Christ'' – Poul Madsen, *The Cross in Colossians* (Gospel Literature Service, 1958).

Promise ''Knowledge puffs up, but love builds up'' (1 Corinthians 8.1b).

DAY 102 He has lost connection with the head (2.19a)

Good Morning, Disciple,

Have you heard the story of the little woodpecker on his first assignment? He had been shown by his Daddy woodpecker how to cling on to the side of a tree and peck. Now it was his turn. Clinging on for all he was worth, he took his first thwack. Just as his little beak struck the bark a bolt of lightning hit the tree and split it in two. As he picked himself off the ground he turned to his father and said, "Now how's that for superior pecking?"

It never ceases to amaze me how susceptible we are to self-delusion. Left to my own devices, I'll fool myself every time. I cannot really tell which is my greater enemy, ego or the evil one. I fear it may be the former, so remind myself that it is safer to glory in Christ than my own experience.

Clearly these pretenders, in wandering into legalism, folk lore and pagan practices, had lost their hold on Christ. Their only hope was to repent and come back to the Lord.

How about ourselves – is there hope for any of us? A thousand times, Yes! How? "Watch your life and doctrine closely" (1 Timothy 4.16) and "fix your thoughts on Jesus" (Hebrews 3.1) who is the "author and perfecter of our faith" (Hebrews 12.2).

Paul shows us how we may hold on to Christ in 1 Timothy 4. He contrasts good food with junk food: "truths of the faith" and "good teaching" versus "godless myths" and "old wives' tales". Be assured of this, your daily study in God's Word is your greatest protection against heresy. One fed on a good diet can soon spot an unwholesome one.

He goes on to show that input should always be balanced by output. Even a diet of good food may lead to obesity unless it is accompanied by physical exercise. But for the Christian physical exercise alone will not do. We must also apply what we learn from God's Word in the nitty-gritty of everyday living. Whereas the ascetic looks to escape from the humdrum of mundane existence, we convert the mundane into a glorious pursuit after "righteousness, godliness, faith, love, endurance and gentleness" (1 Timothy 6.11).

As we train who could be a better coach than our Father? Put your confidence in Him as you meditate on Hebrews 12.1-13.

Quote *Et teneo, et teneor*: I both hold and I am held – Spurgeon's Theological College motto.

Promise "May our Lord Jesus Christ himself and God our Father, who loved us and by his grace gave us eternal encouragement and good hope, encourage your hearts and strengthen you in every good deed and word" (2 Thessalonians 2.16-17).

DAY 103 From whom the whole body, supported and held together by its ligaments and sinews, grows as God causes it to grow (2.19b)

Good Morning, Disciple,

Are you growing? I do hope so. How I have prayed over each of these letters to that end. I want you to grow and to be strong in the Lord. But I want that growth to be real growth. Not a deadly cancerous growth at the expense of the body. Not a pot-bellied growth of malnutrition nor a disgusting obesity from too much food and too little action.

Real growth can only happen if you are in the body, the Church, and in Christ, the head. It is invariably true that when we lose contact with the Church by neglecting fellowship, we lose contact with Christ too. When we lose contact with Christ we always lose, in some measure, contact with the Church. It could not be otherwise. If we are one body we belong together.

If we belong together we must work at building each other up in love. The greatest among us needs the help of others. Albert Einstein once said, "Many times a day I realise how much my own inner and outer life is built upon the labours of my fellow-man, both living and dead, and how earnestly I must exert myself in order to give in return as much as I have received."

Albert Schweitzer, who came from a rich home, spent his life serving as a missionary doctor in Africa. As a small boy he happened to get into a fight with a lad from a very poor home. He won the fight and was about to walk away when the poor boy got up, dusted himself off and said that if he, too, had eaten he would have won. Schweitzer never again wore fine clothes. He refused the luxuries of his inheritance and though he became a fine organist and surgeon, he never forgot the poor.

This is true humility. The spiritual guru would have every one look up to him. What a contrast to the Christ-like man or woman whose only delight is to serve others.

As you read 1 Corinthians 12.12-31 you may like to meditate on what God wants you to do and to be in His Church.

Quote "The fact that God has put us together in the body of Christ is one of His major means of making each of us more like Jesus" – David Jackman, *Understanding the Church* (Kingsway Publications, 1987).

Promise "I have other sheep that are not of this sheep pen. I must bring them also. They too will listen to my voice, and there shall be one flock and one shepherd" (John 10.16).

DAY 104 Since you died with Christ to the basic principles of this world, why, as though you still belonged to it, do you submit to its rules: "Do not handle! Do not taste! Do not touch!"? These are all destined to perish with use, because they are based on human commands and teachings. (2.20-22)

Good Morning, Disciple,

Society, like the Church, tends to flip-flop between the extremes of licence and legalism, permissiveness and puritanism, feast and fast. But the balanced Christian life rejects the extremes of antinomianism (the rejection of all moral law) and asceticism (the rejection of life). You have died to both, says Paul, and that death has set you free, because death severs the bond which binds a slave to his master.

We shall see later how this works in the realm of morality. Here we are at the other end of the spectrum of human behaviour. The heretics offered access to the higher realms of spirituality by self-denial, through crippling rules and regulations. Jesus said of them, "You hypocrites! You travel over land and sea to win a single convert, and when he becomes one, you make him twice as much a son of hell as you are" (Matthew 23.15).

"You took my freedom away a long time ago," said Alexander Solzhenitsyn of the state, "and you can't give it back because you haven't any yourself." That's what Paul is saying here. These blind guides offer you the manacles which they themselves wear.

There is little doubt that the three "do nots" – eat, taste, touch – are all to do with food. I wonder if Mark, one of Paul's prison companions, had told him Jesus" reply to the Pharisees when they complained about His disciples eating food with ceremonially unwashed hands: "Nothing outside a man can make him 'unclean' by going into him. Rather it is what comes out of a man that makes him 'unclean'" (Mark 7.15). Paul says in effect, "Look, as soon as you put that food into your mouth it is going to start breaking down into waste. Don't get trapped back into all this mumbo-jumbo which is destined to the same end. Get on with the business of living the resurrection life – free in Christ."

As you read Mark 7, note that the Old Testament Law was still in operation. Once it was fulfilled in Jesus' death and resurrection the law of the Spirit came into operation. Rejoice in your freedom. Are there still some religious hang-ups from your old life to be rid of? Hand them over to Christ!

Quote "Christianity in its true and highest forms is not a religion of prescriptions but of principles" – Alexander Maclaren, *Expositor's Bible* (Hodder & Stoughton, 1899).

Promise "Therefore, there is now no condemnation for those who are in Christ Jesus" (Romans 8.1).

DAY 105 **Such regulations indeed have their appearance of wisdom, with their self-imposed worship, their false humility and their harsh treatment of the body, but they lack any value in restraining sensual indulgence (2.23)**

Good Morning, Disciple,

Have you heard the story of the lad who came home from Sunday School, sat on a kitchen stool, ordered a diet of grass and tried to touch his toes with his forehead?

"What on earth are you up to?" demanded his mother.

The boy replied, "This morning we heard about a saint called Simon Stylites, who lived up a pole for thirty-six years and could touch his toes with his head more than 1,200 times in succession. Another saint lived on a diet of grass. So I'm going to lick them both. I'll live on this stool for forty years, eat only grass and touch my toes with my head 10,000 times.''

Ten minutes later an exasperated mother expelled her son from her busy kitchen. As he left he muttered, ''I give up. No one could ever be a saint at home.''

This is precisely Paul's point. Unworkable religiosity has nothing to do with the real business of life. It must be exposed for what it is — a sham. Its proponents, for all their harsh treatment of their bodies, do so only for the praise of others or to indulge themselves in self-righteousness. It can only lead to an overbearing bigotry and sophisticated elitism.

The false teachers in the church at Colosse were corrupting the gospel of grace with their self-imposed works. And their descendants are with us to this day, inside and outside the Church, believing that by human effort they can manipulate the spirit world and even God Himself. By self-imposed cruelty to their bodies they actually indulge the flesh and thereby deny true spirituality which depends entirely upon God's grace alone.

If a person's religion does not prepare him for the real business of living in a real world of need then it is mere self-indulgence. ''Religion that God our Father accepts as pure and faultless is this: to look after orphans and widows in their distress and to keep oneself from being polluted by the world'' (James 1.27).

Meditate on the difference between the Pharisee and the child in Luke 18.9-30, then consider why Jesus wanted the rich man to give up his possessions.

Quote ''The zeal of men for superstition is surpassingly mad'' — John Calvin.

Promise '' 'I tell you the truth,' Jesus said to them, 'no-one who has left home or wife or brothers or parents or children for the sake of the kingdom of God will fail to receive many times as much in this age and, in the age to come, eternal life' '' (Luke 18.29-30).

DAY 106   **Since then you have been raised with Christ**
(3.1a)

Good Morning, Disciple,

At last, we break through the "valley of the shadow" of dead religion into the glorious sunlight of Easter hope. Reaffirming his earlier baptismal reference that we have been "made alive with Christ" (2.13), the apostle now shows that godly conduct is based upon our confidence in the resurrection – Christ's and ours.

Shortly after the Russian revolution a mass meeting in Moscow celebrated the victory of the proletariat over Tzarist rule. Anyone who wanted to make a free speech could do so. After many had praised the virtues of atheistic materialism, a shabby little Orthodox priest mounted the platform.

"You have heard the arguments brought forward to prove the new world view," said the undernourished priest. "But, my friends, *Christ is risen!*"

Like an erupting volcano the masses replied with a thunderous affirmation, as they had always done in the Easter service in church, *"He is risen indeed!"*

A few years ago I was privileged to speak at the celebration of one thousand years of Christianity in Russia at the huge First Baptist Church of Leningrad. I wondered whether, after more than seventy years of Communism in which many had suffered much deprivation for their faith in Christ, these people would still remember the refrain. So I began my speech: *"Christ is risen!* As soon as my interpreter translated it into Russian, the whole congregation stood up and shouted back in their mother tongue, *"He is risen indeed!"* The faith had not only survived, it was stronger than ever. The gulags of Stalin's regime had not crushed the Easter hope any more than the stone in front of the tomb could keep our Lord from rising. He is alive, therefore we live.

Charles Kingsley's grave is marked by a marble cross on which are inscribed the words, "We have loved. We love. We shall love." Encompassing these words are three others, "God is love." It is because God loves us that we can have this confidence. We have been raised with Christ.

You have already read most of that great resurrection chapter, 1

Corinthians 15. I have saved the remainder (33-58) for today, so that you can be prepared for the next few days of what I call "living in the light of Easter".

Quote "For the Christian eternal life begins, not on the day a man enters heaven, but on the day eternal life enters the man through the new birth" – Donald Grey Barnhouse, *The Invisible Wall* (Zondervan, 1965).

Promise "So will it be with the resurrection of the dead. The body that is sown is perishable, it is raised imperishable" (1 Corinthians 15.42).

DAY 107 Set your hearts on things above (3.1b)

Good Morning, Disciple,

After the death of King George VI in 1952, Winston Churchill said, "During the last few months the King has walked with death as if it were a companion, an acquaintance whom he recognised and did not fear. During the last few months the King has been sustained, not only by his natural buoyancy of spirit, but by the sincerity of his Christian faith."

How I would have loved to have been a fly on the wall at some of those regular Tuesday meetings between Churchill, the premier, and George, the King. Clearly the life and impending death of the head of state made a profound impression on Churchill.

Compare that with one of the kings of English drama, Oscar Wilde, as he summarised his life. "The gods had given me almost everything. But I let myself be lured into long spells of sensual ease . . . I grew careless of the lives of others. I took pleasure where it pleased me, and passed on. I forgot that every little action of the common day makes or unmakes character, and that therefore, what one has done in the secret chamber, one has some day to cry aloud from the house top. I ceased to be lord over myself. I was no longer the captain of my soul, and I did not know it. I allowed pleasure to dominate me. I ended in horrible disgrace."

"What is done in the secret chamber" – there lies the difference between the character of these two kings. Here's how the Scripture puts it: "Those who live according to the sinful nature have their minds set on what that nature desires; but those who live in accordance with the Spirit have their minds set on what the Spirit desires. The mind of sinful man is death, but the mind controlled by the Spirit is life and peace" (Romans 8.5-6).

The morality of heaven demands the ethics of that Kingdom on earth. As Tolstoy said, "If God and the future life exist, then truth and virtue exist: and man's highest happiness consists in striving for their attainment."

Ephesians 4.17-32 will prepare you to live for Jesus today. Set your heart, as you would set a compass, to head in the right direction – homeward.

Quote "Think of no other greatness but that of the soul, no other riches but those of the heart" – John Quincey Adams.

Promise "And God raised us up with Christ and seated us with him in the heavenly realms in Christ Jesus, in order that in the coming ages he might show the incomparable riches of his grace, expressed in his kindness to us in Christ Jesus" (Ephesians 2.6-7).

DAY 108 Where Christ is seated at the right hand of God (3.1c)

Good Morning, Disciple,

Have you ever seen anyone killed? Even to watch someone die of natural causes is traumatic enough. But to witness the stoning to death of a man like Stephen, as Paul (the young Saul) did, must have been so ghastly as to have imprinted itself in every detail upon his mind. He would certainly have remembered the final words of Christianity's first martyr which sent the crowd berserk and sealed his fate: "Look, I see the heaven open and the Son of Man standing at the right hand of God" (Acts 7.56).

No doubt Dr Luke, who was with Paul during his captivity (3.14), had also related to him why those words were like a red flag to a bull. It dated back to when Jesus used Psalm 110.1 to show the Pharisees that the Messiah, the Christ, was not David's son but God's own Son sitting at His right hand (Matthew 22.43-45).

It was this claim to deity which ensured death on a cross for Jesus. When the chief priests asked him if he was the Christ, Jesus answered ". . . from now on, the Son of Man will be seated at the right hand of the Mighty God." They understood the image; that is why they went on to ask, "Are you the Son of God?" (Luke 22.69). When He answered in the affirmative, death was the only verdict they could give short of falling down to worship Him.

Why should Paul's readers seek what is above? Because that is where their Lord and Master rules, "far above all rule and authority, power and dominion and every title that can be given" (Ephesians 1.21).

The symbolism of His being seated next to the throne was to remind them, and us, that the new life can be successfully lived only so long as we act in harmony with the risen reigning Lord Jesus who is "at the right hand of God and is also interceding for us" (Romans 8.34), representing our needs in the Godhead as a high priest (Hebrews 8.1-2).

As you read Peter's Pentecost sermon, Acts 2.14-41, you will surely want to meditate on what special gift Jesus gave to you from His position, "exalted at the right hand of God".

Quote "Our Father refreshes us on the journey with some pleasant inns, but will not encourage us to mistake them for home" – C. S. Lewis, *The Business of Heaven* (Harcourt Brace Jovanovich, 1984).

Promise "To him who overcomes, I will give the right to sit with me on my throne, just as I overcame and sat down with my Father on his throne" (Revelation 3.21).

DAY 109 **Set your minds on things above, not on earthly things (3.2)**

Good Morning, Disciple,

I'm sure you have noticed how the way trees lean in exposed places demonstrates the direction of the prevailing wind. Likewise the mind reveals the bent of the prevailing culture.

To understand what Paul is getting at here we must look back within the letter. There we see that the earthbound mind is hostile towards God both in behaviour (1.21) and in belief (2.8). A person is as a person thinks. This is universally true for every age. This is why the new Christian is called to conform no longer "to the pattern of this world, but to be transformed" – by what? The renewing of the mind!

Swami Shivanda of India used to tell his disciples what at first sight looks almost Christian: "Kill the mind and then, and only then, can you meditate." Modern gurus of Transcendental Meditation, with their mind-blocking mantras, and the New Agers' reliance upon intuition are the direct descendants of those in Asia Minor, who by the "cunning and craftiness of men in their deceitful scheming" blew infant Christians off course.

We are not called to bypass the mind but to renew it (Romans 12.2). With all the treasures of wisdom and knowledge hidden in Christ (2.3), we are to devote our attention to where He is. We are not to look inward but upward. "We take captive every thought to make it obedient to Christ" (2 Corinthians 19.5). Empty the mind? That is not Christianity!

Paul is not advocating the kind of other-worldliness which leads to being so heavenly-minded that we are of no earthly use. On the contrary, when our attitude becomes as Christ's, we come right down to earth like He did (Philippians 2.5-11) to do the will of our Father. Isn't that what Paul prayed? That we be filled with the knowledge of His will through all spiritual understanding, in order that we might live a life worthy of the Lord (1.9-10). Christ-like thinking will lead to Christ-like action.

Far from being other-worldly, Paul is laying the foundation for the very practical issues of Christian morality, church life, home and family, work and witness, which will occupy our thoughts to the end of this book.

I am quite convinced that the battle for Christianity in the twenty-first century will be in the arena of the mind, both in belief and behaviour. As you meditate on 1 Corinthians 1.18-31, think about what it means to be a fool for Christ.

Quote "The Kingdom of God is not a Christianised society, it is the divine rule in the lives of those who acknowledge Christ" –

John Stott, *Issues Facing Christians Today* (Marshall Morgan & Scott, 1984).

Promise "I will instruct you and teach you in the way you should go; I will counsel you and watch over you" (Psalm 32.8).

DAY 110 For you died and your life is now hidden with Christ in God (3.3)

Good Morning, Disciple,

Before his eventual conversion the philosopher Mortimer Adler explained why he was not a Christian. "That's a great gulf between the mind and the heart. I was on the edge of becoming a Christian several times, but I didn't do it. I said that if one is born a Christian, one can be light-hearted about living up to Christianity, but if one converts by a clear conscious act of the will, one had better be prepared to live a truly Christian life. So you ask yourself, are you prepared to give up all your vices and the weaknesses of the flesh."

Well, of course, he's right in one thing but wrong in the other! Becoming a Christian for him and everyone else demands a "conscious act of will", a giving up of anything which dishonours the Lord. On the other hand, he makes the common assumption that it is different for those who are brought up in Christian homes. It is not! God has no grandchildren, only sons and daughters, all of whom by a conscious act of the will surrender to the claims of the gospel.

This involves, for everyone, death to the old sin-nature, burial in baptism and a brand-new life – all in Christ (2.11-13). Only the one who is truly dead to the old life can share in the new life. That will affect every area. As Tertullian, the North African lawyer of the second century, put it, "At every forward step and movement, at every going in and out, when we put on our clothes and shoes, when we bathe, when we sit at table, when we light the lamps, on couch, on seat, in all the actions of daily life, we trace upon our forehead the sign" (the cross).

Paul may be getting in one last dig at the gnostics in his reference to our life being "hidden" with Christ in God. We are not left to discover other ways to God. We are, says Paul, already there – in Christ, who is, of course, in God (John 17.21).

Riding my bike this morning, I saw little spring lambs in the Cotswold meadows. As soon as they saw me they bolted for their mothers, where they could be not only protected, but fed. What a lovely illustration, I thought. When we come under attack, what do we do? Back to the one who loves us, there to be protected and fed as we grow towards maturity.

Turn to the shepherd this morning, as you meditate on John 10.1-18.

Quote "Through your birth, O Christ, you shape all things afresh, making them new once more and leading them back again to their first beauty" – from the Orthodox Church Feast of Christmas Liturgy.

Promise "Dear friends, now we are children of God, and what we will be has not yet been made known. But we know that when he appears, we shall be like him, for we shall see him as he is" (1 John 3.2).

DAY 111 When Christ, who is your life, appears, then you also will appear with him in glory (3.4)

Good Morning, Disciple,

When Columbus left the shores of Spain in 1492 to look for a new route to the East Indies, the coins in his pocket bore the inscription *ne plus ultra* – "no more beyond". All the known world had been settled.

When the Santa Maria returned to Spain sceptics would not believe Columbus's stories of unknown lands, until he showed them the new foods, gold and native Indians he had brought back. Now the coins were restruck with just the words *plus ultra* – "more beyond".

It's the same with heaven. Only one has come from there and He has made it known. We have believed His report. And we who believe have been raised with Him, are hidden with Him, and when He returns to earth in power and glory, we shall be revealed with Him (3.1-4).

For this to happen we must either die and go by direct route to be at "home with the Lord" (2 Corinthians 5.8); or, if we are still alive on earth at His coming, we shall be caught up with Him in the rapture, which will herald His coming in glory (1 Thessalonians 4.17). It is at that "second coming" that we who believe shall appear with Him. Our message to the world now and then is: *plus ultra* – "more beyond".

We do not know the timing of His return (Matthew 24.36). But we should live each day as though it were our last, not in fear, but in the spirit of the apostle who said, "For to me, to live is Christ and to die is gain" (Philippians 1.21).

Lord Shaftesbury wrote, "I do not think that in the last forty years I have lived one conscious hour that was not influenced by the thought of our Lord's return." That's how it should be. Why, even the creation, so sadly abused by man's sinfulness, "waits in eager expectation for the sons of God to be revealed" (Romans 8.19).

How then should we live? Surely "everyone who has this hope in him purifies himself" (1 John 3.3), "so that when he appears we may be confident and unashamed before him at his coming" (1 John 2.28).

As you read more about His coming in 1 Thessalonians 5.1-11 you may like to meditate on the trio in verse 8 – faith, love and hope.

Quote "My greatest desire is to live today in anticipation of tomorrow and be ready to be welcomed into His home for all eternity" – Dr Billy Graham, *Facing Death and the Life After* (Word, 1987).

Promise "And when the Chief Shepherd appears, you will receive the crown of glory that will never fade away" (1 Peter 5.4).

DAY 112 Put to death, therefore, whatever belongs to your earthly nature (3.5a)

Good Morning, Disciple,

By now it's no doubt becoming second nature to you, when you spot "therefore" in the text, to look and see what it is there for. Clearly the moral demands of this and the next few verses would be an impossibly high standard without the motivation of all that Christ has done for us, outlined in earlier verses.

The original readers may have studied these verses for their baptism, so that they understood what it meant to be buried with Christ in baptism (2.12) and "dead to sin but alive to God in Christ Jesus" (Romans 6.11). But what is true in salvation language must also become true, progressively, in the practical arena of life. Putting to death bad habits is a daily exercise.

Our motivation is Christ. We walk where He walked. "If anyone would come after me," He said, "he must deny himself and take up his cross and follow me" (Mark 8.34). Where self has been enthroned, Christ must become King.

Christ has achieved our salvation single-handed, but we must work with Him at sanctification. With the help of the Holy Spirit, we are to put to death whatever belongs to our earthly nature. "If you live according to the sinful nature, you will die; but if by the Spirit you put to death the misdeeds of the body, you will live" (Romans 8.13). We have the choice. We make our lives either into a spiritual brothel, by taking what belongs to Christ and prostituting it (1 Corinthians 6.15), or into a temple in which the Holy Spirit takes up residence (1 Corinthians 3.16).

Such morality is pooh-poohed by the world. We fight, therefore, not only against "the flesh" and the schemes of the devil, but against cultural norms as strong today as in first-century pagan society.

Such morality is as revolutionary as Gorbachev's Perestroika. He said of it, "Perestroika is a revolutionary process . . . We simply have no right to relax, even for a day . . . Revolution requires the demolition of all that is obsolete, stagnant and hinders fast progress."

Shall we be less determined in our following of Christ?

1 Peter 4.1-11 will show that we have not advanced far in twenty centuries. But the change begins, not with society, but with you and me.

Quote "Never in history has there been a revolution in which it was possible to lay down one's arms and rest on one's laurels after victory" – Lenin, quoted by Mikhail Gorbachev in *Perestroika* (Harper & Row, 1987).

Promise "And we, who with unveiled faces all reflect the Lord's glory, are being transformed into his likeness with ever-increasing glory, which comes from the Lord, who is the Spirit" (2 Corinthians 3.18).

DAY 113   Sexual immorality, impurity, lust, evil desires (3.5b)

Good Morning, Disciple,

I sometimes wonder if our western society has taken too many steps backwards towards our pagan past. There is little doubt that the Judeo-Christian morality which was the basis of our laws has been eroded by an incessant attack from permissive psychology and humanism. The reservoir of high principle has all but dried up, leaving a society sickened by its own excesses. Christianity breaks in on this mass self-indulgence to say: there is a better way.

To understand this verse fully we should start at greed (which we will look at tomorrow) and work our way outwards, from the inner craving of the heart to our behaviour. Covetousness is the fork in the road which leads us ever away from God's path into paths of ever-increasing sinfulness. It's what goes on in the heart which determines the action; hence the warning of Jesus that "anyone who looks at a woman lustfully has already committed adultery with her in his heart" (Matthew 5.28).

Sexual immorality and impurity cover every kind of sexual sin from relationships outside marriage to homosexuality, incest, rape and pornography. But choosing evil desires in preference to godly desires is not just in the sexual area. Jesus says it is "desires for other things" which, weed-like, choke the Word, making it unfruitful (Mark 4.19).

The question is, who will win whenever you or I come to that fork in the road? God or sin? Here's a verse to keep in mind: "Do not let sin reign in your mortal body so that you obey its evil desires. Do not offer the parts of your body to sin, as instruments of wickedness, but rather offer yourselves to God, as those who have been brought from death to life" (Romans 6.12-13). If we do not submit to Christ, at that point we shall, almost inevitably, choose the wrong path with all its consequences.

The Lord, in His mercy, never leaves us to our own devices. His Holy Spirit will equip and enable us to live holy lives, but we are to play our part by self-control (1 Thessalonians 4.4) and avoidance (1 Corinthians 5.9).

By the way, if you have fallen, take heart. "If we confess our sins,

He is faithful and just and will forgive us our sins and purify us from all unrighteousness" (1 John 1.9).

Try Ephesians 5.1-21 for today's reading. I love the opening verses and I want you to enjoy them, too.

Quote "We are called to be people of conviction, not conformity; of moral nobility, not social respectability" – Martin Luther King, *Strength To Love*.

Promise "Being confident of this, that he who began a good work in you will carry it on to completion until the day of Christ Jesus" (Philippians 1.6).

DAY 114   Greed, which is idolatry (3.5c)

Good Morning, Disciple,

Do you see why yesterday I called covetousness the fork in the road? Idolatry is going after something other than God, because it seems to be more important or valuable than God Himself. Greed is not only associated with money. It is the desire to have more. More than is due; more than is right or fair; more of what belongs to someone else. It may be his wife, in which case it may lead to adultery, divorce, the break-up of a home and the further disintegration of society. It may be somebody's possessions and may lead to theft or even murder. I have a feeling this is why God put it at the bottom of His Ten Commandments. It is the one sin which can cause us to break every other commandment right up to number one, "You shall have no other gods before me (Exodus 20.3). It is the very reason Jesus warned, "You cannot serve both God and Money" (Matthew 6.24).

I am sure you have noticed what the "therefore" in verse 5 is there for. Gratitude is the answer! When we are truly thankful for what God has done for us, we become content. When we are contented we can put greed to death. You may be certain of this, the world cannot give you anything which will add one iota to what you have in Christ. That is what Aristotle Onassis found. Though he was the richest man in the world, in his lifetime he said, "I climbed to the top of the financial tree and when I got there found nothing."

The birth of the Church at Pentecost gave the world a people of generous spirit. "No-one claimed that any of his possessions was his own, but they shared everything they had" (Acts 4.32). How refreshing! But within a generation greed had begun to affect the young Church. It was one thing to have false teachers peddling the Word of God for profit (2 Corinthians 2.17) and exploiting the Church with myths and fairy tales (2 Peter 2.3), but the problem went even deeper than that. Like some notable examples in our recent past, the leaders of the church at Ephesus had become so greedy for money that Paul had to write to Timothy with very specific instructions and warnings about money.

You can read about this in 1 Timothy 6.3-21 as a timely reminder of the corrupting nature of greed. Meditate especially on verse 18. It is God's antidote.

Quote "Materialists mistake that which limits life for life itself" – Leo Tolstoy.

Promise "But godliness with contentment is great gain" (1 Timothy 6.6).

DAY 115   Because of these, the wrath of God is coming (3.6)

Good Morning, Disciple,

There are many, sadly even in the Church, who will tell you not to worry about hell. I agree with them. You should not worry about hell, if you are walking with the Lord as a believer. If you are not – you should worry.

To the person who objects to the doctrine of hell, C. S. Lewis responds: "In the long run the answer to all those who object to the doctrine of hell is itself a question. "What are you asking God to do?" To wipe out their past sins and, at all costs, to give them a fresh start, smoothing every difficulty and offering every miraculous help? But he has done so on Calvary."

God never changes His standard of justice to suit our standards, but He longs to welcome us home when we repent. On the other hand, if we will not repent, God's wrath remains implacable. "Let no one deceive you with empty words," says Paul. "God's wrath comes on those who are disobedient" (Ephesians 5.6). The good news is to be preached from the roof tops: "Whoever believes in the Son has eternal life" (John 3.36). But it is never to be preached without the corresponding truth: "Whoever rejects the Son will not see life, for God's wrath remains on him" (John 3.36). We have no authority to proclaim the good news if we disbelieve the bad news, for the Scriptures declare both to be true. Paul asks the most devastating question in the whole Bible when he probes our souls with these words: "Do you not know that the wicked will not inherit the Kingdom of God?" (1 Corinthians 6.9).

Are you among those who have "turned to God from idols" (idols of greed, evil desires, etc.) to serve the living and true God, and to wait for his Son from heaven, whom he raised from the dead – Jesus who rescues us from the coming wrath" (1 Thessalonians 1.9)? I do hope so; with all my heart, I hope so.

Right back on day six I asked you to meditate on what you had been saved from (Romans 1.18-32). This morning you may like to focus your attention and prayers on Romans 2.1-16.

Quote "Only he who has experienced the greatness of God's mercy can understand something of how great His wrath must be" – Peter O'Brien, *Word Biblical Commentary – Colossians* (Word Books, 1982).

Promise "For God so loved the world that he gave his one and only Son, that whoever believes in him shall not perish but have eternal life" (John 3.16).

DAY 116 You used to walk in these ways, in the life you once lived. But now you must rid yourselves of all such things as these (3.7,8a)

Good Morning, Disciple,

The Old Testament is full of examples of the symbolic use of clothing to represent personal characteristics. So, for instance, Job says, "I put on righteousness as my clothing; justice was my robe" (Job 29.14). And King David prayed that his accusers might be "clothed with disgrace and wrapped in shame as in a cloak" (Psalm 109.29). Even

Isaiah, when prophesying about the Lord Jesus, declared that "righteousness will be his belt and faithfulness the sash around his waist" (Isaiah 11.5).

This was carried over into the New Testament. The Christian is called to strip off like an athlete ready for the race (Hebrews 12.1), and here in Colossians we have the same symbolism, but in a baptismal context. As I said earlier, the teaching of chapter three was most likely a preparation for baptism.

When a candidate went down to the river or lake to be baptised, he would wear his oldest and dirtiest clothing. These symbolised the old life. As Isaiah said, "All our righteous acts (good works) are like filthy rags" (Isaiah 64.6). When the new Christian entered the water he left his old clothes on the bank. He was then plunged under the water, "buried with Christ", and came up, "raised with Christ", to receive a white robe. This symbolised the new life and new behaviour. We shall never know, but I wonder if the baptised came up singing a chorus, "My soul rejoices in my God. For he has clothed me with the garments of salvation and arrayed me in a robe of righteousness" (Isaiah 61.10). Why, I can almost hear Paul's baptismal sermon! "Since we belong to the day, let us be self-controlled, putting on faith and love as a breastplate, and the hope of salvation as a helmet" (1 Thessalonians 5.8).

There is also a possible reference here to our circumcision in Christ. As we have seen earlier (day 91), "In Him you were also circumcised, in the putting off of the sinful nature" (2.11). Both our baptism and our circumcision are acts of God's grace which demand an act of our will in present behaviour. "Let us put aside the deeds of darkness and put on the armour of light" (Romans 13.12).

Meditate this morning on James 2.14-26. It highlights the need for right action coupled to faith.

Quote "The unexamined life is not worth living" – Socrates.

Promise "He who overcomes will, like them, be dressed in white. I will never blot out his name from the book of life, but will acknowledge his name before my Father and his angels" (Revelation 3.5).

DAY 117 Anger, rage, malice, slander and filthy language from your lips (3.8b)

Good Morning, Disciple,

I was tempted to call these "sins of the lips", until I re-read the words of the Lord, "The things that come out of the mouth come from the heart" (Matthew 15.18). And there lies the key to this load of rubbish.

The Greek word *orge* used here for anger is the same word used of the Lord's anger, or wrath, in verse 6. That should immediately tell us that, of itself, it is not sin. In fact, there are said to be 375 instances of God's anger in the Old Testament. God's anger is not sin, it is *at* sin, just as we ought to be angry when we see blatant injustice, or pollution, or homelessness. Such an anger is constructive and creative. But when anger is targeted at another person, whether it is expressed or not, it is a sin. It needs to be dealt with in the same way as all sin. Confess it and drop it. Don't take it into the next day (Ephesians 4.26).

Rage, *thumos*, is more concentrated – compressed anger, if you like. It explodes. We say, "He's the sort of man who is always 'blowing his top.' " Both kinds of anger are equally destructive.

Malice, *thakia*, is a nasty piece of work. It is that ice-cold Macbethian meanness which wishes and connives harm, and is so morally indefensible.

For slander the Greek word is *blasphemia* from which we get our English, blasphemy. You can see the connection straight away. To slander or defame God's name – so much in vogue today, especially in the popular arts – is to be guilty of blasphemy. But when it is directed at another it is called slander.

The final word is *aischrologia*. It covers every kind of foul, bad and abusive language, smutty stories and innuendo. The Christian's speech will show, as well as his behaviour, that the old life has been cast off and a new order begun. As Dr Henry Brand put it, "You can use your background as an excuse for present behaviour only until you receive Jesus Christ as your personal Lord and Saviour. After that you have a new power within you that is able to change your conduct" – and your speech.

James 3 has much more to say about the tongue which I know you will find as challenging as I do. Let's make it a matter of prayer to put off the temperamental sins and put on the Holy Spirit (Galatians 5.22-23).

Quote "The theories we live are the ones we really believe" – R. C. Sproul, *Lifeviews* (Fleming H.Revell Co., 1986).

Promise "A quick-tempered man does foolish things" (Proverbs 14.17a).

DAY 118 Do not lie to each other (3.9a)

Good Morning, Disciple,

Augustine said, "When regard for truth has been broken down or even slightly weakened, all things will remain doubtful." How right he was. All of us, even the most blatant liars, share the desire not to be deceived.

In the context of his letter, however, Paul is not speaking about society in general, but about honesty within church relationships – that Christians should not lie to one another. The clue to why is found in his letter to the church at Ephesus, written at roughly the same time as this one to Colosse. "Therefore each of you must put off falsehood and speak truthfully to his neighbour, for we are all members of one body" (Ephesians 4.25). Here we have a "therefore" – and when we look to see what it's there for, all is revealed. Some in the church were backsliding into their old ways. In their lust for more they were drifting back into ignorance, darkness and the muddled thinking of their former lives (Ephesians 4.17-19). "You didn't come to know Christ like that," says Paul, "you heard and were taught the truth that is in Jesus! Why go back into lies?"

We may only conjecture, but I think it is a safe assumption that the lies of the false teachers, with their empty philosophy, their fine sounding but untrue arguments and idle notions about what they claimed to have seen in visions were devaluing the very truth of God itself. Hence Paul's strong assertion that what they had heard from Epaphras was "the word of truth" (1.5), God's grace in all its truth (1.6). So this is more than just an exhortation to honesty. It is also a clear warning not to tell lies about spiritual experiences.

Augustine developed from the Scriptures an eight-fold distinction between lies. The worst are lies uttered in the teaching of religion, and at the other end of the scale are lies which hurt no one and might save someone from physical defilement. Yet even a lie which saved a person's life was not to be praised. "It is enough that the deception should be pardoned," he said, "without its being made an object of laudation."

The Holy Spirit, who lives in you, is the Spirit of truth (John 14.17). Even though "no deceit was found in his mouth" (1 Peter 2.22), Jesus was accused. See how He answered in John 8.31-59 and as you meditate ask God, the Holy Spirit, to fill you with His truth.

Quote "It is easy to tell a lie but hard to tell only one. The first must be thatched with another or it will rain through" – (source unknown).

Promise "I tell you the truth, if anyone keeps my word, he will never see death" (John 8.51).

DAY 119 Since you have taken off your old self with its practices and have put on the new self (3.9b,10a)

Good Morning, Disciple,

Arthur Kanedereka supported the guerrilla movement fighting for nationalist rule in what is now Zimbabwe, encouraging young black men to join the armies operating from Zambia and Mozambique. When he became a Christian he was haunted by the atrocities inflicted on both sides of the conflict. He met with other believers, including the prime minister's son, Alec, in what they called a Cabinet of Conscience to discuss the future and to pray for peace.

One day Arthur announced that he would go over the border to meet with Nkomo and Mugabe in a fresh bid for peace. His Christian friends warned him that he was likely to be killed. He answered their protests by saying with a smile, "I'm not afraid to die . . . What matters is what we are living for when death meets us."

He not only went on his mission. He achieved more than anyone previously and looked like bringing the warring factions together for peace talks. His murder delayed what he had worked for, but not for long. The rest is history.

Just before Arthur's untimely death, Alec Smith recalls remarking that he had shaved off his beard – the symbol of an African nationalist politician. Arthur stroked his shiny chin and said, "This year I want to have a quiet Christmas and see what more I need to shed from my life to become more like Christ." How right he was. What matters is what we are living for when death meets us. He never saw Christmas but he saw Christ.

People sometimes tell me they find it impossible to imagine that I have been in prison or lived the wild life of my youth. I answer them, "New nature – new behaviour." "If anyone is in Christ, he is a new creation; the old has gone, the new has come!" (2 Corinthians 5.17). The Adam nature must die and be buried before the Christ nature can take over.

The act of baptism symbolised this truth vividly as the candidate received the white robe, displacing the rags of the past. "For all of you who were baptised into Christ have clothed yourselves with Christ" (Galatians 3.27). What an audacious thought!

The Christ-clothed life is the theme of Romans 13. I would encourage you to spend good quality time meditating on it this morning.

Quote "There are but two men seen standing before God, Adam and Jesus Christ; and these two men have all other men hanging at their girdles" – Thomas Goodwin.

Promise "Instead, speaking the truth in love, we will in all things grow up into him who is the Head, that is, Christ (Ephesians 4.15).

DAY 120 Which is being renewed in knowledge in the image of its creator (3.10b)

Good Morning, Disciple,

Salvation is a rich mixture of what Christ has done for us and what the Spirit continues to do in us. Being made new in Christ is a finished process so far as regeneration is concerned, but "Inwardly we are being renewed day by day" (2 Corinthians 4.16).

When I was studying for the ministry at Spurgeon's College I had to preach a trial sermon, to be followed by a helpful critique from appointed students. As I waited nervously, my first censor stood to give his opinion. "We'd like to thank Mr Goodwin for his sermon today," he said, much to the delight of everyone there. The point was not lost on me. Frank Goodwin was the minister of my home church, which was close to the college. Unconsciously I had picked up his mannerisms and style of preaching. Without knowing it, I had become like him.

On another occasion, when I was ordering some stationery, the elderly stock-keeper said in obvious surprise, "Jackopson? You're not Charlie Jackopson's boy, are you?" This old-timer had been friends with my father, who died when I was only fifteen months old. "Cor!" he said, "You're the spittin' image of your dad. You talk like him. Everything about you is Charlie Jackopson." How could this be? I had never known my father. The answer, of course, lies in the genes. He had passed on something of himself.

These two illustrations may help explain what Paul is getting at. Adam was formed in the image of God with God's breath (spirit) in him (Genesis 1:26-27; 2:7). This image was broken when the Adam man sinned, so his sons and daughters were born in Adam's image (Genesis 5.1-3) and the deformed image of God (Genesis 9.6).

Christ came to re-form that image of God in the new man – the Christian. He was the new Adam and his offspring would be "transformed into his likeness" (2 Corinthians 3.18) and conformed to His image (Romans 8.29). There you have the history and theology of salvation: formed; deformed; reformed; transformed; conformed.

I had become like Frank Goodwin because I knew him. And this is how we are renewed to be like Jesus. The breath of God's Holy Spirit is breathed into us at our spiritual birth, but we must get to know Him through His word and a daily relationship.

In Hebrews 2, see how Jesus became like us in order that we might become like Him.

Quote "The highest Christian love is not devotion to a work or to a cause, but to Jesus Christ" – Oswald Chambers, *The Place Of Help* (Christian Literature Crusade, 1935).

Promise "Therefore we do not lose heart. Though outwardly we are wasting away, yet inwardly we are being renewed day by day" (2 Corinthians 4.16).

DAY 121   Here there is no Greek or Jew, circumcised or uncircumcised, barbarian, Scythian, slave or free, but Christ is all, and is in all (3.11)

Good morning, Disciple,

The rulers of Laos and Vietnam in pre-colonial days worked out a very successful tax arrangement in the unmarked border areas. Those who ate short-grain rice, built their homes on stilts, and decorated them with Indian-style serpents were considered to be Laotians. Others, who ate long-grain rice and built their homes on the ground with Chinese style dragons adorning them, were considered to be Vietnamese. Nationality was determined by the cultural values they displayed.

Such should be the case for all who profess faith in Christ. Our citizenship is in heaven where "every tribe and language and people and nation" (Revelation 5.9) will be represented. Whatever barriers exist on earth will be broken down in God's Kingdom.

Our lives should display the cultural characteristics of heaven. Without the work of Christ in our hearts we would reflect the world's divisiveness, based on nationality, religion, race, culture, status, sex, etc. But within God's family that isn't even an option. "Anyone who claims to be in the light but hates his brother is still in darkness" (1 John 2.9).

Christ had broken down the dividing wall of hostility between Jew and Gentile (Ephesians 2.14), but the little church at Colosse was evidently experiencing some friction over Jewish customs. Maybe the Greeks looked down their noses at the barbarians whose faith was less sophisticated – especially Scythians, whom the Jewish historian Josephus called "little better than wild beasts". Paul's allusion to slaves may provide yet another clue as to why he says his purpose is that "they may be united in love" (2.2).

This list is not exhaustive. Elsewhere he says that in Christ there is neither male nor female (Galatians 3.28), so the Christian man could not recite the daily thanksgiving of the pious Jew, "Lord, I thank you that I am not a Gentile, a slave or a woman." Salvation is open to all, because "there is no difference . . . the same Lord is Lord of all and richly blesses all who call on him, for "Everyone who calls on the name of the Lord will be saved" (Romans 10.12-13).

Yesterday you read about Jesus your brother. Today as you meditate on 1 John 2 you may like to consider, "Who is my brother?"

Quote

He drew a circle that shut me out
Heretic, rebel, a thing to flout.
But love and I had wit to win,
We drew a circle that took him in.
— Edwin Markham, *Poems of Edwin Markham*,
ed. Charles Wallis (Harper Row).

Promise "He is the atoning sacrifice for our sins, and not only for ours but also for the sins of the whole world" (1 John 2.2).

DAY 122 Therefore, as God's chosen people, holy and dearly loved (3.12a)

Good Morning, Disciple,

As one who has made his own fair share of blunders, I take a perverse delight in reading of somebody else who boobed. Back in 1946 a referendum in Italy changed the constitution from a monarchy to a republic. The deposed King Umberto II was about to board his aeroplane at Ciampino Airport on his way to exile in Portugal. At the last moment he remembered that he had not handed the accounts over to the Privy Purse staff. Calling an aide he said with a wave of his hand, "Don't forget the accounts. Give them to the people over there."

The aide thought he was referring to the crowd of well-wishers standing behind the Privy Purse staff. In Italian the word "conti" is the same for both count and account, and he thought the King was making a parting gesture. That is how the whole crowd became ennobled with the title and are to this day called the Counts of Ciampino.

What a blunder! Not so the titles given to us today. "Chosen people, holy and dearly loved" are neither empty titles nor an accident of Paul's pen. They are, first, a fulfilment of prophecy. "I will show my love to the one I called 'Not my loved one'. I will say to those called 'Not my people', 'You are my people'" (Hosea 2.23). His people is, of course, Israel. Who, then, are these who were not His people but are now included? The Church! The bride of Christ.

Paul has deliberately taken the very titles bestowed on ancient Israel and transferred them over to the Church. The Jews were familiar with the words in Deuteronomy 7.6-8 that God's people were holy, chosen and loved. This is reinforced by that introductory word "therefore". It points us back to the previous verse where Jew and Gentile are one.

But look beyond the privilege of belonging and being loved to that little word "holy". We are called to be different. Israel had been given "most favoured nation" status to become the vehicle for God's grace. She accepted the status but reneged on her duty. Shall we do the same? Or will our lives show something of Jesus Christ and His message to the world? That's really the question Paul is asking. What a privilege! What a responsibility!

Read Matthew 5.1-20 and meditate especially on the salt and light.

Quote "Our progress in holiness depends on God and ourselves – on God's grace and on our will to be holy" – Charles Colson, *Mother Teresa* (Zondervan, 1983).

Promise "For there is no difference between Jew and Gentile – the same Lord is Lord of all and richly blesses all who call on him" (Romans 10.12).

DAY 123   Clothe yourselves (3.12b)

Good Morning, Disciple,

We have seen already that baptism is a symbol of putting off the old life with its practices (3.9). The old worn-out garments of sin must be replaced with a new wardrobe.

You will recall that at the baptismal service the old rags were left on the river bank and as the candidate came out of the water he or she received a clean white robe to symbolise the new life in Christ. The imagery was borrowed from the Roman Empire, where only the true-blooded citizen of Rome could wear the white toga. Slaves and foreigners could wear only coloured togas, to distinguish them from citizens.

Just as the responsibility for taking off the old clothes is our own, so is that of reclothing ourselves in the image of Christ. It is, in fact, a command to the whole Church, in much the same way as Jesus

Himself commanded us to "love each other" as His followers (John 15.12). While this does not absolve us from loving the unbeliever it is primarily an instruction to the Church. As Paul said elsewhere, "Let us do good to all people, especially to those who belong to the family of believers" (Galatians 6.10). The love we practise at home is the nursery from which a stronger strain may be transplanted into society.

One Sunday at the chapel service at my daughter Ruth's school I heard the Bishop of Truro, Michael Ball, give one of those sermons beloved by scholars for its brevity. He talked about our Lord's command to love one another and gave a most useful insight into the word "command". In the Greek the word has three meanings, he said. It means, first, an instruction to be carried out in obedience to the one who commanded it. Secondly, it is a commission, rather like a commissioned officer in the army who is there to represent and carry out the will of his commander-in-chief. Thirdly, it is a proclamation to others that this is the will of the one who made the command.

Isn't that what we are called to, as we respond to this instruction to clothe ourselves? We must obey the command. As we do so, we fulfil our commission to become more and more like Jesus and so we become God's commercial to the world.

Yesterday you began looking at the Master's Sermon on the Mount. Read on to the end of Matthew 5, and meditate especially on verses 43-48.

Quote "Our choice is a coat of paint on the outside or a dye to permeate the whole" – source unknown.

Promise "Carry each other's burdens, and in this way you will fulfil the law of Christ" (Galatians 6.2).

DAY 124 With compassion (3.12c)

Good Morning, Disciple,

"Have a bowel", the ancients might have said in much the same way as we say, "have a heart", meaning to care. For them the intestines were the seat of the emotions. So the Greek word for compassion is, literally, "bowels of mercy" or more politely, "mercy in the inner parts".

Where you place it anatomically doesn't really matter, so long as you show it. Compassion is the first of the designer label clothing of the Kingdom, exhibited and modelled supremely in Christ, who "when he saw the crowds, he had compassion on them, because they were harassed and helpless, like sheep without a shepherd" (Matthew 9.36). The inner man determines the outward action. You never sense with Jesus any ulterior motive to His care. It is always recognisable by the hallmark of genuine compassion. So when a man comes to Him with a dreadful skin disease, He flies in the face of the religious and medical practice of His day. "Filled with compassion, Jesus reached out his hand and touched the man" (Mark 1.41).

Such compassion is often costly. Andy Warhol knew this. He confessed to *Newsweek*, "When I got my first TV set I stopped caring so much about having close relationships . . . you can only be hurt when you care a lot."

One person in our own generation who has exemplified this Christ-like quality over and above most of us is Mother Teresa of Calcutta. As the wizened old lady clothed in white cares for the dying beggars, she says, "These people have been treated all their lives like dogs. Their greatest disease is a sense that they are unwanted. Don't they have a right to die like angels?" What drives a person to such sacrificial service? An inner tenderness which has been touched by the grace of God!

How much easier most of us find it to tell a person what to do with his problem than to stand with him in his pain. Compassion is rarely expressed in words alone. "Suppose a brother or sister is without clothes and daily food. If one of you says to him, 'Go, I wish you well; keep warm and well fed', but does nothing about his physical needs, what good is it?" (James 2.15-16).

Compare this with the Good Samaritan (Luke 10.25-37), then see if you can re-write that story with modern characters in a modern context. It's powerful when you do!

Quote "Nothing can atone for the insult of a gift except the love of the person who gives it" – Old Chinese proverb.

Promise "Then the King will say to those on his right, 'Come, you who are blessed by my Father; take your inheritance, the kingdom prepared for you since the creation of the world'" (Matthew 25.34).

DAY 125 Kindness 3.12d

Good Morning, Disciple,

The command "Be kind and compassionate to one another" (Ephesians 4.32) is, I believe, a recognition that kindness is not a natural characteristic. In fact, it is the opposite to greed, which we looked at in an earlier letter. Greed is rampant selfishness, whereas kindness is a fruit of the Spirit (Galatians 5.22) and an expression of love (1 Corinthians 13.4). Bishop Moule called it "the character which offers sympathy and invites confidence".

Several years ago, when I was helping a band of hippy travellers, I told them that I was going to Darlington the next day. "Darlington," exploded Carol, "that's where my mum and dad live." She pleaded that I should take her and her new-born baby with me. I agreed to do this but faced a problem. I had made an arrangement to go via Wimbledon where I was to have breakfast with Sir Cyril and Lady Black.

The next morning when we arrived in Wimbledon I knocked at the door and explained to Lady Black that the dishevelled, shoeless mother was a hippy from the Peace Convoy. "Oh, bring her in," chirped Lady Black with a genuine welcome and without any hint of condemnation.

When eventually we resumed our journey to the north Carol kept saying, "And she's a Lady – he's a Sir – and they invited me in for breakfast." Such was the impact of this act of simple kindness that Carol's heart was softened to receive Christ as her Saviour.

We in the Church are not always so kind. John Stott in his book *Issues Facing Christians Today* tells of one sad occasion when a lady turned up at a country vicarage to ask for some help. The vicar, no doubt a busy man and slightly out of his depth, told the woman that he would pray for her. She later wrote this poem:

I was hungry
     and you formed a humanities group to discuss my hunger.
I was imprisoned
     and you crept off quietly to your chapel and prayed for my release.
I was naked
     and in your mind you debated the morality of my appearance.

I was sick
  and you knelt and thanked God for your health.
I was homeless
  and you preached to me of the spiritual shelter of the love of God.
I was lonely
  and you left me alone to pray for me.
You seem so holy, so close to God
  but I am still very hungry – and lonely – and cold.

Our kindness and compassion are the litmus test of true spirituality, as you will see when you read Matthew 25.31-46.

Quote "You can never warm a man's heart while his feet are cold" – William Booth

Promise "He who is kind to the poor lends to the Lord, and he will reward him for what he has done" (Proverbs 19.17).

DAY 126 Humility, gentleness (3.12e)

Good Morning, Disciple,
  If pride and greed are the twin columns at the entrance to Satan's abode then humility is the very gate of heaven. I have kept these two graces together because in Scripture they are paired as qualities of Christ. He said, "Take my yoke upon you and learn from me, for I am gentle and humble in heart, and you will find rest for your souls" (Matthew 11.29).
  In classical Greek this word was unknown except as a term of derision. To be humble was to be timid. Indeed, Paul uses it in that sense when he says to the Corinthians, "By the meekness and gentleness of Christ, I appeal to you – I, Paul, who am *timid* when face to face with you" (2 Corinthians 10.1). Our Lord introduced a new meaning to the word which we need to rediscover today. The media have brainwashed this generation to believe that might is right. Manliness is portrayed as a musclebound machismo. Arrogant, foul-mouthed self-glorification is paraded as the desirable norm. Many would be amused at Paul's words, "Be completely humble and gentle" (Ephesians 4.2).

Robert Henrich put his finger on the pulse when he rhymed, "In man ambition is the commonest thing; each one by nature loves to be King." This is no less true in the Church than in the world, for the self-willed man will always tend towards pride and aggression. As we have seen already, the false teachers were filled with pride cloaked as humility. Sham humility is pride with the odour of death around it. Real humility is a Christ-like character with the aroma of life about it. It was said of Eric Liddell, the Olympic runner and missionary to China whose story was told in the memorable film *Chariots of Fire*, that he was "ridiculously humble in victory, and utterly generous in defeat".

Meekness, translated in the NIV as gentleness, is the twin of humility. They are never far apart. According to the Beatitudes it is the meek who inherit the earth (Matthew 5.5). The Greek word *praotes* was often used as an adjective to describe a wind as being gentle, or a colt just broken in, or even a poultice, soothing and healing. The stronger a wind, the more damage it causes; a horse uncontrolled is of no use to its master for pleasure or work; and a poultice too hot or roughly applied will do more harm than good.

As you read Daniel 1 this morning you will see a true man of God at work – courteously courageous and infectiously humble.

Quote "Nothing is so strong as gentle men; nothing so gentle as real strength" – St Francis of Sales.

Promise "When pride comes, then comes disgrace, but with humility comes wisdom" (Proverbs 11.2).

DAY 127   And patience. Bear with each other (3.13a)

Good Morning, Disciple,

"Patience is a virtue, possess it if you can; never found in women and seldom in a man." Whenever I quote that in my house there are squeals of protest from the three ladies in my life!

Once again the Greek helps us with our understanding. *Makrothumia* broken down looks like this: *makros* = long; *thumos* = anger or temper. Put them together and you get the clearest possible picture, long-tempered as against short-tempered. You will remember that anger and rage were left on the river bank of baptism with all the other "filthy rags". The other word, *anechomia*, translated in the NIV as "bear with each other", means to put up with or endure.

Earlier we saw that these two qualities were part of Paul's prayer for the believers (1.11), and in Ephesians 4.2 they are linked again with an interesting qualification: "Be patient, bearing with each other in love." How shrewd! Even such good qualities as long-suffering and patience can be misused unless they are tempered with love.

Once again the Lord is our model, both in living and in dying. Patience is one of God's supreme attributes; He is "slow to anger, abounding in love" (Exodus 34.6) and "patient with you, not wanting anyone to perish, but everyone to come to repentance" (2 Peter 3.9).

Paul clearly wants to avoid an inquisition and unnecessary conflict. He has dealt with the false teaching by using the only effective antidote – the word of truth. The Scriptures never advocate the kind of wishy-washy tolerance which says, "It doesn't matter what you believe so long as you're sincere." However, once heresy is nailed, patient teaching and careful instruction (2 Timothy 4.2) are needed so that the truth will have long-lasting impact. The newly-strengthened must use their spiritual muscle to "bear with the failings of the weak" (Romans 15.1).

I saw a profound example of this in the lives of two close friends who took into their home a young lass who had come to Christ at the Glastonbury Festival. Her background in the drug sub-culture and poor home environment have made her both unreliable and unpredictable. She has a real love for the Lord and for her foster parents but glue-sniffing had her hooked for almost a year. Again and again this couple would take six steps forward and seven steps back, always ready to start at square one all over again.

As you read James 5.7-20 use the picture there of the farmer waiting for harvest to focus your attention on whatever it is that makes you impatient. Then pray about it.

Quote "Our patience will achieve more than our force" – Edmund Burke.

Promise "The Lord is gracious and compassionate, slow to anger and rich in love" (Psalm 145.8).

DAY 128   And forgive whatever grievances you may have against one another (3.13b)

Good Morning, Disciple,

Everyone says that forgiveness is a lovely idea, but how few attain its high ideal when there is something to forgive. It seems we would rather live with the poisonous consequences of malice and resentment, as we harbour feelings of self pity and revenge, than forgive as we have been instructed to do. Too soon, this personal hostility spreads like an uncontrolled fire through gossip and self-justification, until people have taken sides and made reconciliation that much the harder to achieve.

Forgiveness, therefore, should be swift and decisive, no matter what the balance of right or wrong. This does not mean condoning the offence. Let sin be sin. But it cannot be exposed as such unless it is first forgiven. When we come together in reconciliation as brothers and sisters we can see who and what the real enemy is.

If you are offended, forgive. If you are at fault, confess. In fact, Jesus said you cannot go to the Father unless you do (Matthew 5.23-24).

When responding to those who wrong us, we always have a choice between the flesh, the soul and the Spirit. The flesh lashes out with physical or verbal abuse and adds sin to sin. The soul by the control of will and emotions patches up the quarrel and forgives on a horizontal plane, man to man, woman to woman, but lasts only so long as no further offence occurs. But the Spirit-controlled person controls the body and the tongue, forgives on the horizontal plane as an act of deliberate obedience, and goes on to seal the matter in heaven, on the vertical plane.

When Jesus prayed from the cross, "Father, forgive them," He was forgiving those around Him on the horizontal plane and calling for their forgiveness in heaven, on the vertical plane. When we lift the sin to God for His forgiveness we may not then dredge it up again and hold it against our brother or sister.

I love Psalm 103. It puts forgiving others into its true perspective. When you have meditated on it for a while try this. Wherever you see His action of forgiveness, love and compassion put your own name; and put the name of someone who has wronged you where you see the personal pronoun.

Quote "Any resolution of a dispute apart from the Spirit life amounts to a compromise, a negotiated settlement, a cease-fire, or a best guess" – Gene Edwards, *Preventing a Church Split* (Christian Books, 1987).

Promise "(The Lord) forgives all your sins and heals all your diseases" (Psalm 103.3).

DAY 129   Forgive as the Lord forgave you (3.13c)

Good Morning, Disciple,

After World War I, when much of Belgium lay in ruins, a small class of children were taken to a wayside shrine to pray. They began to pray the Lord's prayer, ". . . Give us this day our daily bread and forgive us our trespasses as we . . ." Then looking around them at the devastation of war, and then at their teacher, they faltered. From behind them came a strong, steady voice, ". . . as we forgive those who trespass against us." They turned and there before them was King Albert.

He had learned through the bitter experience of war what Jesus taught, and Paul here repeats, that the forgiveness which we receive is the motivation for the forgiveness we offer to others. The other side of that coin is that when we forgive we release forgiveness. As Jesus said, "When you stand praying, if you hold anything against anyone, forgive him, so that your Father in heaven may forgive you your sins" (Mark 11.25). We see a vivid example of this in the death of the first Christian martyr. Did Stephen perhaps remember the words of Jesus from the cross, "Father, forgive them" (Luke 23.34), when he prayed as the stones were being hurled, "Lord, do not hold this sin against them" (Acts 7.60)?

The nature of God's forgiveness "in Christ" (Ephesians 4.32) is complete, as we have already seen (2.13). The word used there and here is the same, meaning to "make a gift of the wrong", giving it back as a cancelled debt. In fact, Jesus uses this very picture when He tells the parable of the cancelled debt (Luke 7.41-42).

The tense shows that our obligation to forgive is continuous. When a person says, "I can forgive but I'll never forget," it is an act of rebellion against Him who removed our sins "as far as the east is from the west".

Peter asked Jesus, "How many times shall I forgive my brother when he sins against me? Up to seven times?" The rabbis taught that forgiveness should be given three times, so Peter doubled their quota and added one for good measure. But he hadn't reckoned on the mathematics of heaven. "I tell you not seven times but seventy seven times" (Matthew 18.22), or, as some manuscripts have it, seventy times seven, 490! The number is not important because love "keeps no record of wrongs" (1 Corinthians 13.5).

I wonder what lessons you will learn as you read Matthew 18.15-35. I imagine we shall never exhaust the mine of God's grace in forgiving us.

Quote "Christ did not overcome evil with evil; He overcame evil with good. Although crucified by hate, He responded with aggressive love" – Martin Luther King.

Promise "(The Lord) redeems your life from the pit and crowns you with love and compassion" (Psalm 103.4).

DAY 130 And over all these virtues put on love, which binds them all together in perfect unity (3.14)

Good Morning, Disciple,

In the third century AD when rabbis sought to find one Scripture upon which the whole of the law could rest, they settled on Proverbs 3.5-6: "Trust in the Lord with all your heart and lean not on your own understanding; in all your ways acknowledge him, and he will make your paths straight." If you were to ask me for one verse from the New Testament on which the whole work of God rests for the believer, I would suggest Galatians 5.6: "The only thing that counts is faith expressing itself through love."

Certainly love received the Lord's vote as the greatest commandment (Matthew 22.37-40). Paul seconds that with the assertion, "The entire law is summed up in a single commandment, "Love your neighbour as yourself" (Galatians 5.14).

It is the "most excellent way" in the gifts of the Spirit (1 Corinthians 12.31). It heads the list of the fruit of the Spirit (Galatians 5.22).

Remember, we are still looking at our clothing – our new wardrobe.

We have put on Christ-like compassion, kindness, humility, gentleness, patience, forbearance and a forgiving spirit. Now on goes the outer garment – love! In other words, "Clothe yourselves with the Lord Jesus Christ" (Romans 13.14).

The Greeks used four words for love, each with a different connotation. *Philos* was used for friendship, camaraderie. *Eros*, from which we get our English word erotic, is sexual love. *Philadelphia* is fraternal love such as we have in a family. Then there is *agape*, love that comes from God.

No doubt there is an implied contrast here with the elitist false teachers hiving off into their secret meetings. Such an "in group" could only hope for friendship at a level of *philos*. At worst they could split the Church, as has happened so often when individuals get high on their pet doctrines.

Love is the gel that binds everything together. Have you ever been to a ladies' knitting circle? Each of the ladies knits squares in all colours and shades from left-over wool. These are then sewn together to make a blanket. That's the picture we have here. Love sews all the virtues together to make this outer garment.

What happens when love is missing? I'll leave you to answer that as you meditate on 1 Corinthians 13 – God's love song.

Quote "Love is the crown and coping stone of the Christian character" – F. B. Westcott, *A Letter To Asia* (Klock & Klock, reprint, 1981).

Promise "God is love. Whoever lives in love lives in God, and God in him" (1 John 4.16).

DAY 131   Let the peace of Christ rule in your hearts, since as members of one body you were called to peace (3.15a)

Good Morning, Disciple,

When I read, "You were called to peace," I'm always tempted to add a little rider, "not to pieces". That is really the message Paul is trying to get over to this church which has suffered disruptive influences which undermined the authority of a faithful pastor and caused division. They were in pieces, torn apart and in need of peace

– peace with God in Christ and, equally important, the peace of God.

As we saw way back in chapter one, God's great peace plan has been established. We, who were hostile towards God, have been reconciled to Him by the blood of Jesus on the cross (1.20-22). We have peace with God.

Why then do so many Christians suffer anxiety illnesses like anyone else? Part of the answer lies in the fact that they do not have the peace *of* God. Jesus promised, "Peace I leave with you; my peace I give you. I do not give to you as the world gives" (John 14.27). The world gives advice and pills, psychoanalysis and exorbitant bills for hypnosis and other stress-reducing therapies. Now, I'm not saying that the doctor should not prescribe drugs when necessary. Far from it! But all the doctor can do is to treat the symptoms. What God will do deals with the core.

He has given His Holy Spirit to strengthen our weaknesses. The fruit of the Spirit is love, joy, peace, etc. (Galatians 5.22). Notice the catalogue of ills which precedes this promise. Anyone who lives a life of careless abandon with regard to God's principles must not be surprised when doubts, fears and anxieties invade the mind. But when our lives exhibit the fruit of the Spirit and the virtues of Christ, we shall know the full measure of peace.

Prayer, too, is an essential element. Notice the progression from anxiety through prayer to peace in those much loved words of the apostle, "Do not be anxious about anything, but in everything, by prayer and petition, with thanksgiving, present your requests to God. And the peace of God, which transcends all understanding, will guard your hearts and your minds in Christ Jesus" (Philippians 4.6-7).

Paul's reference to our being members of one body makes it clear that the context here is peace in the Church. A Church that had suffered from self-inflicted wounds needed, as we do today, the continuous controlling influence of Christ's peace.

If Christ can still a raging sea and calm a possessed lunatic, then surely He can cope with you and me. Why don't you read about that in Mark 4.35 to 5.20. Meditate especially on 5.16 in contrast to 5.3-5.

Quote "When there is peace in the heart there will be praise on the lips" – Warren W. Wiersbe, *Be Complete* (Victor Books, 1981).

Promise "Be of one mind, live in peace. And the God of love and peace will be with you" (2 Corinthians 13.11).

DAY 132   And be thankful (3.15b)

Good Morning, Disciple,

Here we go again with one of the great themes of this letter: be thankful. You can tell what kind of a Dad Paul would have been, can't you? "Now don't forget when you leave the party to say, Thank you for having me."

Gratitude is a rare commodity. Perhaps it is a sign of the times, for the Scripture predicts that ingratitude will be one of the hallmarks of the "terrible times in the last days" (2 Timothy 3.1-2). The instruction to become a thankful people is not just to make God feel good (though if it does who would begrudge Him that!), it is to lay the foundation for contentment, service, love and peace. It is to make a moral choice between the Christ-like clothing in the wardrobe of this letter and the ever increasing levels of depravity in a time when "people will be lovers of themselves, lovers of money, boastful, proud, abusive, disobedient to their parents, ungrateful . . ." (2 Timothy 3.2-4). And so it goes on, in stark contrast with the qualities of love listed in 1 Corinthians 13, the fruit of the Spirit in Galatians 5.22 and the virtues of Christ. If ingratitude was the reason for man's slide away from God (Romans 1.21-32) then thankfulness must surely be the first step on the ladder out of the abyss.

Every Sabbath in the synagogue of Israel, the congregations recited Psalm 95, "Come, let us sing for joy to the Lord; let us shout aloud to the Rock of our salvation. Let us come before him with thanksgiving.' As they recounted His dealings with them and His awesome creative power, they were brought back to the point of thankfulness.

When invited to preach in churches I sometimes go around the whole congregation asking them to name one thing for which they are truly thankful. There is laughter as we do this and the occasional tear, but it is a moving and enriching experience to hear the responses. "Thank you for my new job"; "Thank you for my church, and Mrs Jones, who baked a cake for me when I was ill"; "Thank you for my food," says one lad who looks as though he would enjoy anything;

"Thank you for my wife," says another – I never knew a wife that didn't like to hear that; "Thank you for the Lord Jesus"; "Thank you that I am saved."

If we are thankful we need to express it. "Through Jesus, therefore, let us continually offer to God a sacrifice of praise" (Hebrews 13.15).

Psalm 95 would be a good training ground in how to compose a prayer of thankfulness. Why don't you meditate on it for a while, then spend some quality time thanking God for what He has done in your life.

Quote "Praise opens the door to more grace" – John Wesley.

Promise "Enter his gates with thanksgiving and his courts with praise; give thanks to him and praise his name" (Psalm 100.4-5).

DAY 133 Let the word of Christ dwell in you richly (3.16a)

Good Morning, Disciple,

When you study the Bible by yourself, here are some helpful steps to bear in mind. They are taken from an excellent introduction to studying the Scriptures written by my good friend Andrew Green.

Step one. What does the passage actually say? Someone has said you can make the Bible say anything you want it to. Yes, and people do! Heretics are not confined to the remote past. They are among us now. It is probably true to say that all heresy starts with a careless handling of God's Word. While God speaks through the Scriptures to each generation, we must read it in its original context. What did the author mean? What did those who first read it understand it to mean? What did it say in its original language? If you don't know Greek, you'll need a commentary – get advice from a trustworthy leader before buying one.

Let's use today's text as an example. My commentary tells me that the word translated "dwell" has various shades of meaning, such as "indwell" or "live in". But live in whom? You as an individual, or you as the whole Church? In this instance it could mean either within you or among you. Both, of course, are necessary. To grow up in your faith you need to be in a church which teaches and preaches God's

Word. But you must do your part by studying at home if it is to dwell "richly" in you.

Step two. What does the text mean in the context of the whole passage and the whole Bible? Let's try that here. The immediate context tells us to let peace rule in our hearts. Add to that the Word of Christ. So we have peace and the Word living in and among us. Is there anything else? This is where other Scriptures come to my aid. Paul told Timothy, "You yourselves are God's temple . . . God's Spirit lives in you" (1 Corinthians 3.16). So now we have Peace + Word + Spirit. We need both the Word and the Spirit if we are going to know inner peace and peace in our churches.

Step three. Application – what does this teach me for today? Here, I'd say, we are being encouraged to know God's Word thoroughly and reject man-made myths, traditions and philosophies. A diet of these leads to starvation. The Word of Christ leads to spiritual wealth undreamed of.

Meditate on Psalm 119 – any two sections you like. They will all endorse what has been said.

Quote "Scripture comes like a sword to interpret us" – Andrew R. Green, *The Authority of Scripture* (Kingsway, 1990).

Promise "The unfolding of your words gives light; it gives understanding to the simple" (Psalm 119.130).

DAY 134 As you teach and admonish one another with all wisdom (3.16b)

Good Morning, Disciple,

Do you have any idea how important yesterday's letter was? Permit me to be really unsubtle and spell it out. *It was crucial.* I want you to be so excited about God's Word that you will have an insatiable appetite to study it and come closer to the Lord by understanding it properly.

You may like to try this test. Using the principles which I borrowed from Andrew Green's book, *The Authority of Scripture*, let's unpack this text.

The first step is to ask, "What does it mean in its context?" Well, there are three words which we've already met: teach, admonish and wisdom. You remember how, in 1.28, Paul said, "We proclaim him, admonishing and teaching everyone with all wisdom"? But he is not at Colosse and neither is Pastor Epaphras, so he says in effect, continue to work out your own salvation. You don't need a priest. You've got the Word of Christ, now share it among yourselves. He has given them in written form what to date they had only heard from Epaphras. So this and the other Scriptures from the Old Testament were to be the solid basis for teaching and correction and indeed the answer to his own prayer in 1.9 that they may be filled with the knowledge of His will, through all spiritual wisdom and understanding. The heretics only have an "appearance of wisdom" (2.23) and an empty "deceptive philosophy" (2.8). Getting the hang of it?

Let's go on then to step two. Does any other Scripture throw light on the text? Yes, of course, there are many, but let me suggest two insights by way of example.

Paul's letters to Timothy are written into a similar situation. Actually, it was much worse. There is no evidence in Colossians that the heretical ne'er-do-wells were leaders, whereas at Ephesus, where Timothy was ministering, it was the teaching elders who had gone astray, both morally and in their theology. So as a corrective Paul instructs Timothy to return to sound methods of teaching. "The things you have heard me say in the presence of many witnesses entrust to reliable men (bypassing the corrupting elders) who will be qualified to teach others" (2 Timothy 2.2). Now read on to see how he is going to do this – using the Scriptures, "teaching, rebuking, correcting and training in righteousness" (2 Timothy 3.15-16). Do you see the admonishment there?

Now, how about application? Tell you what – I'll leave that to you. How would you apply this to yourself and to your church?

Go back to Psalm 119 and again choose two sections to meditate on.

Quote "One proof of the inspiration of Scripture is that it has withstood so many years of poor teaching" – A. T. Robertson.

Promise "God's word is not chained" (2 Timothy 2.9).

DAY 135 **And as you sing psalms, hymns and spiritual songs with gratitude in your hearts to God (3.16c)**

Good Morning, Disciple,

A few years ago we had an extension built on to our house by a Christian builder, Mervyn. For weeks the noise of hammer and cement mixer blended with Mervyn's vast repertoire of hymns and choruses. I even learned some new ones. It was great!

Now, of course, not everybody can go round their daily chores singing, though it would be fun to see what would happen if Mervyn were to spend a day at the Stock Exchange or in the House of Commons.

Scripture is full of song and heaven rejoices to the sound of music. At the creation, "The morning stars sang together and all the angels shouted for joy" (Job 38.7) and in heaven "they sang a new song" (Revelation 5.9). Even Jesus, moments before He left the upper room to take those fateful steps to Gethsemane, sang a hymn with His disciples (Matthew 26.30).

Tertullian sheds some light on our text. He noted in around 200 AD, "After water for the hands, and lights have been brought in, each is invited to sing to God in the presence of the others from what he knows of the Holy Scriptures or from his own heart." Song seems to have had a dual role in the early Church, as a tool for teaching and a vehicle for spontaneous praise. It is probably unhelpful to try to unwrap the meaning of psalms, hymns and spiritual songs beyond saying that all forms of music were to be employed in worship. In the Ephesian parallel we have, in contrast to drunken carousing, the influence of the Holy Spirit upon music: "Be filled with the Spirit. Speak to one another with psalms, hymns and spiritual songs. Sing and make music in your heart to the Lord" (Ephesians 5.19).

Isn't that the balance we need? The word of Christ and the Holy Spirit in songs of gratitude with sufficient content to teach the truth, and filled with joy and praise to express our hearts. Incidentally, I love the literal meaning of the word translated "gratitude": "grace singing". Let's have more of it.

Cliff Richard says, "Why should the devil have all the best music?" Music is neutral. It is what you do with it that determines whether it is debased or lofty.

Read about one of the most explosive songs ever recorded, in Acts 16.16-40. Then follow the example of St Mervyn and sing a song!

Quote "Let us sing a hymn and spite the devil" – Martin Luther King.

Promise "Yet a time is coming and has now come when the true worshippers will worship the Father in spirit and truth" (John 4.23a).

DAY 136 And whatever you do, whether in word or deed, do it all in the name of the Lord Jesus (3.17a)

Good Morning, Disciple,

Did you hear about the prison chaplain who ended his chapel service with the words, "Go out in peace to all the world"? Five hundred inmates rushed for the door!

Maybe he could have chosen a wiser benediction but he had the right idea. Christianity must be lived out in the real world. For the Christian prisoner, and thank God there are some who like me have come to know the Lord in gaol, it means living it out on the wing where the going is tough. The same goes for all of us, whether inside the Church, with its challenging relationships, or outside in the world, with all its pressures to conform to ways, goals, and standards which are alien to Christ. Private devotion or public worship which does not prepare us for that is in some way deficient.

In the UK every civil, legal and military authority can be traced back to the throne. Everything they do is done in the name of the Queen. In the same way the believer has confessed the name of the Lord Jesus Christ (Romans 10.9) and given allegiance to Him. Therefore, all should be done and said in His name. This has very practical implications. If we cannot put the name of Jesus to an action, then that action is out of the question. If we cannot say something and then immediately follow it with "in the name of Jesus", then those words should not pass our lips. After all Jesus Himself said, "By your words you will be acquitted, and by your words you will be condemned" (Matthew 12.37). This is what Paul meant when he said, "Now that faith has come, we are no longer under the supervision of the law" (Galatians 3.25). The standard we aim for is much higher. So when someone glibly excuses his poor behaviour by saying, "We are no longer under the law," he shows that he has totally misunderstood the consequences of his faith.

This will have special relevance over the next few weeks when we look at the Christian at work, at home and in the world.

As you read 1 John 2.1-17 keep in mind verse 3 and remember that "his commands" are not the same as the "rules and regulations". The one comes from God, the other comes from man.

Quote "When we do everything in our Lord's name we shall constantly be revelling in the sunshine of our gratitude to the heavenly Father" – R. C. H. Lenski, *The Interpretation of Paul's Epistles, Colossians* (Augsburg Publishing House, 1937).

Promise "But thanks be to God! He gives us the victory through our Lord Jesus Christ" (1 Corinthians 15.57).

DAY 137   Giving thanks to God the Father through him (3.17b)

Good Morning, Disciple,

This is the fifth occasion we have come across the theme of thanksgiving. Quite remarkable, isn't it, that we should have so much gratitude from a prison cell. But then it is often the darker experiences of life which bring the greatest contrast of laughter, love and thankfulness.

Consider, for instance, Martin Rinckart, a pastor in Eilenberg in Saxony. He remained there throughout the Thirty Years' War, refusing to abandon his post even when disease and famine threatened his life. The pestilence of 1637 ravaged the population packed within the walled city, and he buried 4,480 people, including this own wife.

Many stories are told of his heroism and generosity. Once when a general demanded a bounty of 30,000 thalers, and Rinckart had pleaded in vain for the impoverished people, he said to his flock, "Come, my children, we can find no mercy with man; let us take refuge with God." There, on their knees, they sang a hymn of assurance, "When in my hour of utmost need." So moved was the general that he reduced the levy to 1,350 thalers. It is against this backdrop of gutsy service in the real world that Rinckart penned the words:

> Now thank we all our God, With hearts and hands and voices,
> Who wondrous things hath done, In whom His world rejoices;
> Who from our mother's arms, Hath blessed us on our way
> With countless gifts of love, And still is ours today.

You can spot an additional thought in the parallel verse in Ephesians. "Always giving thanks to God the Father for everything, in the name of our Lord Jesus Christ" (Ephesians 5.20). Have you got it? "Always . . . for everything." And again, "Give thanks in all circumstances, for this is God's will for you in Christ Jesus" (1 Thessalonians 5.18). In redundancy? Yes! In sickness? Yes! When somebody deliberately harms me? Yes!

In the flesh we could not do it, so notice in each place the little rider, "in Jesus Christ", "in the name of our Lord Jesus Christ", "through him". When we are able to say thank you through Jesus we are showing our total dependency on Him. The focus of our lives is taken away from self with all its fears and anxiety, and fixed on Him who is able to do all things. We are able to declare, whatever the circumstances of life, "Thanks be to God. He gives us victory through our Lord Jesus Christ" (1 Corinthians 15.57).

Enjoy Psalm 92 and meditate on verse 8.

Quote "Praise drives out the darkness and turns on God's light" – Wesley Duewel, *Touch the World Through Prayer* (Francis Asbury Press, 1986).

Promise "For he will command his angels concerning you to guard you in all your ways" (Psalm 91.11).

DAY 138 Wives, submit to your husbands, as is fitting in the Lord (3.18)

Good Morning, Disciple,

The word submit means to "arrange under rank" and has to do with divine order, not only in the home but everywhere in God's

Kingdom. For instance, we are all to submit to "the governing authorities" (Romans 13.1). The natural world has been placed under the authority of humans (Psalm 8.6-8). Within the Church the young submit to the old (1 Peter 5.5), we all submit to Christ as head (Ephesians 1.22) and "to one another out of reverence for Christ" (Ephesians 5.21), notwithstanding our equality in Him. Even our Lord, though equal with the Father (John 5.18), humbly submits Himself to the Father's will (John 6.38).

So when Paul asks wives to submit to their husbands, it has nothing to do with the superiority of the one nor the indignity of the other, for in Christ both are equal.

But, says a Christian lady, I'm better than my husband at certain things. Fine, that's not in question. I have two daughters who can knock spots off me educationally and in many other ways, but they delight to humour me, as much as I delight to love them. I have given my wife the responsibility of managing our financial affairs because she's so much better at it than I am. Indeed, the Scripture says they are to "manage their homes" (1 Timothy 5.14).

I repeat, it is not a matter of equality, but a matter of order. God has placed the husband in a position of loving authority over the home, not to tyrannise or degrade or humiliate but to establish it under Christ's supreme Headship (Ephesians 5.24). The man who insists that his wife submit to him not only shows his moral inferiority but has lost the battle already. The wife's submission will be voluntary or it will be not at all.

The key lies in the motive – because it is "fitting in the Lord" and "so that no one will malign the word of God" (Titus 2.5), and in the case of an unbelieving husband that he might be won to the Lord (1 Peter 3.1).

One of my Sue's favourite Bible passages is Proverbs 31. It is fascinating. Who says women are the inferior sex – certainly not the Bible. Read it this morning – I know it will thrill you.

Quote "No man can love his wife in the way God requires until he bows in the presence of his Master and confesses that he needs divine help" – Selwyn Hughes, *Marriage As God Intended* (Kingsway, 1983).

Promise "Let us not become weary in doing good, for at the

proper time we will reap a harvest if we do not give up"
(Galatians 6.9).

DAY 139 Husbands, love your wives and do not be harsh with them (3.19)

Good Morning, Disciple,

If you are married then you will want the very best for your home life, and I can assure you that when you put *all* these biblical principles to work, happiness is the reward. You can actually build heaven into your family life even when the outward circumstances appear to be chaotic.

When Christ is head of the home, the nearer you get to Him the nearer you get to each other. For the sake of order the man is given the delegated responsibility of being head of the family, and is given two commands to guide all his actions. Love your wife – do not be harsh.

Don't be harsh with your wife does not just mean, don't be aggressive. It means to be actively gentle, kind, patient and all those thoughtful, Christlike qualities which every Christian ought to show to another.

In Ephesians 5.25-32 the command to love is given an additional condition: "As Christ loved the church and gave himself up for her." How did Christ love the church? "He made himself nothing" (Philippians 2.7); the very opposite of what Western culture believes a man should do and be. The husband must work to feed and care for his own (Ephesians 5.29; 1 Timothy 5.8), but if he simply uses that as an excuse for ambitions which take him up, up and away from his family, then the price is too high.

Jesus took on the "nature of a servant" (Philippians 2.7). Service, humility and sacrifice are God's role-model for the Christian husband. It would be a perverse woman indeed who would exchange such for the empty goal of feminine superiority.

The wise and Christlike man will be considerate (1 Peter 3.7), and do as Christ has done, by delegating the everyday management of the family to his wife (1 Timothy 5.14), on the basis of shared decision-making and mutual confidence (Proverbs 31.11). He will "praise her", "reward her" (Proverbs 31.29, 31), and do everything in his power to "please his wife" (1 Corinthians 7.33). He will not only show her love in action but he will tell her, more often than he imagines necessary, "I love you". The only thing he can do for her that Christ could not do for the church, is to say, when he is in the wrong, "Darling, you're right! I'm sorry." That's a man!

Read all about it in Ephesians 5.22-31 and if you are a married man, go right now and tell your wife what she needs to hear.

Quote "Love without leadership can result in chaos. And leadership without love can result in tyranny" – Dan Benson, *The Total Man* (Tyndale House, 1977).

Promise "He who loves his wife, loves himself" (Ephesians 5.28).

DAY 140 Children, obey your parents in everything, for this pleases the Lord (3.20)

Good Morning, Disciple,

"Pleases the Lord"? Parents are not particularly offended by it either!

Remember, this apostolic instruction was addressed to believing families in the Church. Therefore, the "in everything" obedience is tempered by the condition "in the Lord". Hopefully, no Christian parent would ask a child to do something which was contrary to God's will. In the unlikely event of that happening, however, appeal must be made to the higher authority: "We must obey God rather than men!" (Acts 5.29). The believing son or daughter should first talk the matter over with both parents, and if there is still an impasse, ask permission to discuss the matter further with a church leader. Only as a last resort should family discipline be taken outside the home, with the possible exception of parental abuse.

The Christian child, of whatever age, must obey, not just because Dad says so or because Mummy's a nag, but because obedience to the command gives God pleasure. Even a child can in this way "live a life worthy of the Lord and may please him in every way" (1.10).

In Ephesians 6.1-3 Paul gives three answers to the child's favourite question – "Why?"

Because "this is right". It is the God-given responsibility of Christian parents to teach their children by precept and example that which is right, pleasing to God and appropriate in society.

Another reason is that it "may go well" with them. I suspect he has two things in mind. Firstly, the wellbeing of the home – after all, no child is really happy when under the cloud of punishment. Flouting parental discipline creates an unhappy environment for everyone. He may also have the child's future in mind. If a youngster persists in disobedience a bad habit is formed, which will affect life at school and beyond.

The third reason is that they may enjoy a long life on the earth. Gone are the days when a father, under Roman law, could kill his child for disobedience. But a rebellious lifestyle still has its dangers. The young man who wraps his joy-ride around a lamp post and the lass who dies of Aids because of intravenous drug abuse reached their destinies by a thousand refusals to be disciplined.

Meditate on Hebrews 12, which has much to say about self-discipline.

Quote "Obedience to parents is the stepping stone to obedience to God" – Everett Harrison, *Colossians – Christ All Sufficient* (Moody Press, 1971).

Promise "Listen, my son, to your father's instruction and do not forsake your mother's teaching. They will be a garland to grace your head and a chain to adorn your neck" (Proverbs 1.8-9).

DAY 141 Fathers, do not embitter your children, or they will become discouraged (3.21)

Good Morning, Disciple,

What is the very best thing that parents can do for their children? As I've stayed in family homes around the world I have observed that children are as close to their parents as their parents are close to each other. So the best thing is for parents to love each other and stay together. After all, "Has not the Lord made them one? . . . And why one? Because He was seeking a godly offspring. So guard yourself in your spirit and do not break faith with the wife of your youth. 'I hate divorce,' says the Lord God" (Malachi 2.15-16).

So do kids in most cases.

I'll tell you something else I've noticed. Parents who make unreasonable demands on their partners invariably make the same demands on their children. Some parents make no demands at all and that is equally damaging. One young man in prison told me he was sure his parents did not give a fig about him, because "They never said No." It is rather like Adonijah, King David's delinquent son, of whom it's said, "His father never interfered with him by asking, 'Why do you behave as you do?'" (1 Kings 1.6).

Neglect and bullying can have the same effects. More often though the problem is one of inconsistency: fluctuating between unwise spoiling and unloving nit-picking.

Here Paul wants to balance yesterday's instruction to young people. The father, or mother for that matter, who constantly makes unreasonable demands or nags must not be surprised if their child either rebels, or loses all natural spirit and becomes a timid wallflower.

Paul adds, "Bring them up in the training and instruction of the Lord" (Ephesians 6.4). Note that this is the father's responsibility, but it's too often delegated to the mother. To fulfil it, Dad needs to spend time with his children. Comedian Bill Cosby says, "I made a lot of money and I've given lots of it to charities, but I've given all of myself to my wife and the kids, and that's the best donation I'll ever make."

I almost called off our wedding just two weeks before the event. I told Sue that being a husband and a father scared me because I'd never had a Dad of my own. I soon discovered that if I knew God as Father all I had to do was ask His help and put into action what I saw of His fatherly love. It works! And when I have failed I have asked my daughters to forgive me.

Take a look at Psalm 127 and pray about home building.

Quote "Don't take the heart out of a child" – Jay E. Adams, *Christian Living in the Home* (Presbyterian & Reformed Publishing Co., 1972).

Promise "Train a child in the way he should go, and when he is old he will not turn from it" (Proverbs 22.6).

DAY 142   Slaves, obey your earthly masters in everything (3.22a)

Good Morning, Disciple,

Try to imagine what it was like to be a slave. He had no right to own anything, not even his own children, for just as a hen laying an egg surrenders it to its owner so the slave must give up everything to his master. To be caught as a runaway slave often meant death.

How could Paul tolerate such an obvious evil? But his purpose was not primarily to change society but to change hearts, which of course would eventually change society. By concentrating on the gospel and its demands for a change in behaviour, he planted the seed which grew through the centuries until it blossomed and bore fruit through the lives of Christian men like William Wilberforce.

Paul's immediate concern is not to sound a call for abolition, but to address the real issue facing both slaves and slave owners who had become Christians. Elsewhere he had recommended that where it was possible for slaves to be free, they should be (1 Corinthians 7.20-23). Indeed, this very letter to Colosse was to be carried by Tychicus accompanied by Onesimus, a runaway slave who had become a Christian. Onesimus would carry with him a personal letter to his own Christian master in which Paul appeals for him to be received back as a brother. Paul addresses the subject here in the context of family order, since most slaves, who made up about half the entire population, were household servants, many of them highly educated.

What relevance does this have for us today? The principles spelt out to Christian slaves and masters act as a remarkably timeless foundation for all work. Both in the home and in the work place, order creates harmony. Respect for authority is a Christian testimony today just as it was then. Christian bosses should not be treated with less respect because they are brothers (1 Timothy 6.1-2). Unbelieving and harsh managers are to receive the same respect as those who are good and considerate, and employees should even be ready to suffer for the sake of Christ (1 Peter 2.18- 20).

We may be protected by contracts of employment, but that does not mean we can live by lower principles. If anything, our improved lot should make us even more diligent – the very best of workers in whatever our chosen sphere.

As you read Mark 19.32-45, focus your meditation on verse 43 and ask yourself how you can apply this principle at work.

Quote "It is not so much what you do each day – it's what you get done that counts" – Will Rogers, Myron Rush, *Management, A Biblical Approach* (Victor Books 1984).

Promise "Those who sow in tears will reap with songs of joy" (Psalm 126.5).

DAY 143   And do it not only when their eye is on you and to win their favour but with sincerity of heart and reverence for the Lord. Whatever you do, work at it with all your heart, as working for the Lord, not for men (3.22b, 23)

Good Morning, Disciple,

The key to this big chunk is in the last six words: "For the Lord, not for men". Though the employee (or slave) is to obey and respect his earthly boss, that boss has only an earthly authority. The Christian looks to a higher authority – the Lord Jesus Christ in whom he lives, to whom he relates and for whom he works. Work for him is worship, fulfilling part of God's original mandate to take care of his creation (Genesis 2.15, 28).

John Stott's classic statement should be set over every place of work: "Work is the expenditure of energy (manual, mental or both) in the service of others, which brings fulfilment to the worker, benefit to the community, and glory to God." Get the motive right and the practice will follow.

When the Christian worker sees beyond his boss to the Lord, the community and his own personal fulfilment, there is no place left for skiving and clock-watching, half-heartedness and dishonesty. This does not mean that he will become a workaholic. To be intoxicated by work is every bit as self-indulgent as the glutton or the drunkard. The converse, however, is equally true. As Harold Mayfield put it, "Rest and play are the desserts of life. Work is the meal. It is only a child who dreams of a diet of desserts alone."

Some believers have wondered whether they should use their positions at work for evangelism. You might expect me, as an evangelist, to say yes to that; after all, it can be quite a large lake of somewhat captive fish. Although one cannot make hard and fast rules, I'd say that at work an employee is contracted to do the work, not to evangelise. My doctor, for example, when faced with a patient whose problems are not purely medical, will sometimes ask the patient if he would like to speak to a minister – though he is perfectly qualified to speak on spiritual matters himself.

The most important witnessing opportunity at work is not necessarily the sharing of the gospel, but Christlike behaviour: submission to authority, a cooperative disposition, courtesy, humility and honesty (Titus 2.9-10).

Look out for these qualities in the life and work of Joseph as you meditate on Genesis 39.

Quote ''God even milks the cows through you'' – Martin Luther.

Promise ''So I saw that there is nothing better for a man than to enjoy his work, because that is his lot'' (Ecclesiastes 3.22).

DAY 144 Since you know that you will receive an inheritance from the Lord as a reward (3.24a)

Good Morning, Disciple,

Every Monday since I came to this Cotswold hideaway, almost three months ago, Rita has come in from the village to vacuum and change the sheets for me. She is paid to do this by the owner of the apartment but as this is the last day I shall see her I gave her a thank-you box of chocolates – a bonus. I would not share that information with you except that it is such a timely illustration for our text this morning. I have never known anyone, no matter how much they are being paid already, to say no to a bonus.

These Christian slaves, and for that matter, all of us who are in Christ, are already assured of heaven because of what Christ has done for us on the cross. But now for the bonus, which must have blown the minds of these slaves in the Lycus Valley. There is more to come. Good behaviour in serving Christ is to be rewarded with an even greater inheritance! These who could not even own property, who could leave nothing to their offspring, are now told, "You have heaven, plus." The reward is for both "slave and free" (Ephesians 6.8), employer and employee, based on service.

I wonder in the light of what Paul has said about "men-pleasing eyeservice" whether he had in mind the words of our Lord when He said, "Be careful not to do your 'acts of righteousness' before men to be seen by them. If you do you will have no reward from your Father in heaven" (Matthew 6.1). On the other hand, when we give with pure motives, "Your Father who sees what is done in secret, will reward you" (Matthew 6.3, 4). Or again, "Love your enemies . . . Then your reward will be great" (Luke 6.35-6).

The two stages in Galatians 4.7 help explain the concept. "So you are no longer a slave (to the Law), but a son; and since you are a son, God has made you also an heir." The analogy is not a perfect one but may shed some light. A child adopted into a family does nothing before the event to earn that privilege. It is an act of love by the adopting parents, but thereafter the child is expected to take a full share in the responsibilities as well as the privileges of being a son or daughter.

In the light of this, read Matthew 25.14-30 and meditate on verse 21.

Quote "Salvation is according to grace, judgment is always according to works, good or bad, for believer and unbeliever alike" – Peter T. O'Brien, *Word Biblical Commentary* (Word Books, 1982).

Promise "You will be repaid at the resurrection" (Luke 14.14).

DAY 145 It is the Lord Christ you are serving (3.24b)

Good Morning, Disciple,

If at any time you visit the Louvre in Paris, bypass the crowds hunting down the Mona Lisa and find Jean-François Millais' painting, The Angelus. At sunset, as the Angelus rings over the fields, two peasants stop to pray. Christ has broken into the humdrum of work.

You may be a teacher with a class of boisterous kids, a bricklayer building an extension, a nurse in a psychiatric ward, a solicitor, a banker, an artist, a bus driver – whatever you are doing today, do it for the Lord. You are as close to Him in the ordinary decisions of the workaday world as you ever are in church.

Donald Wildman tells of a church in the United States which was looking for a church caretaker – a janitor, in their parlance. The minister suggested an unemployed man called Anderson. "But he's no good," protested the trustees, "he's known to be workshy." When, however, it became clear there were no other candidates, the minister was given permission to employ the town loafer.

After the man had been working at the church for a while folk noticed a change. He no longer wore his tattered clothes but a smartly pressed uniform. His sullen face broke more and more often into a happy smile. He became polite and even asked if he might join the church, for, through his work, he had come to know Christ as his Saviour. Before long he was taking on new chores. A year later he asked if he might teach in the Sunday School.

The minister left the church to serve in another town but some years later returned to conduct some special services. He was met at the station by a trustee who told him, "This weekend you are to stay with Mr Anderson." The minister looked puzzled. "I know what you are thinking," smiled the trustee, "but Mr Anderson is a highly respected member of our church and community. He is president of the bank. A wealthy uncle left him a fortune but, do you know the greatest miracle of all, Mr Anderson still teaches his Sunday School class and acts as church janitor in his spare time. He often says, 'God cleaned my life and my soul, and as long as I live I will personally see that his house is kept clean.'"

Peter has some uncomfortable things to say about the work place and our responsibility to society (1 Peter 2.13-25). Focus on one of his sayings for your meditation.

Quote   Before the door our welcome Master stands,
Tells us the ripened grass requires our hands.
– Stephen Duck, "The Thresher's Labour"
in *Penguin Book of English Verse* (Penguin, 1982).

Promise "God has made you also an heir" (Galatians 4.7).

DAY 146　Anyone who does wrong will be repaid for his wrong, and there is no favouritism (3.25)

Good Morning, Disciple,

I sometimes have to chuckle as I study my commentaries on Colossians. Today, for instance, some of them argue that the judgment in this text applies to the slaves, others suggest it is aimed at the masters, whilst others tentatively plump for the middle of the middle ground.

Two men robbed a jewellery store. One was a lawyer, the other a school drop-out. When sentenced, the lawyer received ten years and the youngster three years. The lawyer's defence argued that this was unfair, but the judge explained that the lawyer was under greater responsibility to be an example of the law. What do you think? God's judgment is on a much higher plane. He judges with no partiality.

Perhaps some of the commentators have missed the clues. First, the sentence begins with the word "anyone" and ends with "there is no favouritism". Doesn't that seem pretty all-inclusive? Second, in the parallel passage in Ephesians, Paul says that "both their master and yours is in heaven, and there is no favouritism with him" (Ephesians 6.9). Surely there is the same equality in judgment as there is in rewards, where Paul says the Lord gives to both slave and free (Ephesians 6.8). Clearly the God whose name is Justice is neither biased nor swayed by outward appearance. "For we will all stand before God's judgment seat", where "every knee will bow . . . each of us will give an account of himself to God" (Romans 14.10-12).

The One who gives salvation as a gift and rewards those who do good is the One before whom we must all give an account. "We must all appear before the judgment seat of Christ, that each one may receive what is due to him for the things done while in the body, whether good or bad" (2 Corinthians 5.10). As F. F. Bruce states in his *Colossians* commentary: "It may be difficult to understand how one who by grace is blessed with God's salvation in Christ will, nevertheless, be requited for wrongdoing before the divine tribunal, but it is in accordance with biblical teaching that judgment should 'begin with the household of God' (1 Peter 4.17), and even if the tribunal is a domestic one, for members of the family of God, it is by no means to be taken lightly."

As you read 1 Corinthians 3 in the context of Paul's plea for unity, you will see some relevant teaching in verses 11-15 which should form the basis of a useful meditation.

Quote "Justice is a habit of mind, productive of fair dealings" – Aristotle.

Promise "Behold, I am coming soon! My reward is with me, and I will give to everyone according to what he has done" (Revelation 22.12).

DAY 147 Masters, provide your slaves with what is right and fair, because you know that you also have a master in heaven (4.1)

Good Morning, Disciple,

It would be very easy to read this statement and ask, Why didn't the apostle go further and call for emancipation? We look with the benefit of that near-perfect science of hindsight, but compare Paul's statement with the most advanced thinkers of his era. In Plato's ideal Commonwealth a master would be able to execute his slave for the most petty misdemeanour. Aristotle regarded a slave as "the physical implement of his master's mind, being to his owner as an ox might be to a person too poor to afford a slave". A common proverb may have had special relevance to Onesimus, Philemon's runaway slave who was most likely a Phrygian: *Phryx plagis emendatur*, "You school a Phrygian with a whip."

It is almost impossible for us to appreciate the daring of Paul's instruction. Taken with his early statement of equality in Christ between Phrygian and Greek, slave and free, it was nothing short of revolutionary.

The master is reminded that in Christ he is himself a slave, with a master in heaven. Therefore, the golden rule is particularly appropriate – do unto others as you would have them do to you. The Ephesian parallel makes this plain. There it says, "Masters, treat your slaves in the same way". In the same way as what? The same as the Lord treats both slave and free: rewarding everyone for the good they do (Ephesians 6.8-9).

Paul had launched a torpedo which centuries later would hit its mark. This one verse did more than any other sentence in the history of man to scuttle the evil of slavery. Not only so, it is the foundation upon which modern industrial law, trade unionism and the best company practice toward employees is based. To do what is right and fair, just and equitable, is the accepted goal of all civilised work practice. This is the seed from which it all grew.

The Scripture studiously avoids the temptation to tamper with particular institutions, social or political, as they relate to nations in any age. If it is to speak to every nation in every age, it is the principles, even the undeveloped principles of verses like this one, which will have greater effect than going headlong into revolution with all guns blazing.

As you read Paul's moving letter to Philemon – you'll find it just in front of Hebrews – keep this verse (Colossians 4.1) in mind. Then meditate on verse 18. Pray about your work, whether you are an employer or an employee, or even unemployed, that God will help you to live by these principles.

Quote "Yet shall I temper so – justice with mercy" – John Milton, *Paradise Lost*.

Promise "Maintain justice and do what is right, for my salvation is close at hand" (Isaiah 56.1).

DAY 148 Devote yourselves to prayer (4.2a)

Good Morning, Disciple,

Are you as intimidated as I am by the biographies of men like Paul Y. Cho, Watchman Nee, Hudson Taylor and the like? Christians in the Far East do seem more inclined to pray. Perhaps that is one of the reasons why even under the most oppressive Communist regimes the faith has flourished.

In *The Flying Scotsman*, the biography of Eric Liddell, the Olympic runner who became a missionary to China, Sally Magnusson records the secret of his life to be constant prayer. As a prisoner during World War II Liddell was a source of strength and encouragement as well as being a witness for Christ among the other inmates. A fellow Christian there recalled, "Eric was a man of prayer not only at set times; he talked to God all the time, naturally, as one who enters the "School of Prayer", to learn this way of inner discipline. He seemed to have no mental problems; his life was grounded in God, in faith, and in trust."

In such men the twentieth century meets the praying origins of the Christian faith. Luke testifies that "They (the new church) devoted themselves to the apostles' teaching and to the fellowship, to the breaking of bread and to prayer" (Acts 2.42).

The disciples, of course, had experienced three years with the Master of prayer. He understood more than any other the practical and spiritual dynamic of prayer, of being constantly in touch with His Father. "Very early in the morning, while it was still dark, Jesus got up, left the house and went off to a solitary place, where He prayed" (Mark 1.35); "Jesus went out to a mountainside to pray, and spent the night praying to God" (Luke 6.12). Like His disciples, we learn better from His example than from any exhortation.

I believe as an evangelist that prayer is the missing ingredient in so much contemporary evangelism, and yet this is the very context in which the apostle pleads, "Devote yourselves to prayer" (Colossians 4.2) – public prayer, private prayer, all kinds of prayer.

Jesus taught much on the subject of prayer. I wonder, as you read Luke 18.1-17, how many lessons you can learn from Him? Jot them down and meditate on them. Then, of course, you will want to pray about them, so that they become indelibly a part of your own consistent prayer life.

Quote "When God intends great blessings for His people He sets them praying" – C. H. Spurgeon.

Promise "Then you will call upon me and come and pray to me, and I will listen to you. You will seek me and find me when you seek me with all your heart" (Jeremiah 29.12-13).

DAY 149 Being watchful and thankful (4.2b)

Good Morning, Disciple,

I do hope that if you have not yet begun to witness to others about your faith in Christ, you will do so. Over these next few weeks I want to help you to share your faith lovingly, sensitively and clearly with your friends and relatives as opportunities open up.

The very best preparation you can make, as we saw yesterday, is in prayer. But why has Paul slipped in this word "watchful"?

The origin of the phrase "watch and pray" most likely dates back to when the Jews were rebuilding the walls of Jerusalem on their return from exile in Babylon (Nehemiah 4). Threatened with attack, the builders worked with their trowels in their hands and a sword at their sides. "We prayed to our God," says Nehemiah, "and posted a guard day and night to meet this threat."

Jesus Himself used the term when pointing forward to His second coming: "Be always on the watch, and pray" (Luke 21.36). "If he comes suddenly, do not let him find you sleeping. What I say to you, I say to everyone: 'Watch!'" (Mark 13.37).

Jesus used the words again in the Garden of Gethsemane. He told Peter, "Watch and pray so that you will not fall into temptation. The spirit is willing, but the body is weak" (Matthew 26.41).

Paul warns the Church to defend itself with spiritual armour and the word of God and says, "Pray in the Spirit on all occasions with all kinds of prayers and requests. With this in mind, be alert and always keep on praying for all the saints" (Ephesians 6.18).

Being watchful, then, has something to do with seizing the opportunities while there is still time; being alert in the face of temptation, especially that of sleeping on the job; and watching out for Satan's schemes. Remember Peter's warning: "Be self-controlled and alert. Your enemy the devil prowls around like a roaring lion looking for someone to devour" (1 Peter 5.8).

One more thought. When you pray, watch out for the answers so that you know what to be thankful for. I have a sneaking suspicion that if God were to answer on the basis of what we remembered we'd asked for, the answers would be few.

1 Thessalonians 5 takes up all these themes, so you cannot do better than to meditate there this morning.

Quote "Two wings are necessary for the soul to reach God's throne – prayer and praise" – Wesley L. Drewell, *Touch the World Through Prayer* (Francis Asbury Press, 1986).

Promise "Do not be anxious about anything, but in everything, by prayer and petition, with thanksgiving, present your requests to God. And the peace of God, which transcends all understanding, will guard your hearts and your minds in Christ Jesus" (Philippians 4.6-7).

DAY 150 And pray for us too that God may open a door for our message (4.3a)

Good Morning, Disciple,

How often I've heard my wife say, "Darling, I can't be in six places at once," as I thoughtlessly pile one more thing onto her heavy schedule. Ah, but you can! If you are a praying man or woman you can be in Africa with your missionary friend; you can be in prison as the men gather for chapel or in the House of Commons when an important debate is going on; you can be in hospital alongside your sick friend. Such is the wonderful power of prayer. As Paul said, "Join me in my struggle by praying to God for me" (Romans 15.30).

No doubt Paul had in mind Timothy and the other brothers, whom he calls fellow prisoners and co-workers, when he says, "Pray for us." Spiritual praying, he knew, is not an attempt to manipulate God so that man's will is done in heaven, but a humble willingness that God's will may be done on earth. Therefore, he does not ask for release from prison, but that the gospel would spread right there in prison, or should I say, house arrest.

That God was able to do this is clear: "For two whole years Paul stayed there in his own rented house (in chains!) and welcomed all who came to see him. Boldly and without hindrance he preached the kingdom of God and taught about the Lord Jesus Christ" (Acts 28.30-31). Many Christians who might otherwise have been timid became courageous witnesses (Philippians 1.12-14). Another answer to these prayers is the very letter we are studying, which has spread the gospel throughout the world.

It is God's work and it is He who opens the doors. What He opens "no-one can shut" (Revelation 3.7). Let me suggest five doors you can pray open in the lives of those you want to reach with the message.

1. That their eyes may be opened to see Jesus for who He really is (Luke 24.31). 2. That their minds will be open to understand the message, for "the god of this age has blinded the minds of unbelievers"

(2 Corinthians 4.4). 3. That the Scriptures, which contain the real message of Christ, may be opened (Luke 24.32). 4. That hearts will be open to receive Him who says, "I stand at the door and knock" (Revelation 3.20). 5. That the Lord will open your mouth to tell others (Ezekiel 29.21).

As you read Acts 16.6–40 you will see how this prayer life works out in practice.

Quote "Prayer is not overcoming God's reluctance, it is laying hold of His willingness" – Richard Trench, Archbishop of Dublin (1807-1886).

Promise "For I will give you words and wisdom that none of your adversaries will be able to resist or contradict" (Luke 21.15).

DAY 151   So that we may proclaim the mystery of Christ, for which I am in chains (4.3b)

Good Morning, Disciple,

I wonder how you or I might fare if we were sent to prison for our faith in Christ. The seventeenth-century preacher John Bunyan, when told by the authorities that if only he would stop preaching he would be released from prison, replied, "If I am out of prison today, I will preach the gospel again tomorrow, by the help of God." Twentieth-century Christians have been no less determined to go on preaching, even within prison. As the poet Lovelace put it, "Stone walls do not a prison make, nor iron bars a cage."

The mystery Paul proclaimed "is that through the gospel the Gentiles are heirs together with Israel, members together of one body, and sharers together in the promise of Christ Jesus" (Ephesians 3.6). It was for preaching this that Paul was in prison. When he told a Jewish crowd in Jerusalem that God had told him to preach the gospel to the Gentiles, they shouted, "Rid the earth of him! He's not fit to live!" (Acts 22.21-22). If only he had been content to be a Jewish Christian like the others, he could have been free, but this universal gospel was not negotiable. It had landed him in prison but it must not be imprisoned. He was in chains but it must not be chained. This mystery must be revealed, this gospel proclaimed.

When two Christians were about to be burned at the stake in Oxford for preaching the gospel, Ridley, the younger of the two, showed some signs of fear as the tormentors prepared to light the fire. Latimer charged him with the words, "This day we shall light such a candle in England by God's grace, as, I trust, shall never be put out."

In the second century Polycarp, Bishop of Smyrna, was also faced with denying his faith or certain martyrdom. He boldly stated, "For eighty-six years I have been his slave and he has done me no wrong; how can I blaspheme my King who has saved me? . . . Let me tell you plainly – I am a Christian."

Neither chains nor death can hold back the gospel – but apathy and disobedience may. We who are called by God must be no less faithful to the task of knowing the gospel clearly and proclaiming it fearlessly.

As you read Acts 24, just one of Paul's adventures, see how the Lord is able to have His gospel shared with the highest officials in the land.

Quote "It is only a valid faith if it can be shared" – David Augsburger, *Witness is Witness* (Moody Press, 1971).

Promise "By standing firm you will gain life" (Luke 21.19).

DAY 152 Pray that I may proclaim it clearly, as I should (4.4)

Good Morning, Disciple,

By now you are grasping some of the foundations of the faith and growing as God intends you to grow. You may even be sensing His call to share this faith but may not know where to begin. Well, whether you are called to be a preacher or, like every believer, called to be a witness, you must be prepared to give an answer to everyone who asks you "to give the reason for the hope that you have" (1 Peter 3.15) in Christ Jesus.

Even the apostle Paul asks for prayer that he may proclaim the gospel clearly, because he knows only too well the cunning of the evil one who, as we have seen in the parable of the sower (Mark 4.1-20), is able to snatch, starve or strangle the tender faith of the untaught convert. True faith must be founded on the "word of truth – the gospel" (1.5) and built up stage by stage according to the "word of Christ" (3.16).

In my little booklet *Hope Now* I have set out a scheme which I would like to pass on to you over the next few days. I have based it all on this letter to the Colossians. (It's available from Hope Now Ministries, 14 Chetwynd Drive, Bassett, Southampton, SO2 3HZ.) We'll start on that tomorrow. Today, let me leave you with some practical words of advice.

First, recognise that even Paul, who knew this Word so clearly through the revelation given to him, still calls for prayer that he may have an opportunity to proclaim it and, when that chance comes, to do it in a way that people can understand. Wouldn't you say that if Paul needs this prayer, we do, too? Enthusiasm unchecked by a wholesome dependence upon God's Holy Spirit and His Word can make you one of those windbags, full of hot air, that we encountered in chapter 2.

Secondly, hold on to your own relationship with the Lord Himself. Remember, it is He that men and women are called to respond to, not a neat set of propositions to which they give an intellectual nod of the head. When you walk with the Lord, others will want to walk with you.

There is no better person qualified to teach in the school of witnessing than the Master Himself. See how many lessons you can jot down in your notebook as you read of His encounter with a Samaritan woman, John 4.1-42.

Quote "The world is my parish" – John Wesley.

Promise "'Come, follow me', Jesus said, 'and I will make you fishers of men.'" (Mark 1.17).

DAY 153 Pray that I may proclaim it clearly, as I should (4.4)

Good Morning, Disciple,

Before we look at the content of the gospel message, let me remind you of the four steps necessary for anyone coming to faith in Christ.

I call this HUB-S – the hub of salvation. Hearing – Understanding – Believing – Surrendering.

Paul asks the crunch question, "How, then, can they call on the one they have not believed in? And how can they believe in the one of whom they have not heard? And how can they hear without someone preaching to them?" (Romans 10.14).

The Colossian Christians not only "heard the word of truth, the gospel" (1.5), but they "understood God's grace in all its truth" (1.6) from a faithful evangelist who taught them (1.7). This is surely the point of Paul's prayer request. Hearing a jumble of ill-defined ideas, even though they may all be true, will not help the honest seeker come to faith. Nor will it serve as a secure foundation when the winds of "hollow and deceptive philosophy" begin to blow. Preaching and teaching are both necessary for reaching a lost world. Oh, for more evangelists with a brain in their head and fire in their belly!

Having heard and understood the gospel he or she will either believe or not believe. At first sight this would seem a matter of choice, but the longer I have preached, the more convinced I am that there is no choice. A person either believes what he has heard or he doesn't believe. He cannot manufacture faith. If faced with all the evidence he still cannot believe, the only recourse is to pray for God to give him faith to believe. At this point, when a person has heard, understood and believed, the lifelong process of surrender to Christ as Lord begins (1.18).

I would urge you not to get involved in the futile debate about whether this decision is yours or God's. All you need to know is that the gospel freely given demands surrender to Christ as both Saviour and Lord. At some point in the process of salvation there is a decision of the will or all the imperatives of Colossians are empty sham.

So there we have it, HUB-S. We are going to stay on this subject for a few days, so don't be alarmed when you see the same text come up tomorrow.

As for today, James 4 has some superb practical advice to keep you in meditation for as long as you've got time.

Quote "The very nature of God demands a universal mission" – Michael Green, *Evangelism in the Early Church* (Hodder & Stoughton, 1970).

Promise "Everyone who calls on the name of the Lord will be saved" (Romans 10.13).

DAY 154 Pray that I may proclaim it clearly, as I should (4.4)

Good Morning, Disciple,

What I am about to share with you is the heart of the matter: the very purpose for which I have written to you day after day for five months. My calling is "to prepare God's people for works of service, so that the body of Christ may be built up" (Ephesians 4.12).

Have you noticed as we have studied together how giving our God is? I counted forty-five different gifts in chapter 1 alone. It is as if He is saying, "All of this is yours and there's even more stored up for you in heaven."

There are four specific salvation gifts which I've put into an acrostic: H.O.P.E.

Heaven is opened to you. We were disqualified from heaven because we were alienated from God by our sinful behaviour (1.21). Not even a whole mountain of self-imposed religiosity and good works, the like of which we looked at in chapter 2, could save us, "He only could unlock the gate of heaven and let us in." It is "the Father, who has qualified you to share in the inheritance" (1.12).

Offenders are forgiven. We who were trapped by our sin and guilt before God have been freed and forgiven (1.14), so that we may stand before God on the day of judgment, "holy in his sight, without blemish and free from accusation" (1.22).

Peace with God is restored by Jesus "making peace through his blood shed on the cross" (1.20). Not only are we reconciled to God (1.22) but we are also given the power of the indwelling Christ to be at peace with each other and in our own hearts (3.15).

Finally, we are *empowered by God* to live for His glory (1.11). We have been given the "full riches of complete understanding" (2.2), and "fulness in Christ" (2.10), indeed, the very energy of Christ working in us and through us (1.29).

Doesn't that make it clear? Just remember H.O.P.E. – Heaven, Offenders, Peace, Empowered – and hang your thoughts and the

Scriptures on them, and you have step one in a "pattern of sound teaching".

Now, having looked at God's way, take a look at the chaos which can be caused by going man's way. In Jude, just before Revelation, you see what happens when men speak their own word from wrong motives. Watch and pray!

Quote "Only as we believe IN Him (Jesus) and allow Him to flow through us by His Spirit will men and women whom He is drawing to Himself respond" – Stephen Olford, *The Secret of Soul Winning* (Moody Press, 1963).

Promise "When calamity comes, the wicked are brought down, but even in death the righteous have a refuge" (Proverbs 14.32).

DAY 155   Pray that I may proclaim it clearly, as I should (4.4)

Good Morning, Disciple,
   The gospel we are called to proclaim hangs neatly on the acrostic F.A.I.T.H.

> **F**acts concerning Jesus
> **A**bsolute God
> **I**nnocent man
> **T**ook our sins to the cross
> **H**e is alive that we might live

By now you will see the paramount importance of having faith in knowable and transferable *facts* – not fanciful religious opinions and cults. It is the Jesus of history, the self-revelation of God, we are to believe in.

There are two things folk need to know about who the real Jesus is. First, He is the *absolute God*. "In Christ all the fulness of the deity lives in bodily form" (2.9).

The second flows out of the first. If He is the absolute God, He has all the attributes of God, most notably His sinless nature. He is the *innocent man*. But wasn't He put on a cross, a sort of ancient gallows? Listen to what those who condemned Him have to say.

Pontius Pilate pronounced Him innocent three times (Luke 23). Nor could Herod find any evidence of guilt (Luke 23:15). Judas Iscariot said in a fit of remorse, "I have sinned by betraying innocent blood" (Matthew 27:4). When Jesus asked, "Can any of you prove me guilty of sin?" (John 8.46), none could. The whole historic record of His behaviour is summed up in the words that He was "tempted in every way, just as we are – yet was without sin" (Hebrews 4.15). Both His deity and His innocent humanity are affirmed.

Again there are two things He has done for us. First He *took our sins to the cross*, so that we might stand on the day of judgment, "holy in his sight, without blemish and free from accusation" (1.22).

Finally, *He is alive*, "the firstborn from among the dead". I love that, because if He's the firstborn then there's a second born, a third born and so on. I don't know what my number was but I do know that as a young man in a cell in Winchester Prison I trusted Christ to give me new life and I have never regretted it. And if you've trusted Him, "God made you alive with Christ" (2.13). This is the F.A.I.T.H. we preach.

Using the fingers of one hand you could learn that outline and always have a starting point for sharing your faith. Now see how Peter did it in Acts 4.1-31 and meditate on verse 12.

Quote "His concern was not with programmes to reach multitudes, but with men (and women) whom the multitudes would follow" – Robert Coleman, *The Master Plan of Evangelism*" (Power Books, 1963).

Promise "The one who raised the Lord Jesus from the dead will also raise us with Jesus" (2 Corinthians 4.14.)

DAY 156 Pray that I may proclaim it clearly, as I should (4.4)

Good Morning, Disciple,

Today I want to show you how to introduce someone to the actual step of becoming a Christian. You have shared with them the message of H.O.P.E. You have shown how the gospel of F.A.I.T.H. grows from that root of H.O.P.E. Now for the fruit – L.O.V.E.

As God brings conviction by the power of the Holy Spirit, you can use these four letters to show one who is ready how to take that crucial step of faith.

I usually ask my contact whether they have understood what I have said so far. If they have, I ask, "Do you believe what you have heard?" If they say "yes" again, I introduce them to L.O.V.E. by saying, "God did all that for you because He loves you – 'God demonstrates his own love for us in this: while we were still sinners Christ died for us' (Romans 5.8). Love needs a response from the object of that love – from you. The only adequate response to love is L.O.V.E."

If they appear hesitant I usually give them a copy of my booklet *Hope Now*, and I ask them to take it home and read it prayerfully. But if they are ready to move on I introduce them to the "L" of L.O.V.E. and say, "The first thing God wants you to do, is to *love Him*. Jesus said the greatest commandment is to 'Love the Lord your God with all your heart' " (Matthew 22.37).

Then I introduce the O – *Obey Him as Lord*. Jesus said, "If anyone loves me, he will obey my teaching" (John 14.23). Repentance, I explain, turning away from the self-life, is the first step in submitting to Jesus as Lord (2 Peter 3.9; Colossians 1.18). I ask if they are ready and want, with all their heart, to do that.

If they do I introduce them to V – *Voice a prayer of faith* – and invite them to pray out loud after me, a phrase at a time, or to pray their own prayer in silence.

Lastly, E – *Enter into God's family*. Usually we look together at John 11.25 to discuss the matter of assurance, and I give them a copy of my booklet *Grow Now* and a nurturing Bible Study. (Both are available from Hope Now Ministries, 14 Chetwynd Drive, Bassett, Southampton, SO2 3HZ.)

Spend some time with Jesus this morning in John 14. It is an absolute treasure trove.

Quote "Loving God is man's unique privilege; that is why we are special. He put us in the centre of His picture and made all the Universe around us the frame" – Billy Hanks, Jr, *Everyday Evangelism* (Zondervan, 1983).

Promise "He who loves me will be loved by my Father, and I too will love him and show myself to him" (John 14.21).

DAY 157 Be wise in the way you act towards outsiders (4.5a)

Good Morning, Disciple,

"Every Christian has the Holy Spirit, but the Holy Spirit doesn't have every Christian," said A. W. Tozer. Certainly the apostle had no illusions about the imperfections which are common to us all. Hence the need for this gentle reminder that behaviour will have an effect on our witness, one way or another.

We must be careful to live in a way which attracts and doesn't repel, so that when we witness by our words, our lives do not scream out in contradiction. In a sense everything Paul has spoken of − a life lived in Christ at home, at work and in the church − is included here. It is not putting another face on for the sake of the unbeliever but having a truly Christ-like character. As one dying soldier in the Crimean War said to Florence Nightingale, "You are Christ to me."

It is my privilege to lead a team of Christian workers and witnesses to serve and evangelise the 100,000 or more guests at the annual Glastonbury Pop Festival which attracts a somewhat diverse blend of humanity to Somerset's Vale of Avalon, and includes many of the hippie travelling community.

In 1990 the then Bishop of Bath and Wells, now Archbishop of Canterbury, visited the site to welcome the many guests to his diocese.

As we entered one of the bus homes in the "travellers' field" I noticed that he kicked his boots off at the door: a courtesy which he could well have forgotten in the shabby, dirty surrounds of a hippie camp. I know his sensitive, warm-hearted wisdom was appreciated.

It was a special joy to me because two years earlier our bus hosts had been enraged by the behaviour of some young "hippie" Christians who had been witnessing to them. "I'll be ready to listen," Phil had told me, "when your converts give up smoking dope."

In fairness to them, they were very young Christians, more zealous than sanctified, but their behaviour offended those they were trying to win and diminished their effectiveness. I'm glad to say that when I told them of Phil's remarks they were convicted by the Holy Spirit to give up "pot" and are now serving the Lord with ever increasing wisdom and no less zeal.

As you read Philippians 4, jot down some of the virtues which will add to your appeal.

Quote "How we live reveals our deepest convictions about life" – William Temple.

Promise "Let love and faithfulness never leave you . . . then you will win favour and a good name in the sight of God and man" (Proverbs 3.3-4).

DAY 158 Make the most of every opportunity (4.5b)

Good Morning, Disciple,

You can tell Paul is an experienced evangelist. He knows that sometimes, when enthusiasm would make us careless of people's feelings, we need to remember, "Be wise in the way you act toward outsiders". But when we are spiritually dull and oblivious to the fate of the unconverted, he says, "Make the most of every opportunity" (4.5). Wisdom and daring, sensitivity and boldness. How rare it is to find those qualities held in balance. Yet that's precisely what Paul did, in the footsteps of his Master, the Lord Jesus. Do you not see in them both a remarkable strength of mind and determination, a sort of controlled recklessness in achieving their goals?

The Emperor Nero may have "fiddled while Rome burned" – but Paul burned while Nero fiddled. Even while he was in chains he made converts in Nero's own household (Philippians 4.22). You may be sure that they didn't just happen. It took as much courage to preach then as it does in many hard situations today.

I remember speaking at a ministers' fraternal in Edinburgh, where one of the pastors said to me, "Edinburgh's an awfully hard place to evangelise." To which I replied, "Show me a place that isn't. I've travelled around the world and haven't found one yet." Evangelism is an act of the will, that seeks to make God's love in Christ known to every man and woman, "When it's convenient and when it's inconvenient" (2 Timothy 4.2 NEB).

Today, at the silver wedding anniversary of my brother and sister-in-law, my seven-year-old nephew spent three or four hours asking me questions about God. With so many relatives to talk to it would have been easy to fob him off with some glib answer, but in another year or two he may not want to ask spiritual questions. I may long then for an opening to share the love of Christ but find only a closed door. The opportunity was today, and whether he was seven, seventeen or seventy, it had to be seized. Who knows where it might lead. As Helen Lenore Kromer put it:

> One man awake can waken another;
> The second can waken his next door brother.
> The three awake can rouse the town,
> By turning the whole place upside down.
> The many awake can make such a fuss,
> That it finally wakens the rest of us!
> One man up, with dawn in his eyes, multiplies.

Read Matthew 10.1-32 and then read the words of Jesus in Matthew 28.18-20. Pray for an opportunity to speak for your Lord today.

Quote "Evangelism and social action are like the two blades of a pair of scissors or the two wings of a bird" – *Evangelism and Social Responsibility*, The Grand Rapids Report (Paternoster Press, 1982).

Promise "Now go; I will help you speak and will teach you what to say" (Exodus 4.12.)

DAY 159 Let your conversation be always full of grace, seasoned with salt (4.6a)

Good Morning, Disciple,

Reading gravestones may seem a morbid pastime but I have to confess I find it quite interesting and occasionally amusing. Who could fail to see the humour in the local hypochondriac who had put on his stone, "I told you I was ill." What about this one:

> Beneath this stone a lump of clay
> Lies Arabella Young
> Who on the twenty-fourth of May
> Began to hold her tongue.

I'd love to know the story behind that. I guess her reputation lived on after her. Jesus didn't say anything about the chatterbox but He did say, "Out of the overflow of the heart the mouth speaks. The good man brings good things out of the good stored up in him" (Matthew 12.34-35). The converse is as true, which is why when Paul talked about a change of behaviour he followed it immediately with instructions about anger, lies and bad language (3.5-8). The talk must match the walk.

"Full of grace" may hold some reference to the gospel of grace, but I'm inclined to think that the context here has to do with enhancing our evangelistic opportunities. Whether preaching the gospel or conversing generally the same applies – watch that mischievous tongue. "Do not let any unwholesome talk come out of your mouths, but only what is helpful for building others up according to their needs, that it may benefit those who listen" (Ephesians 4.29).

"Seasoned with salt" reflects closely the words of Jesus, that those who follow Him are "the salt of the earth" (Matthew 5.13), and this may have been in Paul's mind. However, the term was used at that time generally to mean lively and informed speech, full of wit and wisdom. Strangely our English idiom, to take with a pinch of salt, implies the very opposite. We use it of someone who is unreliable, ill-informed, even dishonest.

Our opportunities for evangelism will always be enhanced if we speak wisely and attractively regardless of who is listening. It was recorded of Jesus that "All spoke well of him and were amazed at the gracious words which came from his lips" (Luke 4.22). He never compromised on the content of His teaching and yet "All the people hung on his words" (Luke 19.48). Should we not aim to speak at all times with the same "gentleness and respect" (1 Peter 3.15)?

As you read Hebrews 13 meditate on verse 15 and ask yourself how you can use your "lips to confess his name".

Quote "Words which do not give the light of Christ increase the darkness" – Mother Teresa of Calcutta.

Promise "Pleasant words promote instruction" (Proverbs 16.21).

DAY 160 So that you may know how to answer everyone (4.6b)

Good Morning, Disciple,

Some time back, Sue and I became friendly with some new neighbours. We had never spoken about spiritual matters to them, but one day when I called to borrow a drill bit, Barry said to me, "Vic, you know a lot about Christianity, don't you?" He went on to tell how the Jehovah's Witnesses had knocked on his door and left both him and his wife, Wendy, in a state of confusion. "Could we come round to your house," he asked, "and talk about the future?"

We were delighted to welcome them for dinner a few evenings later. Barry then dropped his bombshell. He thought the Jehovah's Witnesses had ripped Bible passages out of context to prove their points, so, he said, "If you quote the Bible I want to read it in context – the whole chapter." Six exhausting hours later both Barry and Wendy became Christians.

Not everybody is so demanding, but if your life and conversation are following the pattern we have been studying, people will notice the difference and some will ask questions. Don't worry that you don't know all the answers. None of us do!

Once I picked up a hitch-hiker just outside Derby. As we travelled down the M1 conversation turned quite naturally to spiritual matters and he was asking all sorts of questions. I batted them as best I could until he asked me, "Are there any animals in heaven?" I had never really considered the point so I said, "I don't know." To which he replied, "Thanks."

"Thanks for what?" I asked.

"Oh, just for not knowing," he smiled back at me. You see, people don't want to hear what we don't know. They are more than ready to listen to what we do know, however much or little that may be.

Malcolm, a very young Christian, told me about a time when he was witnessing. Right in the middle of his gospel presentation the person said, "What about the Trinity?" Malcolm had not learned anything about the Trinity so he simply replied, "I don't know anything about the Trinity, but I do know about Jesus." What a good answer. He may not have known the theology but the Holy Spirit taught him how to answer.

Because it touches on some of what we have studied, meditate this morning on 1 Peter 3 and focus especially on verse 15.

Quote "Truth is powerful when it is argued; it is even more powerful when it is exhibited" – John Stott, *Issues Facing Christians Today* (Marshall Pickering, 1984).

Promise "For I will give you words and wisdom that none of your adversaries will be able to resist or contradict" (Luke 21.15).

DAY 161 Tychicus will tell you all the news about me (4.7a)

Good Morning, Disciple,

New believers in their first flush of enthusiasm sometimes ask how they can know if the Lord is calling them to the ministry or to missionary service. My answer is invariably to ask them what they are doing now, where they are. True evangelism always starts spontaneously among those closest and dearest to you. If you have no concern for them, you will never manufacture it for others.

We have an example here in Tychicus of an Asian with special envoy status to the people of Asia Minor, his own folk (Acts 20:4). He goes to the Jerusalem conference with financial contributions to the Jewish poor from the churches in Achaia and Macedonia.

Jesus told the Jews that the gospel must be preached first in Jerusalem, then in all Judea and Samaria and on, ever outward, to the ends of the earth (Acts 1.8). When Gentiles were converted he used the same formula. Start where you are. The Samaritan woman goes straight back to her home town to tell others about Jesus (John 4.28). The demon-possessed man when delivered was told to "Go home to your family and tell them how much the Lord has done for you, and how he has had mercy on you" (Mark 5.19).

We may have a clue to Tychicus' pagan background from his name, which is derived from Tyche, the Greek goddess of fortune. Did he perhaps put his confidence in Lady Luck? Many do so and are disappointed by life's spin of the wheel. When Tychicus put his confidence in the providence of God he found much surer ground.

He was more than a mere postman, delivering Paul's letters to Epaphras (Ephesians 6.21), Colosse, Philemon and Laodicea (4.16). He was an envoy with those two abilities so much in demand, dependability and availability. No doubt Paul has in mind a two-way traffic. Tychicus would be able to fill in the blanks regarding Paul's conditions under house arrest, but he would also return to tell Paul more about the state of the churches in the Lycus Valley. And if the heretics tried to undermine what Paul had written his special envoy could scotch it immediately.

Are you as dependable and available for the tasks which face you right where you are today? As you read about the collection taken up at Corinth (2 Corinthians 8.16-9.11), bear in mind the heavy responsibility carried out by such men as Tychicus and pray that God will help you to be equally worthy of trust.

Quote "As I was returning to earth, I realised that I was a servant not a celebrity" – Colonel James Irwin, astronaut.

Promise "Whoever sows sparingly will also reap sparingly, and whoever sows generously will also reap generously" (2 Corinthians 9.6).

DAY 162 He is a dear brother, a faithful minister and a fellow-servant in the Lord (4.7b)

Good Morning, Disciple,

Leonard Bernstein was asked to name the most difficult instrument to play in an orchestra. Without hesitation he replied, "Second fiddle. I can get plenty of first violinists, but to find one who plays second violin with as much enthusiasm, or second French horn or second flute, now that's a problem. And yet if no one plays second, we have no harmony."

And there's no harmony in the church if everyone wants to be king pin. How did Paul put it? "Do nothing out of selfish ambition or vain conceit, but in humility consider others better than yourselves" (Philippians 2.3). Sadly, instead of carrying out the whole injunction, many prefer to take the first two words only – do nothing!

That would never have done for Tychicus. In a world with

no mail service, it was a long and often perilous journey from Rome, via Ephesus and Laodicea, to Colosse. And yet this man is totally at the service of his brother Paul. He made at least one further visit to Ephesus after delivering this letter (2 Timothy 4.12), and was ready to relieve Titus as an interim pastor at Crete (Titus 3.12).

Little wonder the apostle calls him by these three highly significant titles. He is, before anything else, a brother. No sign here of the professionalism that pulls rank at staff meetings. They are co-workers because they are first bound together in the love of Christ as equal members of God's family.

Tychicus shares the title "a faithful servant", literally faithful deacon, with Epaphras (1.7) and with Paul himself (1.23, 25). It is likely that, rather than serving as deacon in a church, he acted as Paul's personal assistant, thereby releasing him to study, teach and pray.

Paul adds a further title, fellow-servant, or more literally, co-slave. This is a title Paul used for himself and Timothy. Later, probably because of this letter, any church worker from bishop to deacon was called co-slave, to remind them of the need for active and joint obedience to God. There would be no lack of second violins if they were "like-minded, having the same love, being one in spirit and purpose" (Philippians 2.2).

It is a noble calling to serve the Church. Prepare yourself for God's purpose for you by meditating on 1 Timothy 3. Note especially those areas where work is still needed.

Quote "The best exercise for strengthening the heart is reaching down and lifting people up" – Ernest Blevins.

Promise "My Father will honour the one who serves me" (John 12.26b).

DAY 163 I am sending him to you for the express purpose that you may know about our circumstances and that he may encourage your hearts (4.8)

Good Morning, Disciple,

That old ditty about nails went something like this:

For the want of a nail, the shoe was lost;
For the want of a shoe, the horse was lost;
For the want of a horse, the battle was lost;
For the want of a battle, the kingdom was lost;
And all for the want of a horse shoe nail.

One nail which has been lost in many churches is the nail of encouragement. I was fortunate as a young Christian that there were so many older and wiser counsellors who encouraged me through my days of impetuous immaturity. How thoroughly blessed I have been to this day. But I can think of others who have been all but frozen out because of a lack of encouragement. I think of Melvin who joined the church at West Norwood at the same time as I did, but after a while he was missing from Sunday services. When I began asking if anyone knew where he was I met a stony wall of silence. Eventually I tracked him down to a pub in the High Street. "Why don't you come to church any more?" I asked him rather clumsily.

"I come here," said Mel. "I get friendship; I'm accepted for what I am and no one judges me for what I'm not. I can come here every evening, seven days a week. We have lots of laughs. It's better than church. People there don't care."

Paul does not want that to happen at Colosse. He knows that the pen never smiles. However much he may say his purpose is to encourage them, the words will lie flat on the page without the personal touch which Tychicus could bring. The postman would be his personalised letter of encouragement.

Tychicus would convey Paul's circumstances, but I'm quite sure that he would also back up Paul's teaching. The apostle may refute the heresies with boldness, but the opponents of the gospel will not just vanish into thin air. Disruptive people seldom leave just because error is exposed. They will often defend themselves by attacking. Surely a part of Tychicus' encouragement was to stand as Paul's seconder when the letter was read out to the congregation.

You may gain some further insight into this ministry as you read 1 Thessalonians 2.17-3.13. Try to encourage someone today.

Quote "Friendship is a sheltering tree" – Samuel Taylor Coleridge, *Youth and Age*.

Promise "But the Lord is faithful, and he will strengthen and protect you from the evil one" (2 Thessalonians 3.3).

DAY 164 He is coming with Onesimus, our faithful and dear brother, who is one of you. They will tell you everything which is happening here (4.9)

Good Morning, Disciple,

Your morning meditation is again Paul's letter to Philemon. I suggest you read it first and then come back to my letter.

Welcome back! Isn't that a fascinating letter? Just imagine the drama. Somehow the great apostle and the runaway slave are brought together in Rome. Irony of ironies, Paul has already led Philemon, the slave's master, to the Lord, and now the slave, too, becomes a Christian. What should he do?

By Jewish law he was obliged to give him refuge and allow him to live where he chose (Deuteronomy 23.15-16). Athenian law also permitted a slave in danger of his life to seek sanctuary at an altar or at the hearth of a private family. The head of that family was obliged to persuade the runaway to give himself up to his master. If he refused to go back he could be sold at public auction and the money sent to the master.

Paul decides to send the young convert back to his Christian master as a brother in Christ. What a fine example of gracious speech and literary power we see in the letter which the runaway himself hands over to Philemon. Paul could use his apostolic authority to release Onesimus. He had, after all, made it clear that in Christ there is no slave or free. But he knows that growth comes with each spiritual decision. The slave would grow as he decided to do what was right. He must face the music – and that might even mean having a brand of ownership burned on to his face to stop him running away again. The master, for his part, must decide whether to accept his slave back as a Christian slave, or send him back to Paul as a gift (Philemon 13), or release him in the knowledge that he would be more useful as a freed brother.

There is a delightful play on the name Onesimus, which means useful or profitable. Hence Paul's quip, "Formerly he was useless (or non Onesimus) to you, but now he has become useful (Onesimus) to both you and me" (Philemon 11).

Did Philemon release him? I'm sure he did, else we wouldn't have had this letter preserved.

Becoming a Christian does not absolve us from our existing responsibilities. It may even require that we make full restitution for past wrongs.

Look again at Philemon 18 and meditate on the ministry of Paul here and its likeness to what Christ has done for us.

Quote "We are all of us Onesimi" – Martin Luther.

Promise "The truth will set you free" (John 8.32).

DAY 165 My fellow-prisoner Aristarchus sends you his greetings (4.10a)

Good Morning, Disciple,

You know the old saying, "A friend in need is a friend indeed"? Well, here's a friend indeed. The kind who will not only stand by you when the chips are down but be right there, literally, when the ship goes down. Aristarchus was with Paul in that shipwreck off Malta (Acts 27.13-44), and that wasn't his first adventure either. Back at Ephesus he was attacked during a riot (Acts 19.29).

He later accompanied Paul to Jerusalem and when Paul was arrested stood by him on the fateful trip to Italy and on to Rome. That Paul calls him a fellow-prisoner is probably only a euphemism, referring to his temporary captivity in Ephesus or, much more likely, his voluntary house arrest with Paul as a volunteer servant.

Nobody in their right mind goes out looking for trouble or suffering but, as they say, when the going gets tough, the tough get going. Who says Christianity is for weaklings? Certainly not the Bible! We meet here a man who rides the circumstances of life lightly. It is far more important for him to stay at his post than to look after his own security. Duty first!

That has been the hallmark of authentic Christianity in so many areas of life. Take, for instance, the husband who refuses to put his wife, who is suffering from Altzheimer's disease, in a nursing home but loves her even though he is no longer recognised. He dresses her, feeds her and gives her constant attention. A fellow-prisoner.

The father and mother of an autistic child, the wife of a hopeless alcoholic, a daughter confined to home looking after her aging parent, and the many thousands of folk who at great personal cost care for others – they are all, in their own way, fellow-prisoners, who voluntarily deny themselves, and the needs of others and their top priority. Duty first!

This is the very heart-beat of the Christian faith. We follow a Lord who left the realms of glory to taste the cross; to become a fellow prisoner; to stand by us in our hour of need. And He is still with us, a fellow-prisoner in whatever circumstances restrict our lives and hold us captive. Can there be a more honoured title than this?

Are you a sailor? Have a look into Acts 27.13-44 and see how rough the going can get, then pray that the Lord will give you the grace to face the storms in somebody else's life.

Quote "Deliverance consists in placing our course unreservedly in the hands of God" – Dietrich Bonhoeffer, *Letters and Papers from Prison* (S.C.M., 1953).

Promise "If we endure, we will also reign with him" (2 Timothy 2.12).

DAY 166 As does Mark, the cousin of Barnabas. (You have received instructions about him; if he comes to you, welcome him) (4.10b)

Good Morning, Disciple,

Have you ever felt like giving up as a miserable failure? Most of us have! I recall a time in my own ministry when, out of resources to cope and feeling thoroughly depressed, I wanted OUT.

Mark was like that. He had accompanied Paul on his first missionary journey as far as Perga in Pamphylia. Then for no explained reason he left and returned to Jerusalem where his mother, Mary, kept open house for the believers (Acts 13:13; 12:12).

Was he afraid of the opposition? If Mark is the young man who had a narrow escape when Jesus was captured (Mark 14:51-2), then it might explain his reluctance to face new dangers. Was he homesick? Was he backsliding? We simply do not know!

The most important part of his story is not his desertion, nor the fact that this caused a rift between Paul and Mark's cousin, Barnabas (Acts 15:37-39). It is that forgiveness restored a wounded brother – and also gave us the Gospel of Mark.

The Scripture never hides the disagreements in the Church, else it could never point to the power of forgiveness. The one who said, "Forgive as the Lord forgave you" (Colossians 3.13), wrote not out of the ivory tower of personal perfection, but as one who blundered and had to apologise, and at the same time found it in his heart to forgive the failings of his younger brother.

The reconciliation was clearly complete. If the church at Colosse had any lingering doubts about Mark's dedication, the letter would dispel them.

Incidentally, we may have a clue to the disagreement in his name. When Luke introduces him to us he is "John, also known as Mark". John is his Jewish name and Mark his adopted Gentile name. When he deserted he is called by his Jewish name John. Was he perhaps having second thoughts about the spread of the gospel to the Gentiles? After the Jerusalem leaders had settled the matter with Paul, Mark rejoined the team and Luke calls him John Mark. Thereafter, he is called Mark.

Well, as I say, it's conjecture! But the lessons are not. Failure is not the end of the road. Brothers and sisters who disagree even to the point of parting company can be reconciled. Churches must welcome back into the fold backsliders and wounded believers. I wonder what other lessons you will draw from Acts 15:22-41 as you meditate this morning. Why don't you jot them down; they are worth remembering.

Quote "Forgiveness, like dimming our headlights, happens sooner when we take the initiative" – anon.

Promise "If we love one another, God lives in us and His love is made complete in us." 1 John 4.12.

DAY 167 Jesus who is called Justus also sends greetings. These are the only Jews among my fellow-workers for the kingdom of God, and they have proved a comfort to me (4.11)

Good Morning, Disciple,

During World War II when it was essential to have an increase in coal production, Winston Churchill called leaders of the National Union of Coalminers to Downing Street for talks. He told them to envision the Victory Day Parade in London, when the heroes of the armed forces would be honoured. But taking up the rear would be the country's tens of thousands of miners. "When people ask, 'Where were you in the critical days of our struggle?' You will reply – 'We were at the coal face, deep in the heart of the earth.'"

A great leader will always honour all who serve, no matter how high or low. Paul was just such a leader, happy always to commend those who, like Jesus Justus, would otherwise have no mention.

We know nothing about this Jesus Justus beyond the consolation he and Mark brought to Paul as fellow Jewish Christian workers. The fact that he adds, "These are the only Jews," indicates his disappointment with his fellow Jews who, even as Christians, could not break free of their prejudice towards the Gentile world. He is not just whingeing when he says, "At my first defence, no-one came to my support, but everyone deserted me" (2 Timothy 4.6). He had a right to expect that those to whom Jesus had said, "Go and make disciples of all nations," (Matthew 28.19) would indeed go.

Before we judge the Jews too harshly, however, we should ask, indeed I ask myself, how far are we prepared to take the gospel across national and cultural divides? John Mark and Jesus Justus broke free of any concept of racial and religious superiority. This cannot be done without an inner struggle and the likelihood of criticism from one's own folk. No one counts the name "betrayer" lightly.

Little wonder then that these two are singled out for praise and obvious affection. They, like Paul, were outsiders among their own. But when people ask, "Where were you in the time of struggle?" they will answer, "At the face with our team leader."

Where will you be when the chips are down? As you read about Peter's awful denial in Luke 22.54-71, ask yourself what you would have done. Pray for courage.

Quote "In the books of heaven they don't write the name of
your denomination, they just write the names of people" – Juan
Carlos Ortiz, *Living With Jesus Today* (S.P.C.K., 1982).

Promise "Repentance and forgiveness of sins will be preached in
His name to all nations, beginning at Jerusalem" (Luke 24.47).

DAY 168 **Epaphras, who is one of you and a servant of
Christ Jesus, sends greetings. He is always wrestling in prayer
for you, that you may stand firm in all the will of God,
mature and fully assured. I vouch for him that he is working
hard for you and for those at Laodicea and Hierapolis (4.12,
13)**

Good Morning, Disciple,

I was tempted to break this up, but the two verses belong together
as a portrait of a pastor. Notice how closely this Gentile is related to
the work and Christian character of Paul, or more correctly, how close
they are brought together in Christ.

They share honourable titles. Epaphras is called a servant, a slave
of Christ Jesus; a title given only to Paul (Romans 1.1) and Timothy
(Philippians 1.1). But we are all called to serve in the new way of the
Spirit (Romans 7.6) and can aspire to this high office, servants, slaves
of Christ Jesus and fellow-slaves in His service (1.7).

Like Aristarchus, he is also called a fellow-prisoner (Philemon 23).
This may mean that he has voluntarily placed himself under house
arrest to serve Paul, or possibly he is awaiting the same fate as the
apostle.

But it is not just titles which bind them. Here are two pastors in
complete harmony: the ideal model for a pastoral team. Both wrestle
in prayer constantly. Did Paul have Epaphras in mind when he said,
"We have not stopped praying for you"? I think so! Both labour and
pray (1.29-2.1) towards the same end: that the believers should stand
firm in the faith, "rooted and built up" in Christ (2.7).

This suggests three lessons for any Christians working together in
team situations. 1. Have the same clearly defined biblical goals. 2.
Pray together, constantly, fervently and definitely, for those whom
you are called to serve. 3. Remember that the servant is not greater

than his master. Jesus said, "The Son of Man did not come to be served, but to serve, and to give his life as a ransom for many" (Matthew 29.28). If we must have titles, then let ours be fellow-servants of Christ Jesus. I am quite confident of this, that if teams would only function as praying, working servants on an agreed agenda we would not have some of the tragic conflicts which sometimes erupt.

See more of what the Master has instructed on this vital subject of persistent praying in Luke 11.1-13 — and put it into practice!

Quote "The first sign of the heavenly call is an intense, all-absorbing desire for the work" — C. H. Spurgeon, *Lectures to My Students* (Passmore & Alabaster, 1890).

Promise "Ask and it will be given to you; seek and you will find; knock and the door will be opened to you" (Luke 11.9).

DAY 169   Our dear friend Luke, the doctor (4.14a)

Good Morning, Disciple,

Blessed is the man who can call his doctor his friend. Our family doctor is one of our closest and dearest friends, so I can understand Paul's affection for the "beloved physician".

Luke, the only Gentile writer of Scripture, wrote both the Gospel according to Luke and the Acts of the Apostles. Legend has it that he was the unnamed disciple on the road to Emmaus when the risen Lord gave His Old Testament Bible study. Later, legend portrays him as an artist. Yet however attractive, we must treat all legends with a pinch of salt.

That he was a detailed historian and investigative journalist we do have ample evidence (Luke 1.1-3a).

By God's plan and providence, Dr Luke and Mark, the author of the second Gospel and close disciple of the apostle Peter, were both together with Paul in Rome, at least when this letter was written and possibly again later (2 Timothy 4.11). What conversations the three had we may only conjecture, but it might help explain the close parallel between the two Gospels. They were, after all, written much later. No doubt Luke picked up useful information from both of them for the details he gives in Acts.

Luke actually joined Paul on the second missionary journey. Was this, I wonder, because Paul had been taken ill earlier (Galatians 4.13)? Even though Paul prayed for the healing of others, he seems not to be averse to the learned skills of the physician. How grateful he must have been when this intelligent, sensitive doctor gave up his promising career to travel widely, and over many years, for the Lord.

We are able to tell precisely when Luke was with Paul by what are called the "We passages" in Acts. Luke dramatically switches to the first person plural whenever he is present in the action. Catch up on some of that action in Acts 20.1-13 and notice the introduction of "we" in verse 6. Notice too the eye for detail in this short account. Praise God for such a writer of the authentic word.

Quote "Medicine is in its right place when it sets out to deal with the body and the mind. But it is the task of religion – of the Christian religion – to deal with the 'whole man'" – Dr Martin Lloyd-Jones, *The Doctor Himself and the Human Condition* (Christian Medical Fellowship Publications, 1982).

Promise "I tell you the truth, unless a kernel of wheat falls to the ground and dies, it remains only a single seed. But if it dies, it produces many seeds" (John 12.24).

DAY 170 . . . And Demas send greetings (4.14b)

Good Morning, Disciple,

Have you ever been tempted to give up the struggle of being a Christian? None of us knows what our reactions would be if faced with torture or death for Christ. Even those closest to the Lord Jesus in His earthly ministry failed the test in His hour of greatest need. "All the disciples deserted him and fled" (Matthew 26.56). And towards the close of Paul's ministry, he records: "At my first defence, no-one came to my support, but everyone deserted me" (2 Timothy 4.16).

Sticking at it when the going gets tough takes courage, so we should not criticise those who, faced with overwhelming hostility, fail the test of loyalty. But such was not the case with Demas, who was once a "fellow-worker" (Philemon 24). His backsliding was a matter of choice. "Demas," says Paul with more than a touch of pathos, "because he loved this world, has deserted me and has gone to Thessalonica . . . Only Luke is with me" (2 Timothy 4.10-11). There we have it – for love of the world.

We may speculate. What was it in the world which lured Demas away? Craving after an old sinful habit (1 John 2.16)? Was it money? He would not be the first, nor the last, to fall for that. "For the love of money is a root of all kinds of evil. Some people, eager for money, have wandered away from the faith and pierced themselves with many griefs" (1 Timothy 6.10).

I would like to think that Demas repented and that we shall meet him in heaven. We have already seen how John Mark came back. The Scripture is silent when it comes to Demas.

I love the thrill of motor racing. You never quite know which cars are going to make it to the end. A car will make an unscheduled pit stop and you think, he's out of it. But then the car which seemed to have retired is back on the circuit. We must pray for our backsliding friends that they come back on circuit and follow to the end when, with us, they can say, "I have finished the race, I have kept the faith" (2 Timothy 4.7).

There are many things hard to grasp in your meditation this morning. So take time to read Luke 14.25-35 carefully and prayerfully.

Quote "Collapse in the Christian life is seldom a blow out; it is usually a slow leak" – Paul E. Little.

Promise "Do not work for food that spoils, but for food that endures to eternal life, which the Son of Man will give you. On him God the Father has placed his seal of approval" (John 6.27).

DAY 171 Give my greetings to the brothers at Laodicea, and to Nympha and the church in her house (4.15)

Good Morning, Disciple,

If you are reading from the old King James version of the Bible, don't worry too much that it reads "Nympha and the church in his house". Just as in our English language the girl's name Georgina is sometimes shortened to George, so the masculine Nymphrodorus of the ancient world could be shortened to Nympha, making it the same as the girl's name. In writing, the confusion would be cleared up by the pronoun "his" or "her". The problem in this instance is that some of the early manuscripts had "his" and the majority of better manuscripts had "her". On balance of probability the later translators have plumped for "her house". It doesn't really matter.

Christians met in homes for the first two or three hundred years. At Philippi they met at Lydia's home (Acts 16.15, 40), at Corinth, with Gaius (Romans 16.23), and wherever Aquila and Priscilla moved, their home became a church (1 Corinthians 16.19; Romans 16.3-5). Perhaps this is why one of the qualifications for ministry in the New Testament church was hospitality (Titus 1.8).

In Britain in recent years there has been a return to the idea that church is wherever Christians meet, whether in cathedral or chapel, church or home. The house-church movement has served as a useful reminder that our homes are to be open for the Lord's use.

Our homes and churches, as bricks and mortar, blend in with the structures which surround them. We, on the other hand, must stand out in sharp contrast to those unbelievers who live around us. Not as prigs and prudes with a "holier than thou" attitude which offends, but as Christ-like examples of love, generosity and neighbourliness which will attract interest and enquiry.

Paul's injunction to "practise hospitality" (Romans 12.13) is one way in which neighbours can be reached with the gospel. I recall an occasion when a neighbour started asking spiritual questions. I invited him and his wife to our home for dinner where we could continue this discussion and that very evening they both heard the gospel and were ready to receive it in the comfort of our living room.

Paul has some excellent principles for families who want to be witnesses in their communities. See if you can list some of these for action as you read 1 Timothy 5.1-25. Pray that your home will become a testimony of Christ's love.

Quote "We have been inhabited by the hospitable Christ" – Karen Burton Mains, *Open Heart, Open Home* (David E Cook Publishing, 1976).

Promise "Everything is possible for him who believes" (Mark 9.23).

DAY 172 **After this letter has been read to you, see that it is also read in the church of the Laodiceans and that you in turn read the letter from Laodicea (4.16)**

Good Morning, Disciple,

It is my experience in life that most personal conflicts between folk are caused by a lack of communication. Reconciliation is achieved, more often than not, by bringing all parties together for a time of open discussion.

We know nothing of the relationship between the churches of Laodicea and Colosse, or indeed, of the third fellowship across the valley in the spa town of Hierapolis. Clearly, they were all working together, functioning from various homes in the three towns. Communication between them was essential.

The Colossians are to deliver their letter to Laodicea and collect a second letter from there to be read in their own assembly of believers. There are many theories about the identity of that letter but it was most probably the letter addressed to Ephesus, a sort of round-robin circular epistle to be read in all the Asian churches. Tychicus, its bearer, would inevitably pass through both Ephesus and Laodicea on his way to Colosse. We have also seen how each of the letters seems to act as a commentary on the other.

Both are to be read aloud in public in the same way that the Old Testament Scriptures were also read aloud in the Jewish synagogues. Such public readings were always accompanied by teaching and an opportunity for the listeners to ask questions. This is a practice I would love to see reintroduced in contemporary churches.

One sure test of whether or not you are in the church of God's choice, is the emphasis placed there on reading and learning from the Bible. If it is not honoured as God's Word but merely placed on a par with other books, you are unlikely to go to it for the "teaching, rebuking, correcting and training in righteousness" for which God purposed it (2 Timothy 3.16).

I wonder whether the apathy and consequent backsliding at the church in Laodicea was a result of just this very thing. Judge for yourself as you read Revelation 3.14-22. Pray for your minister as he prepares to teach next Sunday, that he will be faithful in the delivery of God's Word, and that you will be faithful to receive it and act upon it. Why not take a notebook and make notes on the sermon so that you can remember what is said.

Quote "We have hungered to be masters of the Word, much more than we have hungered to be mastered by it" – Donald A. Carson, *Hermeneutics, Authority and Canon* (Inter-Varsity Press, 1986).

Promise "The word of the Lord stands forever" (1 Peter 1.25).

DAY 173 Tell Archippus: "See to it that you complete the work you have received in the Lord." (4.17)

Good Morning, Disciple,

How appropriate it is that, as we near the end of this book, we address the matter of completing tasks assigned to us by the Lord. For me this is the fulfilment of a commission to write this book for you, so that you may have a solid foundation upon which your spiritual life may grow. For you this is the end of a study which has lasted almost six months. Congratulations for sticking at it.

Archippus is called a fellow-soldier in the letter to Philemon and is likely to be a member of Philemon's household, possibly a son. Here he is instructed to keep on keeping on with the task assigned him, right to the end.

Commentators suggest many ideas on what that task was. It seems unlikely that he was a deacon. Perhaps he was pastor of the Laodicean church, or interim pastor of all three churches in the absence of Epaphras.

Because I am an evangelist I like to think that Archippus was gifted in evangelism and church planting. It's just the kind of greeting that anyone writing to the church where I am in membership might give at the end of a letter: "Tell good old Vic Jackopson to keep up the good work of evangelism." One further clue may be in Paul's view of his own hardships and ministry: "I consider my life worth nothing to me, if only I may finish the race and complete the task the Lord Jesus has given me – the task of testifying to the gospel of God's grace" (Acts 20.24).

Max Sinclair had a fulfilling Christian ministry when a head-on car crash left him with a broken neck and paralysed. His ministry seemed to be at an end. "I saw myself in a wheelchair, Sue feeding me, pushing me along, washing me," he lamented. "Would I ever speak . . . again? What about my God-given ministry?" God had other ideas! Max went on to make a "one in a thousand" recovery, and now has an even wider ministry with the organisation he founded, Christian Viewpoint For Men.

As you read Acts 28.16-31, see how Paul kept to his task right to the end, regardless of the consequences. Pray that you will too.

Quote "Ministry is not something we do for God; it is something God does in and through us" – Warren W. Wiersbe, *Be Complete"* (Victor Books, 1981).

Promise "Let us not become weary in doing good, for at the proper time we will reap a harvest if we do not give up" (Galatians 6.9).

DAY 174 I, Paul, write this greeting in my own hand. Remember my chains. (4.18a)

Good Morning, Disciple,

I have written most of these letters from the quiet of the Cotswold village of Sherborne, in the comfort of a borrowed apartment far away from the "madding crowd". What a contrast with Paul's situation. When he had finished dictating, his secretary passed him the pen so that he could sign his own name to authenticate his authorship and avoid the proliferation of forgeries which had already occurred even as early as his letter to Thessalonica (2 Thessalonians 2.2, 3.17).

He could not do this without the physical cooperation of the guard to whom he was chained. No doubt, as he wrote, those chains rattled and impeded his writing. Hence his plea – remember my chains! He had prayed for the Colossians; he now invites them to pray for him.

Wherever missionary zeal like Paul's has exerted its influence in the world, it has stirred up controversy and persecution, but with it has come life. Mild, respectable and acceptable Christianity leads to a comfortable, imperceptible death. Emblazoned on the heraldic shield of God's Kingdom are the symbols of Christ: a scourging whip, bloody nails and a cross.

Peter Marshall in *The Light and the Glory* tells the graphic tale of an early missionary to America. In 1642 when Jogues' companions were ambushed by Iroquois Indians, he surrendered. "Could I indeed abandon them without giving them the help which the Church of my God has entrusted to me? . . ." If he died, he said, "It is but a transient death, in order to procure for them an eternal life."

His captors tortured him sadistically, tearing off his fingernails and gnawing his fingers. Though he escaped and became a national hero in his native France, Jogues returned later to become the first ambassador. He returned yet again as a missionary priest, writing to a friend before his departure, "My heart tells me that if I have the happiness of being employed in this mission, I will go and will not return; but I shall be happy if the Lord will complete the sacrifice where He has begun it." He did!

As you read Hebrews 11.24-40 be aware that the sacrifice of faith spoken of there was before Jesus came, while the knowledge of God's grace was still shadowy. Now we have the substance, how much greater should be our faith and our willingness to sacrifice?

Quote "Christianity has always produced its best when under suffering" – Rabbi Lionel Blue.

Promise "The man who loves his life will lose it, while the man who hates his life in this world will keep it for eternal life" (John 12.25).

DAY 175 Grace be with you (4.18b)

Good Morning, Disciple,

For the last time! I hope you have grown deeper in your daily walk as we have shared Colossians. I have certainly enjoyed writing these letters. The real test is whether, in the coming days, your own relationship with the Lord, fellowship with the Church, love within the family and ministry to the world in work and witness are enhanced.

Try to keep a balance between all these areas of your life, and go

on to strengthen each one by constant feeding from God's Word and by daily practice.

This diagram, which I used in the Introduction, is one you may want to come back to again and again, because it shows the foundation upon which Colossians is based and on which you may grow. Notice how, starting with salvation and working in an anti-clockwise direction, God's grace is the starting point of everything and permeates all you do.

"We believe it is through the grace of our Lord Jesus that we are saved" (Acts 15.11), and as we go on living for Him we receive more and more. "From the fulness of his grace we have all received one blessing after another" (John 1.16).

In response, we give ourselves to Him in continuous love and obedience and "grow in the grace and knowledge of our Lord" (2 Peter 3.18).

In our relationship with others, whether at church, in the home or at work, "each one should use whatever gift he has received to serve others, faithfully administering God's grace in all its various forms (1 Peter 4.10), and every conversation should be "full of grace" (4.6), enabling us to witness with confidence to the "message of his grace" (Acts 14.3).

Little wonder then that Paul ends his epistle with these words, "Grace be with you." I join with him in this blessing. "May the God of hope fill you with all joy and peace as you trust in him, so that you may overflow with hope by the power of the Holy Spirit" (Romans 15.13).

2 Corinthians 6 is your final meditation. Keep growing!

Quote "Christ plus anything equals nothing. Christ plus nothing equals everything" – Me.

Promise "God is able to make all grace abound to you, so that in all things at all times, having all that you need, you will abound with every good work" (2 Corinthians 9.8).

Bibliography

* *The Epistle of St Paul to the Colossians*, J. B. Lightfoot (London, Macmillan & Co., 1869)
* *Word Biblical Commentary*, Peter T. O'Brien (Waco, Texas, Word Books, 1982)
* *The Interpretation of St Paul's Epistles*, R. C. H. Lenski (Minneapolis, Minnesota, Augsburg Publishing House, 1937-61)
* *The Cambridge Greek Testament Commentary*, C. F. D. Moule, ed. (Cambridge University Press, 1968)
* *The Cambridge Bible*, H. C. G. Moule, M.A. (Cambridge University Press, 1893)
* *Colossians – A Letter To Asia*, Frederick Brooke Westcott (Minneapolis, Minnesota, Klock & Klock, reprint, 1981)
* *New Testament Commentary*, William Hendriksen (Grand Rapids, Michigan, Baker Book House, 1962)
* *The International Critical Commentary*, T. K. Abbott (Edinburgh, T. & T. Clark Ltd, 1985)
* *The New International Commentary on the New Testament*, F. F. Bruce (Grand Rapids, Michigan, Williams B. Eerdmans Publishing Co., 1984)
The Bible Speaks Today, The Message of Colossians and Philemon, R. C. Lucas (Leicester, Inter-Varsity Press, 1980)
Tyndale New Testament Commentaries, H. M. Carson (London, Tyndale Press, 1960)
The Shepherd of the Stars, Charles A. Trentham (Nashville, Broadman Press, 1962)
The Daily Study Series, Colossians, William Barclay (Edinburgh, St Andrew Press, 1975)
Colossians, Christ All-Sufficient, Everett F. Harrison (Chicago, Moody Press, 1971)
Be Complete, Warren W. Wiersbe (Wheaton, Illinois, Victor Books, 1981)

* *Commentaries with extensive use of the Greek language*

Glossary

Abraham	Genesis 11-25; regarded by the Jews as the "Father of their race"
Adam	Genesis 1-3; the first created man
admonishment	correcting with warning
agnostic	one who professes that it is impossible to know whether or not God exists; from the Greek *agnoeo* meaning to be ignorant
Alpha	first letter of the Greek alphabet; name applied to Christ
angel	a messenger from God; those who are attendant upon God in heaven
apocalyptic	concerning the end of the world; concerning hidden or unknown things; Mark 13, Revelation
apostle	one of the Twelve sent out by Christ to preach His gospel
ascetic	a person who renounces material comforts and leads a life of austere self-discipline as an act of religious devotion
atheist	one who believes there is no God
atonement	Christ's sacrifice on the cross, satisfying God's justice
avatar	descent to earth of a deity in human or animal form in Hindu mythology
begotten	born of
channelling	process of receiving information from some level of reality other than the ordinary physical one and from beyond the "self" as it is generally understood. A "channeller", or medium, usually goes into a trance to establish contact with a spirit, ascended master, higher consciousness, or some other entity, and then receives and repeats messages from "the other side" of the physical world.
Christian Union	a group of people meeting together for Christian fellowship, prayer and the study of God's Word; usually in schools, colleges and places of work
Damascus	a city of Syria; "Damascus road experience" – see Acts 9, Paul's conversion

doctrines	principles or theories presented for acceptance or belief; dogmas
Ecclesiasticus	book of the Apocrypha, containing moral and practical maxims
Elmer Gantry	fictional American evangelist of loose morality
emanation	thing proceeding from a source, especially referring to virtues, qualities, moral powers
enlightenment	a state marked by spiritual insight and freedom from illusory appearances; usually achieved by a period of ascetic behaviour, special teaching and/or act of initiation
Esau	eldest son of Isaac, Genesis 25ff
Eusebius	first-century church historian
evangelism	preaching of the gospel
forgiven	released from the debt, pardoned
gnostic	member of sect believing in gnosticism (see below)
gnosticism	belief that enlightenment comes from discovery of hidden knowledge (*gnosis*) via the practice of mysticism, freeing one from the material world of illusion into the realisation of self-deity
Godhead	being God, divine nature, deity
house group	gathering of Christian people meeting in a home for fellowship, worship and the study of God's Word
incarnate	God come to earth in Christ; what we celebrate at Christmas
Isaac	son of Abraham and Sarah, Genesis 17ff
Ishmael	son of Abraham and Hagar, Genesis 16ff
Jacob	son of Isaac, Genesis 25ff
Joseph	son of Jacob, Genesis 30ff
Jude	author of the New Testament letter, brother of James and possibly of Jesus
justification	the first step in the process of salvation; being made righteous by Christ's sacrificial death (just as if I'd never sinned), and thereby reconciled to God
karma	the sum of a person's actions during the successive phases of his existence, regarded as determining his destiny in future incarnations
King David	second king of Israel, son of Jesse, author of many of the Psalms, 1 Samuel 16-1 Kings 2

Lucifer	(see Satan) Angel of Light
Messiah	original Jewish term translated Christ (means anointed); the expected King who rules God's people
Moses	the leader and lawgiver of Israel
mystery	(of the gospel) See Ephesians 3.6
Nathan	a prophet (2 Samuel 7.2)
Nicene Creed	statement of true Christian faith formed at the Council of Nicaea, AD 325, to settle controversy over images (icons)
Omega	last letter of the Greek alphabet; name applied to Christ
Onesimus	a slave of Philemon's for whom Paul intercedes
pantheism	belief that God is everything and everything is God
patriarch	father of family, tribe or nation; hence Abraham, Isaac and Jacob
phantasm	something apparently seen but having no physical reality; a phantom
Pharisee	ancient Jewish sect of legalists maintaining strict orthodox rules and doctrines
Philemon	a member of the church at Colosse which met in his house; master of the slave Onesimus
Phrygian	an inhabitant of Phrygia, an inland province of Asia Minor
reconciliation	bringing together of two alienated parties; hence God and man
resurrection	raising from the dead
Reuben	son of Jacob and Leah (Genesis 29.32-49.3)
sacrament	a sign, especially in a religious ceremony; for example, baptism, the Lord's Supper
Sadducees	religious group who rejected tradition of elders and denied existence of angels, spirits and resurrection (that is why they were sad you see?) (see Acts 4.1-3, 23.8)
sanctification	the ongoing process by which the Christian gives himself/herself more and more to God by behaviour and devotion
sanctified	made holy
Satan (Lucifer)	means adversary i.e. against God; the Devil
shalom	peace

Son of God	Jesus, the only begotten Son of the eternal God, one of the Trinity
sons of God	all true believers in Jesus Christ
Son of Man	Jesus as the true man
spirit	supernatural, non-material realm
stump of Jesse	offspring of King David's father; poetic term for Jesus
symbiotic	depending upon one another, as flowers need bees to pollinate and therefore give the bees nectar to make honey
theology	study of God and religious truth
Trinity	God the Father, Son and Holy Spirit, the Godhead
universalism	doctrine of universal salvation, that all mankind will eventually be saved regardless of their belief or lack of it